May 2, 2023
National and International Scholarships Office

THE NEW BLACK STUDIES SERIES

Edited by Darlene Clark Hine and Dwight A. McBride

A list of books in the series appears at the end of this book.

AIN'T I AN ANTHROPOLOGIST

ZORA NEALE HURSTON
BEYOND THE LITERARY ICON

JENNIFER L. FREEMAN MARSHALL

UNIVERSITY OF ILLINOIS PRESS
Urbana, Chicago, and Springfield

Library of Congress Cataloging-in-Publication Data
Names: Freeman Marshall, Jennifer L., 1968– author.
Title: Ain't I an anthropologist : Zora Neale Hurston beyond
    the literary icon / Jennifer L. Freeman Marshall.
Description: Urbana : University of Illinois Press, [2023]
    | Series: The new Black studies series | Includes
    bibliographical references and index.
Identifiers: LCCN 2022042716 (print) | LCCN 2022042717
    (ebook) | ISBN 9780252044960 (cloth) | ISBN
    9780252087103 (paperback ; acid-free paper) | ISBN
    9780252054150 (ebook)
Subjects: LCSH: Hurston, Zora Neale--Criticism and
    interpretation. | Hurston, Zora Neale--Knowledge and
    learning. | Anthropology. | BISAC: SOCIAL SCIENCE /
    Ethnic Studies / American / African American & Black
    Studies | LITERARY CRITICISM / American / African
    American & Black Classification: LCC PS3515.U789 Z6926
    2023 (print) | LCC PS3515.U789 (ebook) | DDC 813/.52—
    dc23/eng/20220916
LC record available at https://lccn.loc.gov/2022042716
LC ebook record available at https://lccn.loc.gov/2022042717

For my daughter,
Chloe

Contents

Acknowledgments

Zora Neale Hurston wrote in her autobiography, *Dust Tracks on a Road*, "There are years that ask questions and years that answer." Many years have passed since I first felt "commanded" to pursue answers to the questions raised in this monograph. A native of Atlanta, Georgia, with roots in Central Florida and Durham, North Carolina, my earliest private interest in Hurston's works was shaped by the ways her productions in literature and anthropology could inform a broader understanding of my own personal and larger histories and cultures. However, I never considered her as central or the best; I only knew that, like working a math equation or solving a puzzle, I enjoyed reading and rereading her works in order to experience their beautiful insights and complexities and to further consider the challenges that she crafted.

It was a circuitous and compelling path that led me from undergraduate studies in English to graduate studies in anthropology and then to women's studies with brief stops in various professions along the way. In those early years in different locales and before I committed to this project, I found myself intently and sometimes randomly gathering any useful data toward reading Hurston. As I moved closer to this project in my early graduate studies, when I sat to both read and discuss her work, charged popular receptions were there waiting. Sometimes they offered rote imaginings and new insights and they encouraged more reading. Other times conjectures about Hurston's anthropology and authority, on occasion uttered with resolve, were perplexing, as they removed incentives for future study. Much later I encountered undergraduate students in various disciplines, themselves eager to study Hurston's anthropology, who were frustrated and stymied by conversations they encountered that determined Hurston's anthropology as interesting but flawed. They wondered, How could they move forward in their search for answers if so many with authority had deemed her work impenetrable and problematic? So I initially imagined that this project would largely answer questions about her anthropology even as I framed my questions in terms of her iconic literary status. However, as in life, questions unfold and beckon more questions, and any answers are rarely absolute or final. I now offer this project as it began, with a spirit of curiosity, commitment, community, gratitude, and regard for all the scholars whose work I engage here and all the questions and answers that remain.

Alice Walker's declaration that models are vitally important is true. I thank her and all the dedicated Black feminist scholar-activists-artists for the rough-and-tumble paths that they cleared. I wish to specifically thank those Black feminist scholars who literally created a space at Spelman College (Women's Research and Resource Center) within which I first began to critically explore Black feminist thought: Beverly Guy-Sheftall, Jacqueline Jones Royster, and Johnnetta Betsch Cole deserve my immense gratitude for their support of my undergraduate and graduate research when I returned to Spelman as a graduate research assistant. Johnnetta Cole's example first helped me to imagine the many commitments of a Black feminist anthropologist. Jacqueline Jones Royster encouraged and supported my budding interests in publishing. A very special thank-you is reserved for Beverly Guy-Sheftall, who modeled a scholar-activist life and offered me rooms of my own. In addition, as a graduate research and teaching assistant at Spelman, I met poet Opal Moore, and I thank her for every conversation and for calling me to poet.

Graduate work in medical and urban anthropology at Georgia State University led to research opportunities with Carole E. Hill and Claire E. Sterk. I thank them both for the independent research and fieldwork experiences that informed my studies and early imaginings of this project, especially when my research interest in Hurston as an anthropologist was otherwise met with roadblocks and resistance.

Frances Smith Foster, Carla Freeman, and Pamela Hall read this project during its formative stage at Emory University. I thank each of them for their timely and critical suggestions, questions, and comments. A special thank-you to Frances Smith Foster, who was particularly helpful as I navigated a dense but well-worn path of interdisciplinarity at the heart of so many African American literary and cultural productions. As I searched for answers, she encouraged me to truly listen to my questions and to go far afield. I'm indebted to her for the wise counsel she provided. In addition, I thank Jacquelyn Grant and Dianne M. Stewart for courses that were instrumental in my early consideration of Hurston's anthropological study of religious beliefs. I am also grateful for the time I spent with Berky Abreu, Rudolph Byrd, and Josephine Boyd Bradley (Clark Atlanta University, Africana Women's Studies Program), all now dearly departed. In addition, I thank Virginia Shadron for her backing of my graduate studies. Altogether, they provided self-affirming support for this project.

At Purdue University, I thank my faculty and staff colleagues in English Studies; American Studies; African American Studies; Anthropology; Women's, Gender, and Sexuality Studies; the Black Cultural Center; and the LGBTQ Center for their collegiality. Thank you to Dorsey Armstrong, Robyn Bartlett, Jennifer Bay, Terry Bean, Elena Benedicto, Evie Blackwood, Kristina Bross, Bill Caise, Niambi Carter, Robin Clair, Rosalee Clawson, Candance Croney, Susan Curtis, Barbara Hart Dixon, John Duvall, Joel Ebarb, Arne Flaten, Wendy Flory, Elaine Francis, Mark French, Geraldine Friedman, Kim Gallon, Renee Gibert, Nana Gletsu-Miller, Laurie Graham, Leonard Harris, Shaun Hughes, Chrystal Johnson, Michael Johnston, Lowell Kane, Su'Ad Khabeer, Julie Knoeller, Bob Lamb, Brian Leung, Maren Linett, Al Lopez, Christopher Lukasik, Shannon McMullen, Roseda "Edie" Moffitt, Valentine Moghadam, Daniel Morris, Bill Mullen, Derek Pacheco, Venetria Patton, Nancy Peterson, Nush Powell, Victor Raskin, Krista Ratcliff, Charles Ross, Aparajita Sagar, James Saunders, Patsy Schweickart, Ann Shanahan, Jamie Starr, Matilda Stokes, Sandra Sydnor, Mangala Subramaniam, Dena Targ, Renee Thomas, and Irwin Weiser for your professional support and encouragement in various ways. The great NPG—Cheryl Cooky, Marlo David, and Alicia Decker—you are a cohort like no other, and I'm so very grateful for our friendships and feminist coalitions and for all the fun times we've shared. Guadalupe "Lupita" Acosta Roberts, Cornelius "Neil" Bynum, and Valeria Sinclair-Chapman, thank you each for your friendships and for your immense support as I worked to complete this project and for claiming and honoring a beloved community. I thank *all* of my graduate and undergraduate students over the years, who inspire me with their commitment and dedication. Many thanks to Jolivette Anderson-Douoning, Paula Ashe, Juanita Crider, Casarae Gibson, Aria Holliday, Kaylah Morgan, and Megan Williams. I also must offer a special thank-you to *anyone* who, in support of this project, ever shared a truly folksy conversation or any Hurston memorabilia with me.

For your helpful questions, comments, and community, I thank co-panelists and audiences at the American Anthropological Association, the Association for the Study of the Worldwide African Diaspora, the Modern Language Association, the National Women's Studies Association, the Reception Study Society, the Zora! Fest Academic Conference, and the Zora Neale Hurston Society at Morgan State University, as well as Hurston and Harlem Renaissance conferences at Cleveland State University, North Carolina Central University, and Rhode Island College.

I am indebted to the scholarship of Cheryl Wall and most thankful for the opportunities I had to share my work with her at various conferences. I am eternally grateful for her professional model and for the rich scholarly legacy she left for us all. A deep bow and immense gratitude to Valerie Boyd, who offered supportive words of encouragement and claimed me as Hurston's kin as our paths crossed over many years and during various stages of this project. I also must thank Genevieve West for her collegiality, our timely conference collaboration, and for her continued search in the archives of Zora Neale Hurston.

I am also thankful for the relationships and communities that emerged and were sustained through my memberships in the National Women's Studies Association and the National Center for Faculty Development and Diversity during the completion of this project, including Courtney N. Baker, Beauty Bragg, Terri Francis, Heidi R. Lewis, Melissa Lipold, Elizabeth Prom-Wormley, Theda Rose, and Sunita Sah. A very special thank-you to Evangeline "Vange" Heiliger, Jessica "JMil" Millward, and David Perez II for your steadfast support, good humor, and accountability. Special mention and thanks to Davey Shlasko for providing his careful editorial eye and comments.

The anonymous readers from the University of Illinois Press read my manuscript and offered helpful and precise comments, and I thank them for their time and attention to detail. I thank Larin McLaughlin for her initial endorsement of my manuscript and Dawn Durante for her significant and steady support over many years. My deep appreciation also goes to members of the editorial board of the New Black Studies Series. A very special thank-you to acquisitions editor Dominque J. Moore, copyeditor Jill R. Hughes, senior editor Tad Ringo, and art director Dustin Hubbart for his support as we worked to bring my vision of the book cover to life.

I must acknowledge support from the Andrew W. Mellon Emory Teaching Fellowship and a Southern Studies Dissertation Fellowship at Emory University, which greatly sustained this work. My appreciation, also, to Purdue University's Department of English, the School of Interdisciplinary Studies, and Purdue's Office of the Executive Vice President for Research and Partnerships for supporting the publication of this book with a subvention.

Thank you to Edward Burns, Successor Trustee of the Carl Van Vechten Trust, for so graciously granting permission for my use of the Carl Van Vechten photos of Hurston in this project. Thank you, also, to James C. Freeman for the use of his photos from the Zora! 2013 Outdoor Festival. I am also grateful for the archives at the Library of Congress and for the "Smiling woman" who insisted on being acknowledged during the production of this book. Your knowing grin and chuckle astonished me, and then your outright laughter was a bold reminder, so I will share in your good humor. May we one day know your name.

Amber Hussain, Hosi Karzai and family, Stephanie Krajicek, Kelli Randall, Sherie Randolph, Valerie Ruffin, and Jennifer Thomas: I thank each one of you for your generosity of spirit, incredible support, full-bodied laughter, and long-lasting friendships that truly sustained me as I worked to complete this work.

Jill Gordon Waite, I thank you for the great gift of our everlasting sisterhood. I will forever be grateful for your ongoing support and the many experiences and dreams and girls' trips we've shared through the years. To you and our Breakfast Club family, Donald Bridges and Bruce Morton, thank you for years of friendship, inside jokes, good music, and late-night talks. I looked forward to every retreat as I worked to complete this project, and I'm glad that we never try to make a long story short.

I thank my ancestors and all of my family both near and far for their love and for our countless conversations about our family traditions and folklore. My mother, Victoria J. Phillips, provided faithful words and wisdom and offered a hearing ear as this project neared completion. I thank you for sharing your library, your travels, Lasyrenn, and your mother's activist gardens with me. My father, James C. Freeman, engaged many emerging ideas, told me Floridian folk stories from his youth, and eagerly joined me on road trips to Eatonville. I thank you for your gifts of storytelling, poetry, swimming, photography, and music: *Ye tou' mande pou' toi.* My brother, Jason C. Freeman, you are by far the breeziest brother ever. *Everybody* knows this. Thank you for your support, great wit, good humor, and hero's heart of justice.

I especially want to thank my husband, Derick Marshall, for every moment of his unconditional support. It's been a long and winding journey, and I'm truly grateful that you decided to hold my hand and join me on this walk. Thank you for every encouragement, every fruit, flower, and every wondrous landscape that you've shared with me. To our daughter, Chloe, you have in a very real sense grown up alongside this project. I think one day you'll look and find our smiles and laughter tucked within its pages. It is my greatest pleasure to dedicate this book to you and your brilliant mind and voice.

AIN'T I AN ANTHROPOLOGIST

Introduction

"Twice as Much Praise or Twice as Much Blame"

No one on earth ever had a greater chance for glory. The world to be
won and nothing to be lost. It is thrilling to think — to know that for any
act of mine, I shall get twice as much praise or twice as much blame.
It is quite exciting to hold the center of the national stage, with the
spectators not knowing whether to laugh or to weep.

—Zora Neale Hurston (1928)

The above epigraph, from Zora Neale Hurston's (1891–1960) essay "How It Feels
to Be Colored Me," illuminates Hurston's observations and expectations of the
reception of her work by a complex national audience. At times satirical and
ironic, the essay presciently defines race as a sociocultural construction during
an era when theories regarding racial identity and experience were rigorously
challenged and redefined beyond the prevailing evolutionary arguments of
racial difference. Science (including the fields of physical anthropology) argued
for a biological basis for Black inferiority, while the burgeoning social sciences
offered theories regarding the overwhelming influence of slavery on African
Americans' character and social condition. Often noted for its pronouncement
"But I am not tragically colored," Hurston's essay declares her resistance to
rhetoric from the "sobbing school of Negro-hood," including persistent (and
likely patronizing) appeals to the legacy of slavery that might reduce her everyday life entirely to "the problem" of race in the United States.

Already a published poet and author of several short stories, Hurston was roughly five years from publishing the succession of novels and ethnographies through the 1930s and '40s that would bring her national acclaim. Reviews of that era infamously reveal how her race and gender shaped reader expectations of this later work. However, in 1928 Hurston already understood that her identity as a "colored" woman would inform audiences' reception of her "any act." What she embraces in this essay, in all of its complexity, was the right to feel and be herself, idiosyncratic and sometimes puzzling, like any member of the human race. The essay also stands as a personal statement in which Hurston affirms her power and agency as a writer. Self-defined, she revels in the creative possibilities of her own lived experience, which she offers as ample evidence of the emotional complexity of Black life.[1]

Hurston is a notable twentieth-century American writer, with many of her works taught as classics in twentieth-century American literature, women's literature, and African American literature. The author of a significant corpus produced between the 1920s and the 1950s and spanning many literary genres, her works are now in print and largely accessible after a sustained period of relative critical neglect. Today Hurston's legacy as a popular cultural figure and writer seems firmly secure. However, her "twice as much praise or twice as much blame" presaged a quality of the critical reception of her work in the U.S. academy since the 1970s. Readers might be surprised to find that while she has been largely celebrated as a literary artist within the academy, her critical reception within American anthropology is a far more complicated story. Hurston's ethnographies are often received with more ambivalence within the discipline, in part due to their "experimental" form. Although noted as a progenitor in the fields of African American anthropology and Black feminist anthropology, scholars and students of American anthropology routinely call for more critical assessments of her contributions to the larger discipline.

The oftentimes polar receptions of Hurston's two areas of work are quite remarkable, requiring a careful consideration of the terms of her narrative authority across both fields. Is it inevitable that Hurston's literary authority should eclipse her anthropological authority, or are sociocultural and institutional values and processes at play that shape how we read her work? In order to answer these questions, this book explores Zora Neale Hurston's popular appeal as iconography, her elevation into the literary canon, her concurrent marginalization in anthropology, and her significant, though often overlooked, contributions to American anthropology. My reading of the critical reception of Hurston's life and work across both canons and within popular culture provides a unique chronicle of Hurston's place in American cultural and intellectual life.

On Canons

From the 1970s through the early twenty-first century, shifting and concurrent trends in Black feminist literary criticism, African American literary criticism, raced and gendered debates concerning canon construction in literature, and a privileging of poststructuralist theory as well as feminist responses to poststructuralism reshaped the terms of Hurston's literary authority and her canonization as a writer. When and where Hurston enters the disciplines of literature and anthropology illuminates the racial and gendered politics of academic authority across these many critical developments. The 1970s saw the booming of a body of literary works by Black women writers. Toni Cade Bambara, Audre Lorde, Toni Morrison, Ntozake Shange, Alice Walker, Sherley Anne Williams, and many others published poetry, drama, and fiction in an era shaped by the civil rights movement, the feminist movement, and other "counterculture" movements of this period. The 1980s and '90s saw the "Canon Wars" emerge as a period of intense critical debates concerning the inclusion of diverse cultural and gendered perspectives in higher education. The conflict stemmed from a backlash against the efforts of a newly diversified student body and professorate that worked to transform the curriculum and the larger academy. Scholars worked to expand the historical record regarding the intellectual traditions of a variety of disciplines—publishing critical articles, editing anthologies, and crafting syllabi that would establish new histories of intellectual thought. Black women literary scholars, many of them feminists, were at the cutting edge in these debates concerning the politics, possible methods, and critical pitfalls in transforming the academy and establishing a Black feminist intellectual tradition. In particular, the critical arguments made by Mary Helen Washington, June Jordan, Ellease Southerland, Barbara Christian, Cheryl Wall, Alice Walker, Deborah McDowell, Michele Wallace, Toni Morrison, Hazel Carby, Ann duCille, and Hortense Spillers are among the many noteworthy discussions that offer multiple lenses on the historical contexts that shaped Hurston's distinctive reception in literary studies. Their discussions explore the tensions between literary theory and methods of evaluating literature during the mid-1990s, which, they argue, affected the terms of tradition building and canon making in African American and Black feminist literary studies.

Some scholars note Hurston's rise and how readily available her work is in the late twentieth and early twenty-first century and have made arguments concerning the implications of Hurston's popularity within the academy (West 2005, 236–42; Carby 1990, 89; Prahlad 1999, 567; Boyce Davies 1994, 7–9; duCille 1993, 80; Wallace 1990, 175). Hazel Carby, Ann duCille, and Michele Wallace have directly challenged Hurston's central position in constructions of a Black feminist literary tradition on the basis that it privileges a narrow reading of Black women's experiences as rural and Southern and thereby excludes consideration of other Black women writers or Black literary themes (Carby 1990, 89; duCille 1993, 80–82). Many of these scholars note how Hurston's centrality excludes many of her contemporaries who, not unlike Hurston, had to overcome structural racism and sexism as well as personal misfortune as they worked to survive as writers and to have their work authoritatively received among the numbers of Black men shaping the discourse of the period known as the Harlem Renaissance. For example, Nella Larsen (1891–1964) published two novels: *Quicksand* (1928) and *Passing* (1929). Each of her works, like Hurston's *Their Eyes Were Watching God* (1937), draws on literary conventions of the "tragic mulatto" to create more nuanced portraitures of sex, class, and race in the United States. In addition, Jessie Redmon Fauset (1882–1961), like Hurston, was a prolific writer, with many of her essays and poems published in *The Crisis*. She served as the magazine's literary editor between 1919 and 1926, and she published four novels: *There Is Confusion* (1924), *Plum Bun* (1929), *The Chinaberry Tree* (1931), and *Comedy: American Style* (1933). Larsen's and Fauset's novels focused more prominently on middle-class characters and communities in Northern and international settings; therefore their works would fail to meet the rubric set by early critical essays seeking to define a Black women's literary tradition in terms that favored Hurston's Southern settings and folksy discourse. Hurston becomes the quintessential "Black woman as writer" at the center of the Black women's literary tradition within a context of communal discourses within the academy that shape the terms of her popularity among educators, students, and a wider reading audience.

DuCille describes the trend in Hurston's popularity (and the concomitant marginalization of other Black women writers) as "Hurstonism" (1993, 69, 80–85). Hurstonism forestalls a critical consideration of the works of other Black women writers and reveals "a bias in current critical practice for vernacular theories of African American cultural production" (81).[2] DuCille's use of the suffix "ism" invites me to consider the reception of Hurston's work as involving and informed by "a distinctive system, doctrine, or theory" ("ism"). In order to do so, I discuss Hurston's canonical reception diachronically across several key publications to illustrate more clearly the discussions that critics were having regarding Hurston's work and to situate and imagine receptions of her work. At times this approach makes it apparent who was reading and citing whom, the politics of which are themselves a feminist concern. In addition, I consider how authority and canons are constructed as examples of "symbolic capital" vis-à-vis citation practices and patterns (Lutz 1990), illuminating shifting theoretical contexts and debates that frame Hurston's reception.

Hazel Carby has questioned the critical attention given to Hurston's iconic novel, *Their Eyes Were Watching God*:

> We need to return to the question of why, at this particular moment in our society, *Their Eyes Were Watching God* has become such a privileged text. Why is there a shared assumption that we should read the novel as a positive, holistic, celebration of black life? Why is it considered necessary that the novel produce cultural meanings of authenticity, and how does cultural authenticity come to be situated so exclusively in the rural folk? (1990, 89)

While Carby's questions focus on Hurston's classic novel, the same questions can be asked concerning the larger interest in and popularity of Hurston as an iconic artist prior to and since her ascent into the American literary canon. Answers to Carby's questions lie not only in our "shared assumption(s)" but also in our shared experiences, or receptions, of popular essays, critical reviews, anthologies, and other cultural works that rhetorically shape our consumption and knowledge of Hurston as an authoritative author.

Beyond the field of Black feminist literary studies, sociologists Sarah M. Corse and Monica D. Griffin, in "Cultural Valorization and African American Literary History: Reconstructing the Canon," analyze Hurston's ascension into the literary canon via a discussion of shifts in reviews and "narrative meanings" of Hurston's *Their Eyes Were Watching God*. Their study considers original reviews of the work in 1937 and the period from 1965 to 1980, when the work was re-received via Alice Walker and other Black feminist writers, to subsequent shifts in the "interpretive criteria" that moved it from the margins to canonical, inclusive of institutional contexts and resources (such as literary conferences and dedicated anthologies) (Corse and Griffin 1997, 173–203). Corse and Griffin ask, "Why is it that the expansion of the canon made *Their Eyes Were Watching God* a classic, but left *other texts* in obscurity? We cannot answer this question without reference both to the text itself and to the concrete actions of specific actors" (198; emphasis mine). It is not clear if by "other texts," Corse and Griffin mean other Hurston works or other works within the African American tradition that are excluded from the literary canon. I consider both possibilities toward an understanding of the politics of authority that define Hurston's place in the academic canon, particularly as an extension of feminist subjectivity. I also consider "the concrete actions of specific actors" through an analysis of the rhetorical constructions of Hurston as a privileged "iconic" subject that sometimes reveal her to be a "token" object of study.

In contrast to Hurston's reception as a significant literary figure in the American literary canon, she is a marginalized cultural anthropologist within the field of American anthropology. During the same period that Hurston was being "discovered" by Alice Walker, anthropologists—particularly Black and feminist anthropologists—were making significant critical interventions to expand the anthropological canon in order to reflect a more diverse history of social scientific discovery. Anthropologists Gwendolyn Mikell, Irma McClaurin, A. Lynn Bolles, and Faye Harrison, among others, have called for more critical research about Hurston's contributions to the field of anthropology, and they question why Hurston remains largely marginalized within the field (Mikell [1990] 1999, 66; Harrison 1995, 242; Bolles 2001, 31; McClaurin 2012). In addition, the postmodern or poststructuralist "turn" in the academy resulted in an increased interest in ethnographies as written texts. The traditional or classic ethnographies were then revealed to be highly constructed works tailored for public consumption and, most importantly, for academic and disciplinary authority. Canonical interventions during this era sought to define and evaluate various experimental modes of ethnographic production and produced anthologies that offered counter-narratives of the discipline's theoretical or conceptual history. This shift in how ethnographies were read created a generative moment for the consideration of Hurston's "experimental" ethnographies. However, she remains largely marginalized, if not invisible, in anthologies that define broad histories of anthropological theory and conceptions of cultural processes. In addition to considering Hurston's ethnographic authority within the discipline of anthropology, I consider whether her success as a literary figure and her cultural iconography limit and bias anthropology's reception of her work.

Genevieve West's study of Hurston's receptions during the Harlem Renaissance offers a historical framework that illustrates the sociopolitical contexts of Hurston's rise within the academy, criticisms of Hurston's inordinate and distinctive literary reception, and the increased availability of her work since the 1970s (2005, 251).[3] West observes, "Hurston has become a convenient figure for study" (251), and in a final chapter titled "The Making of an Icon," West notes Alice Walker's discovery of Hurston, describes some of the positive reviews of Hurston's reprints since the 1970s, and references the publication of key anthologies of Hurston's work that led her "to the center of the new canon" (246).[4] Beyond West's analysis of Hurston's reception and duCille's description of "Hurstonism," I consider how Hurston's iconography is both symbolically and materially reinforced by formal and informal discourses and markets. If Hurston has become a convenient figure in both popular and critical cultures, then what rhetorical modes populate and construct Hurston as iconic and revered? What are the "peopled politics" of Hurston's current cultural authority, and how do constructions of her identity shape her significance?

Hurston's polar reception is distinctive but not unusual. Author Toni Morrison found that the reception of her own first novel, *The Bluest Eye* (1970), was complicated by reviews that mapped expectations of cultural authenticity onto her novel in ways that either heightened or diminished her claims to literary authority. Since the publication of *The Bluest Eye*, Morrison's vast body of work has provided critical arguments against the tokenization of Black writers (Morrison 1989), and she authoritatively navigated the contemporary reception of her own work over a career that spanned decades (Boyce Davies 1994, 9–10). However, Morrison says, "In 1970, when I began writing *Sula*, I had already had the depressing experiences of reading commentary on my first novel, *The Bluest Eye*, by both Black and white reviewers that—with two exceptions—had little merit since the evaluation ignored precisely 'the aesthetics only' criteria it championed. If the novel was good, it was faithful to a certain kind of politics; if it was bad, it was because it was faithless to them" (2004, xii). Noting the complicated and complex receptions faced by numerous African American writers of previous generations, including Zora Neale Hurston, Morrison writes, "It may be difficult now to imagine how it felt to be seen as a problem to be solved rather than a writer to be read" (xii–xiii).[5]

Here Morrison alludes to Hurston's literary receptions during the Harlem Renaissance, when white critics largely read Black writers and their fictional characters as representations of racial types. Black critics, hoping to resist caricatures in the fight against racism, urged Black authors to avoid characterizations that might draw easy comparison to these conventional portraits. For example, Hurston's contemporaries—Alaine Locke, Richard Wright, and others—disparaged her literary work for its seeming adherence to motifs of plantation literature. In a review of *Their Eyes Were Watching God*, Locke wrote:

> Her gift for poetic phrase, for rare dialect, and folk humor keep her flashing on the surface of her community and her characters and from diving deep either to the inner psychology of characterization or to sharp analysis of the social background. It is folklore fiction at its best. But when will the Negro novelist of maturity . . . come to grips with motive fiction and social document fiction? Progressive southern fiction has already banished the legend of these entertaining pseudo-primitives whom the reading public loves to laugh with, weep over and envy. Having gotten rid of condescension, let us now get rid of oversimplification. ([1938] 1993, 18)

Richard Wright's scathing review stated:

> Miss Hurston can write; but her prose is cloaked in that facile sensuality that has dogged Negro expression since the days of Phillis Wheatley. Her dialogue manages to catch the psychological movements of the Negro folk-mind in their pure simplicity, but that's as far as it goes. Miss Hurston *voluntarily* continues in her novel the tradition which was *forced* upon the Negro in the theater, that is, the minstrel technique that makes the "white folks" laugh. ([1937] 1993, 17)

As Locke and Wright were regarded as leading Black voices during this era, their criticisms signaled to audiences that their reading interests should seek different modes of the Black experience beyond the folk life of the Southern United States, and they also cursorily dismissed Hurston's abilities as a writer and an adept critic of sociopolitical life. Their significant influence has been attributed to shaping later receptions of Hurston's work, including Darwin T. Turner's 1971 essay "Zora Neale Hurston: The Wandering Minstrel," which Black feminist critics, like Barbara Smith in "Sexual Politics and the Fiction of Zora Neale Hurston" (1978), critiqued for its "contempt and sarcasm" as well as its summary dismissal of Hurston's literary and anthropological work (Smith 1978, 26; Turner 1971, 89–120).

In addition to racially charged and sexist critical receptions, Hurston, like many writers during the Harlem Renaissance, had to contend with another influential audience: white patrons. She received support for her education and early anthropological expeditions between 1927 and 1932 from a variety of sources, including Annie Nathan Meyer and Fannie Hurst. In particular, Charlotte Osgood Mason, a philanthropist of many Black and white artists, had a contractual agreement with Hurston that limited her rights to publish folklore materials she collected. Hurston biographer Robert Hemenway discusses how Hurston would not begin her more productive period of writing and publishing her fiction and anthropology until their relationship ended in 1933 ([1977] 1980, 32–36). Her major fictional and ethnographic works, *Mules and Men* (1935), *Their Eyes Were Watching God* (1937), and *Tell My Horse* (1938), were produced beyond her relationship with Charlotte Osgood Mason, leaving critics to debate the effect this relationship had on Hurston's subsequent body of work (Hemenway [1977] 1980, 35–36).

In the 1970s Toni Morrison met the challenges of her complex literary receptions and negotiations of the white gaze through a "fidelity to my own sensibility," resulting in a distinctive, authoritative, and aesthetically compelling and enduring literary voice (2004, xii-xiii). Hurston, likewise, met the challenge of her receptions through her determined commitment to reveal the complexity of Black life in the early twentieth century in both her literary and her ethnographic work, despite reviews that insisted she do otherwise. She often powerfully foregrounded her own "speakerly" voice and "signifying" rhetorical strategies (Gates 1988, 181–98). In doing so, she both analyzed and modeled the complex intellectual capacity of individuals and communities within the African diasporic oral and literary traditions beyond the limits of patronage, personal challenges, and public receptions.

During the same period that Toni Morrison and other Black women writers were being recognized for their literary talents, Hurston would be heralded in literary studies by African Americanists who defended her work in light of negative reviews by her Harlem Renaissance peers as well as more recent reviews that continued to regard her work in similar terms. Many of these readings rightly referenced Hurston's studies as an anthropologist as influencing her literary work, although they sometimes lent only circumstantial authority to the folkloric/anthropological quality of that work. However, through these readings they chronicled Hurston's life, analyzed her literary modes and complex themes, and interrogated biased receptions of her work through a variety of critical lenses.[6]

"Zora": Iconic Folk Hero

Folklore critic Sw. Anand Prahlad argues that "everyone is the folk, even the critics themselves" (1999, 565). If we consider criticism about Hurston as a folktale that both critics and laypeople share, then "Zora's" story reads something like this: Zora Neale Hurston was an American author and American anthropologist. A prolific writer, she published successful novels, short stories, poetry, reviews, and ethnographies, and she is largely known for her literary representations of Black Southern folk culture in the United States from the 1930s through the 1950s. Her works went out of print in the mid-twentieth century, but the 1970s brought a resurgent and continuing interest in her literary and cultural productions. This revival is often credited to celebrated poet and novelist Alice Walker's critical and creative interest in redressing the erasure of Hurston's contributions to literature and culture. Hurston is largely remembered for telling and writing stories by and about Black Southern folks and for extending her interests in race and culture beyond the United States to the Caribbean. Outside of Hurston's uneven reception within the ivory tower, she is a popular figure who is celebrated for possessing an unadulterated honesty and defying common expectations of what a Black woman from the South should do, especially during the early twentieth century. She traveled without a male chaperone to locations where no "respectable" woman would go. She smoked cigarettes, she had lovers, and she married and divorced three times. Her novels sometimes celebrated the lives of women and men on the fringes of society, and they delved into "exotic" and "taboo" subject matter, from affairs with younger men to esoteric and vilified practices of hoodoo and Haitian Vodou. She wrote novels that foreground the maligned but witty and gifted voices of common folk, and she wrote novels that exposed and condemned gendered violence and that featured female characters experiencing sexual pleasure. For many years, Hurston was exploited by white patrons and neglected or maligned by Black male artists who failed to see the brilliance of her radical love of Southern folk culture. Her wealthy patron, Charlotte Osgood "Godmother" Mason, financed Hurston's collection of folklore but exerted paternalistic control over its publication and presumably delimited her opportunities in literature and anthropology. Alain Locke, known as "The Dean" of the Harlem Renaissance, and fellow author Richard Wright panned her work for not addressing serious sociopolitical themes. Despite these and other obstacles, she published many novels, ethnographies, and plays and kept company with many elite figures of the Harlem Renaissance, but she died alone and in poverty, virtually forgotten.[7] The contemporary acceptance and celebration of Hurston's body of achievements comes rather late, but now her legacy has been rightfully restored. One who dared proclaim herself the "Queen of the Niggerati" with bold irony and irreverence now wears a posthumous crown as one of America's literary greats.[8]

The stories told *about* Hurston are just as compelling and culturally rich as those told *by* Hurston, and these stories form the testament of her iconic place in our cultural memory. Icons inspire ritual use, and the telling and retelling of the above folk story is a collective ritual that asserts racial pride and autonomy against racial oppression, as well as a Black female empowerment that counters the double jeopardy of racism and sexism. Within this folktale, the folk are often imagined to be closer to slavery and Africa, their folk manners and customs suggest traditions from an ever-distant past, regardless of their present context. The folk are also imagined in opposition to raced and gendered American middle-class mores. Hurston's championing of the folk and her irreverent resistance to middle-class mores of respectability inform iconic portrayals of her legacy. Although she is often thought of as embodying the folkloric trickster who outwits and survives through sleights of tongue, Hurston's iconography is strengthened by her "tragic" ending: obscurity, poverty, and a solitary death were the price she paid for her race, class, gender, and irreverent ways. In this tale, Hurston is not simply a chronicler of the folk; she *is* the folk. A native of the rural American South, she offers readers a firsthand and unmitigated representation of Black culture that assumes its humanity and worth.

Hurston's now ritual commemoration, through the folktale of her resurrection, symbolically rights the wrongs of an unjust past. Her contemporary success is a reparation for the historical injustices of racism, classism, and sexism. It also serves a present function: all who participate in the telling of the testament of her cultural resurrection may also be symbolically redeemed from a shared history and experience of racial, gender, and class oppression.

The folktale of Hurston's restoration suggests an inevitability of her exalted place in our cultured imaginations and, subsequently, in the American literary canon. New readers might be unaware of her disappearance from the literary scene, while many credit Alice Walker's essay "In Search of Zora Neale Hurston" (1975a; later known as "Looking for Zora") and her edited collection of Hurston's work, *I Love Myself When I Am Laughing . . . And Then Again When I Am Looking Mean and Impressive: A Zora Neale Hurston Reader* (1979a) with bringing Hurston's work back to academic and popular audiences.[9] Others may have simply gotten secondhand knowledge about her significance; they viewed a televised documentary or listened to a radio program or podcast that described her importance to a diverse audience of consumers. As readers, listeners, and viewers, we experience the constructions of Hurston that these media offer, consciously and subconsciously. We assume her current status is natural, inevitable, and primarily due to the intrinsic value of her scholarly and artistic work. However, this iconic narrative elides another possible narrative that describes how shifting political interests and critical trends within the contemporary academy shaped a distinctive reception of Hurston's work within literary studies during the '70s through the '90s and into the present moment. The iconic narrative also elides a disparate reception of Hurston's work within the field of anthropology that regards her contributions to the field as unauthoritative. Altogether, these incongruent receptions ultimately reveal that embodied representations of race, class, and gender are inextricably linked to cultural and academic authority. Of course, Hurston's iconic folk story acknowledges her shifting reception during the Harlem Renaissance or New Negro period. Due to reviews informed by "criteria" and "blueprints" of the social and political aims of Black literature, Hurston's work was, respectively, in and then out of vogue. W.E.B. Du Bois's "Criteria of Negro Art" (1926) and Richard Wright's "Blueprint for Negro Writing" (1937) advocated particular political perspectives in the production of the arts over the period. *The New Negro* (1925), edited by Alain Locke, heralded the emergence of a new cultural aesthetic that would challenge the racism of "Old Negro" representations of racial identity through cultural productions in the arts and letters. Hurston's short story "Spunk," written in Black dialect, is included in this collection of literary works and scholarly essays. By the time she published *Their Eyes Were Watching God* twelve years later, Hurston's place in the ranks of the New Negro was questioned. As mentioned previously, Alain Locke and other critics decided that her work was not sufficiently political in its representation of the racial conditions of the time and that her use of Black dialect aligned it with plantation literature traditions that conventionally represented Black individuals and communities stereotypically.

Since then, Alice Walker's celebratory treatment of Hurston's work is most frequently credited with having recast Hurston's life and works in more honorary tones. But rarely do we think beyond the story of her rise to iconic and canonical status as a process involving numerous individuals and a complex web of social and material factors, ideologies, and rhetorical arguments. This book explores the dynamic processes between the politics of the academy, theoretical and political movements, market trends, disciplinary movements and traditions, and the interests of individual scholars who shape our understanding of Hurston's work.

Claimed as a Black feminist intellectual icon in the 1970s, largely because of readings of *Their Eyes Were Watching God* as a Black feminist novel, Hurston's current appeal now extends beyond discussions in women's studies or other classrooms and includes her mass consumption by popular audiences. Productions of plays Hurston authored as well as plays inspired by her life and personality have run Off Broadway to positive reviews in the *New York Times*.[10] Magazine articles, newspaper stories, and radio broadcasts about her life and work regularly appear on National Public Radio (NPR). References to folklore sayings she collected and infamously uttered are found in popular media and obscure cyber locations.[11] While many writers have no biographies, Hurston has several. Robert Hemenway's literary biography of Hurston's life, *Zora Neale Hurston: A Literary Biography* was published to critical acclaim. However, Hemenway, a white male, asserted that "a 'definitive' book—that book remains to be written, and by a black woman" ([1977] 1980, xx). Since then a remarkable number of biographies have been published by Black and white women. Valerie Boyd first answered the call and published *Wrapped in Rainbows: The Life of Zora Neale Hurston* (2003), which provided a Black woman's perspective on Hurston's life.[12] Other biographies include Deborah Plant's *Zora Neale Hurston: A Biography of the Spirit* (2007) and *Zora Neale Hurston's Final Decade* by Virginia Lynn Moylan (2011), each offering compelling and different critical and methodological approaches to Hurston's life. To these life stories add Hurston's own infamous memoir, *Dust Tracks on a Road*

FIGURE 1. "Portrait of Zora Neale Hurston in the 1940s." Literate and bold, Hurston holds a book in her lap; a cigarette is deftly balanced in her hand. (*Atlanta Journal-Constitution* via Associated Press)

(1942); some critics say the autobiography is full of more tales and lies than truth. Hurston's subversive charm, bodacious honesty, and selective memory draw readers, like a good detective story, further within the Hurston mystique. Most recently, Hurston's *Barracoon: The Story of the Last "Black Cargo"* (2018); an edited collection of her short stories, *Hitting a Straight Lick with a Crooked Stick: Stories from the Harlem Renaissance* (2020); and an edited collection of her essays, *You Don't Know Us Negroes and Other Essays* (2022) ever enlarge Hurston's legacy with newly discovered works from the archives.[13]

Every icon has a venerated image, and these images become iconic when their symbolic elements are recognizable and easily transferable. Exchanged on T-shirts, bookmarks, candles, posters, finger puppets, and book jackets, Hurston's image is often figured in a traditional or candid portrait featuring her ubiquitous hat and trademark smile, suggesting that she is approachable and agreeable. Writers have noted how images of Hurston as an icon transfix and inspire, animating her more renegade personality.[14] Regarding one such image of Hurston, anthropologist Irma McClaurin writes:

> By enshrining herself in this photograph, Hurston publicly displays a hidden transcript that resists attempts to limit her. The photograph challenges gender

and racial stereotypes on multiple levels with its depiction of a Black woman holding a book and a cigarette. The confluence of all the symbols combined in this portrait can only represent an intentional challenge. Further, Hurston's gaze can best be described as confident, sassy, and defiant. It is not the theatrical Hurston, whom everyone has come to know—someone who is often caught with a huge smile or laugh on her face. It is the self-assured and defiant Hurston, who dares anyone to challenge her right to read and to smoke. Thus, the image forces the viewer to contend with the person in a straightforward manner, and to realize that the image before them is not to be mistaken for theatrics, mimicry, buffoonery, or some aspect of the minstrel tradition, but is a reality—the real deal. For Hurston to have herself photographed this way is her own display of what she called "the featherbed of resistance." The image is a visual discourse that stands in opposition to and defiance of the gendered experiences of multitudes of Black women whose access to upward mobility during this period was extremely limited. (2012, 52)

McClaurin's analysis of this Hurston image suggests an iconography that defies popular perceptions of her accessibility, given that she is largely known as a humorous and irreverent folk heroine of the U.S. South.[15] Other images of Hurston complicate and extend this reading, at least in their form and prevalence. The hard-won release of a United States postal stamp to honor Hurston's legacy was celebrated at the fourteenth annual Zora Neale Hurston Festival in 2003. Part of the United States Postal Services (USPS) Literary Arts Series, the thirty-seven-cent stamp reproduces a portrait of Hurston by Harlem Renaissance "Negrotarian" Carl Van Vechten.[16] The photo freezes Hurston's ready smile. Her head is adorned with either a felt or wool brim and is accented with a single feather set at a "characteristic" angle.[17] Instead of a solid wall behind her, as in the 1934 Van Vechten photo, there is a Florida landscape in the stamp's background added by the stamp's artist to invoke the rural Floridian setting of Hurston's works.[18] Spanish moss hangs from a longleaf pine or live oak, and the sun sets or rises over a lake and marshy grassland. The idyllic pastoral image inverts the common tale of Hurston's life. She is remembered in this image not as a crucified saint but as a resurrected heroine, the setting or rising sun invoking its own mythic allusions of literary immortality, which the stamp series promises not only to Hurston but to its many celebrated authors as well.[19]

In Hurston's stamp an "immortalized" image evokes several iconic photos that record her crowned in a fashionable brim of the 1920s or '30s. The photo from which the stamp's image is reproduced is only one of a series by Carl Van Vechten. Van Vechten, who produced many portraits of Hurston as well as other Harlem Renaissance figures, took the images featured in the stamp in November 1934. Another, less iconic, photo from the same series shows

FIGURE 2. "Zora! Festival 2013, Festival Booth Featuring Zora Neale Hurston U.S. Postage Stamp." Hurston's iconography circulates like the stamp that bears her image. Part of the United States Postal Services (USPS) Literary Arts Series and inspired by *Their Eyes Were Watching God*, the portrait artfully renders a photograph of Hurston by Carl Van Vechten. (Courtesy of James C. Freeman)

Hurston sans the smile. She wears the same hat but her lips are pursed. Her forehead, once smoothed by her smile, is tense and more serious. Hurston thanked Van Vechten in a letter dated December 10, 1934: "The pictures are swell. I love myself when I am laughing. And then again when I am looking mean and impressive" (Kaplan 2002, 324). These dual images of Hurston (figs. 3 and 4) grace the front and back cover, respectively, of Alice Walker's edited collection by the same name, revealing Walker's recognition of Hurston's full humanity and agency as a writer and scholar.

For this book project, which addresses receptions of Hurston's literary and anthropological work and describes her scholarly contribution as an anthropologist, one image of Hurston stands out. It differs from many other widely circulating images, literally attached to a community that she engaged during her research. It is found within a filmstrip of nine images documenting local women and men in Belle Glade, Florida, likely near Lake Okeechobee around 1935 (fig. 5). The last image in the strip is of Hurston (fig. 6). It strikes a subtle balance between candid and portraiture. Hurston wears no hat and her posture bears no obvious attitude, suggesting an unguarded ease. Her smile is relaxed, revealing no "open-faced laughter." Within the frame to the far right, young children are seated against a shed out of the afternoon sun. Hurston likely played with

FIGURE 3. "Photograph by Carl Van Vechten of Zora Neale Hurston, at Chicago, Illinois, November 9, 1934." Hurston thanked Van Vechten for this and the following photo (fig. 4) in a letter dated December 10, 1934: "The pictures are swell. I love myself when I am laughing. And then again when I am looking mean and impressive." The caption "I Love Myself When I Am Laughing . . ." graces the front cover of Alice Walker's edited collection of Hurston's works. (Carl Van Vechten Papers Relating to African American Arts and Letters, Beinecke Rare Book and Manuscript Library, Yale University)

these children as she faithfully collected the songs they sang and the games they enjoyed, as documented in *Mules and Men* ([1935] 1978, 273–74). She stands in the foreground; beyond her a field of either sweet corn or sugarcane, crops common to the area, extends into the distance. Just beyond her, a narrow dust path cuts and curves, connecting the field's foreground and background and giving the photograph both depth and perspective. Hurston's gaze is slightly averted and thus alludes to her indirect approach as both author and anthropologist.[20]

Hurston acknowledged the levity and the gravity of her personhood and her work. Although she loved herself when she looked "mean and impressive," those images are rarely used to signify her as a serious writer and anthropologist who used varied narrative modes, besides humor, in her fiction and essays to discuss cultural dynamics. The elision of this aspect of her iconography is often reflected in how readers read Hurston. John Lowe states in *Jump at the Sun: Zora Neale Hurston's Cosmic Comedy*:

> Many of her critics, from the 1920s till today, have failed to perceive the serious issues that her humor contains and have consequently missed many

FIGURE 4. "... And Then Again When I Am Looking Mean and Impressive" graces the back cover of Alice Walker's edited collection of Hurston's works. "Photograph by Carl Van Vechten of Zora Neale Hurston, at Chicago, Illinois, November 9, 1934." (Carl Van Vechten Papers Relating to African American Arts and Letters, Beinecke Rare Book and Manuscript Library, Yale University)

aspects of her important messages. Dismissing her and her characters as simple or romantic, they underread and undervalue a profoundly serious, experimental, subversive, and therefore unsettling artist who found the complex humorous traditions of her culture worthy of presentation in their own right, but also useful in furthering her preferred method of writing by indirection. (1997, 2)

The impression that Hurston is accessible and funny, even as she describes serious situations, is perhaps why a similar likeness mistakenly circulates as being that of Hurston. A 1930s photograph of an unknown woman wearing a wide-brimmed straw hat and holding a pack of cigarettes is often erroneously referenced as Zora Neale Hurston, although the record of the image on file at the Library of Congress in the Lomax Collection titles the image "Smiling woman, three-quarter-length portrait of unidentified person standing out-doors" (fig. 7).[21] The image has been used to market "Zora Neale Hurston: Jump at the Sun" (PBS 2008), which was billed as "the first definitive feature-length biography about Zora Neale Hurston" and broadcast on the PBS *American*

FIGURE 5. Hurston traveled with folklorists Alan Lomax and Mary Elizabeth Barnacle to collect African American folk songs in Florida. Images from the field include local men and women and anthropologist Zora Neale Hurston in Belle Glade, Florida, 1935. (Lomax Collection, Library of Congress)

FIGURE 6. Zora Neale Hurston, anthropologist, in the field, Belle Glade, Florida, 1935. Her posture bears no obvious attitude, suggesting an unguarded ease. Her gaze is slightly averted and thus alludes to her indirect approach as both author and anthropologist. (Lomax Collection, Library of Congress)

Masters series to wide acclaim across America.[22] The same image also graces an edited collection of short stories written by Hurston as well as an edited collection of folktales collected by Hurston and is found on several educational and university websites.[23] There are two images of the misidentified woman on file at the Library of Congress. In both, she wears a wide-brimmed straw hat. However, in one picture the woman holds a package of cigarettes, and her smile is tentative. In the other picture, the woman holds a single obscured cigarette, her mouth open in full laughter (fig. 8). What does it mean that this image (this woman) can stand in for Hurston? The "smiling woman" and Hurston do not look alike. Apart from being Black women, the only similarity in McLaurin's favorite image of Hurston and the "smiling woman," for example, is that they both hold cigarettes. However, their images are conflated because of Hurston's iconic legacy as the humorous and irreverent folk heroine of the U.S. South. This project works against the impulse of readings that might misread Hurston's humor; notes the import of her signifying knowledge production, especially for readings of her works in anthropology; and works to raise and answer questions that center Hurston's agency, distinctive scholarship, and commitment to readings of culture that foregrounded community.

Those complex and enduring qualities of Hurston's contributions to studying and representing Black communities through the arts, humanities, sciences,

FIGURE 7. This "unidentified" woman
is often misidentified as the iconic
Hurston. "Smiling woman, three-
quarter-length portrait of unidentified
person standing outdoors. 1935.
Summer." (Lomax Collection, Library
of Congress)

and social sciences are what draw visitors to the annual Zora Neale Hurston
Festival of the Arts and Humanities in Eatonville, Florida. In another example of Hurston's iconic import, the many photos that show Hurston crowned
in a fashionable brim of the 1920s or '30s inspired the "HATitude Brunch,"
held annually at that festival. Women (along with men and children) attend
the popular event dressed in their best hats in celebration of Hurston's legacy.
In addition, the festival features scholarly panels, educational programming
for young people, "fine" and folk art exhibits, live music from popular blues
and R&B artists, and dramatic readings and dance performances.[24] Before the
COVID-19 pandemic, the festival annually reported over fifty thousand attendees to Hurston's "hometown" of Eatonville from all walks of life and from all
over the country.[25] The small city of Eatonville is a mere seven or eight miles
from Orlando, and the festival draws visitors from nearby Disney World and
Epcot Center as well as longtime Hurston fans who make the road trip for the
festival alone. Digital and poster traffic signs direct travelers to Hungerford Park,
where the main art exhibits and festival concerts are typically held. Local radio
and TV stations announce the festival's cultural and historical significance.
Folks of all ilk are encouraged to attend the relatively inexpensive events, which
offer something for everyone's enjoyment: music, festival food, folk and fine
art, handcrafted dolls, African-ethnic clothing, used and new books, public
lectures, and people-watching.[26]

FIGURE 8. Although now referenced in the Lomax Collection as the "Smiling woman, three-quarter-length portrait of unidentified person standing outdoors. 1935. Summer," the image of this "unidentified" woman erroneously circulates in popular and academic media. (Lomax Collection, Library of Congress)

I attended the "ZORA! Festival" in 2002, 2003, 2013, and 2016 on site, and in 2021 I attended the hybrid event virtually. During my visits in 2002 and 2003, the setting of the festival was constructed to represent a Southern town with street signs named after famous Hurston characters and settings from her novels. In 2013 and 2016, the festival space featured a section devoted to Caribbean cultural representations and focused on the global dimensions of Hurston's work, reflecting recent popular and academic trends in discussions concerning globalization and transnationalism, and in 2021 the conference featured a Women's Forum Program that focused on building economic networks between women from Africa and the Americas.[27] Hurston is popularly consumed both as a cultural festival and in the form of memorabilia because she is symbolic of Black diasporic heritage, community pride, empowerment, and resistance—themes that are also referenced in much of the early criticism regarding her life and work. When held locally, the festival includes public academic lectures and educational presentations hosted at the local library and churches, but attendance is greatest near the grounds of the Hungerford School, a public school founded in 1897 as a private vocational high school for African Americans. Along E. Kennedy Boulevard, festivalgoers mill about, "window shop" in the open-air market, or purchase food and art from registered vendors—and, of course, they purchase Hurston souvenirs (fig. 9).[28] Although corporate sponsorship is evident on booth rentals and signage around the park and on the center stage, an artsy and lively communal atmosphere pervades the gathering.

Beyond the festivals, publications, and postal monuments, celebrity icons and their public performances also drive a popular interest in Hurston.[29] In addition to Alice Walker's significant efforts to restore Hurston's legacy, actors and Black Hollywood's power couple Ruby Dee and Ossie Davis have lent their celebrity and theatrical skills to readings and dramatic performances of her life and work. In the twenty-first century, mainstream cultural and celebrity icons Oprah Winfrey and Halle Berry have joined Walker, Dee, and Davis to celebrate and enlarge Hurston's legacy. A movie version of *Their Eyes Were Watching God*, produced by Winfrey and starring Oscar-winning Halle Berry in the role of Janie, Hurston's most celebrated heroine, aired on ABC television in 2005.[30] Although met with mixed reviews, "it produced the best numbers for any made-for-TV movie on any network in nearly six years" ("Their Eyes").[31]

Before the mass commercial success of Hurston's work and life story, many readers in the 1970s and 1980s first read Hurston's *Their Eyes Were Watching God* as college and graduate students in African American literary and feminist classrooms. Now new generations of readers (in secondary, undergraduate, and graduate education) read Hurston's classic novel and create a continued demand for her many works. For young readers, there's the biography *Zora Hurston and the Chinaberry Tree* (1994), along with several richly illustrated children's book versions of Hurston's folktales, including *The Skull Talks Back and Other Haunting Tales* (2004), *The Six Fools* (2005), *The Three Witches* (2006), and

FIGURE 9. "A Family and Festivalgoers at Zora! Festival 2013, Outdoor Festival." Music, festival food, folk and fine art, handcrafted dolls, African-ethnic clothing, used and new books, public lectures, and people-watching draw families and friends to the annual Zora! Festival. (Courtesy James C. Freeman)

Lies and Other Tall Tales (2005). The first three were all adapted by children's author Joyce Carol Thomas with illustrations by Leonard Jenkins, Ann Tanksley, and Faith Ringgold, respectively. *Lies and Other Tall Tales* is both adapted and illustrated by Christopher Myers. These works, marketed to a youth audience, ensure that grade school readers are familiar with the fruits of Hurston's anthropological work long before they encounter her fiction in high school and college. HarperCollins published all three of these books, and as a major publisher of Hurston's reprinted works and many other titles about Hurston, it too is a driving force that supports the "industry" that Hurston has become (Carby 1990, 72). Perhaps the most unassuming evidence of Hurston's place in the literary canon, and the subsequent demand for her work, is the availability and marked consumption of a CliffsNotes version of *Their Eyes Were Watching God* that allows procrastinating students to get a quick synopsis of her enduring work (JBHE 2001, 25). The *Journal of Blacks in Higher Education* (JBHE) reported in a 2001 article titled "Black Authors Don't Know They Have Entered the Literary Canon until They See a Cliffs Notes Version of Their Work" that Hurston's *Their Eyes* is an ever-rising best seller:

> The Cliffs Notes version of Zora Neale Hurston's *Their Eyes Were Watching God* is the best seller among black authors. "The Hurston book has been steadily moving up our list of best sellers since its publication in 1995," Greg Tusbach, senior acquisitions editor at Cliff[s] Notes, told JBHE. "This book and Ralph Ellison's *Invisible Man* are among our top 50 best sellers. Ellison's book has been in our top 50 for some time." (25)

As my ethnographic essay illustrates, the contemporary interest in Hurston's work and her life is significant because of the many ways she is celebrated, recognized, and reproduced as iconic. Hurston is a classic icon, a "revered symbol" that actually embodies and enacts both classic and commercial meanings of the term.[32] Whether she is regarded as a symbol of cultural celebration or commercially consumed as required reading on a course syllabus, Hurston and her work move with ease, it seems, across popular and literary-academic borders.

Like the images of Hurston that are subject to various readings of Hurston's personality, including the possibility of mistaken identity, Hurston's "image" has been received in multiple ways by the academic critics who have helped to ensure that her works will be read by future generations. This book considers those complex receptions in American literature and American anthropology, including parallel chronologies that highlight the cultural politics of Hurston's receptions in the past and present. The sheer numbers of critical articles, monographs, and collected works regarding Hurston's work are too numerous to consider in this book alone. In fact, their numbers, particularly in literary studies, underscore her successful position within the American literary canon. This book reviews the ideas of some Hurston scholars and their key writings, texts, and edited collections, and through these I trace patterns in rhetorical arguments that inscribe Hurston into the literary canon and how these same patterns influence her reception in anthropology. The approach has a snowball, if periodic, effect, whereby one reading recommends another and leaves out others. Therefore, I also relied on my assessment of the cultural significance of certain readings as evidenced by their inclusion within and across multiple anthologies and collected readings, which shape their respective fields.

Anthologies define and shore up a critical discourse. In practice, educators assign anthologies because they are accessible and because they represent the breadth of what students should know about any subject. For all of their omissions, they are portable canons. Although educators often supplement anthologies with additional readings to meet their individual interests and course goals, and although scholars research work beyond collected works for new readings about any subject, anthologies remain foundational, authoritative, and highly persuasive. They remain a site whereby one can discern the "anthologizing process" of the inclusion/exclusion of Black women writers (Bell et al. 1979, xxviii; Boyce Davies 1995, 2: 6–7).[33] The other check I made against the inherent bias in the use of a snowball method occurs in my reading of Hurston's receptions within anthropology. Doing so makes it clearer which patterned ways of reading Hurston and her work do and do not travel across disciplinary lines. This method ultimately reveals a complex answer to two fundamental questions that I ask: (1) What are the discourses that shape Hurston's marginalization within American anthropology? and (2) How did we get there?

Chapter 1, "On Firsts, Foremothers, and the 'Walker Effect,'" analyzes assessments of Zora Neale Hurston's literary work by key scholars in Black feminist literary studies and African American studies from the 1970s to the mid-1980s, the period that spans Hurston's reemergence as a celebrated author. My close reading of Hurston's reception revises some common assumptions about her rise to celebrity and delineates how her iconic status was constructed during this period. Many scholars emphasize Alice Walker's significance, but I demonstrate how a number of scholars galvanized the reclamation of Hurston's literary work, including Black studies scholars Mary Helen Washington, June Jordan, and Ellease Southerland, whose path-breaking essays were published in *Black World* between 1972 and 1974. In addition, Black feminist poet and literary critic June Jordan's "Notes toward a Balancing of Love and Hatred" (1974) provides another frame for understanding how Hurston's work found a critical opening within a largely male-dominated African American literary canon.

This chapter also assesses the "Walker effect," showing how Alice Walker's critical and popular endorsement of Hurston, coupled with Walker's own growing literary import, influenced readings of Hurston's writing.[34] Critical receptions of Walker's affinity for Hurston helped to promote the latter to canonical status, and the rhetorical descriptions of Hurston in several of Walker's essays define a number of tropes and motifs that were repeated in subsequent discussions of her work in both literary studies and anthropology. Walker's own literary interests are quite complex, drawing from myriad literary and cultural influences. Her essays produce what Cheryl Wall describes as "worrying the line," such that Black women's literary traditions are not produced in a "strictly linear fashion" but rather "revise" and "subvert" a variety of genre conventions, influenced by multiple and diverse texts that complicate traditional literary genealogies (2005, 13). Wall notes the considerable under-evaluation of Walker's essays, the criticism of Walker's commitment to feminism and politics in her writing, and the ways that she "defines and extends an inclusive literary legacy": Walker's essays reference not only Hurston but also many writers in the African American and American literary tradition, such as Richard Wright and Flannery O'Connor, among others. Acknowledging the ways in which Walker "worries the line," this chapter considers how the ever-increasing circulation of Walker's essays, through both periodicals and trade anthologies, influenced both popular and critical audiences and laid a foundation for Hurston's reputation as a Black feminist and womanist foremother. Walker's most popular essays, in constant circulation, represent Hurston's literary and ethnographic productions as affirmative and authentic Black cultural works and define Hurston's life as representative of *the* Black woman's experience. Notwithstanding the complex themes addressed in Walker's corpus, these works shaped subsequent Hurston's receptions.

Chapter 2, "Signifying 'Texts': The Race for Hurston," illuminates the larger critical contexts of Hurston's canonization, which involved debates, or signifying texts, in a race to produce criticism that was framed in terms of poststructuralist theory. For example, the impassioned critical arguments between Henry Louis Gates, Joyce A. Joyce, and Houston Baker reveal some of the paradigmatic differences between scholars who argued for or against a privileging of poststructuralist or culturalist readings in defining and analyzing works as texts produced by African American scholars. I contend that these debates foregrounded an inordinate focus on Hurston's most celebrated works, which fulfilled requirements for literary authority across these competing critical interests.

My title also signifies on Barbara Christian's "The Race for Theory" (1987), which argues that Black literary criticism has been influenced by poststructuralist theories in ways that might delimit and even restrict the critical project of

African American literary studies. Supporting and extending Christian's thesis, I show that the race for theory included a concomitant "race for Hurston" to the exclusion of other Black women writers. I trace this race for Hurston in some of the critical literature in order to reveal what Toni Morrison describes as the "brand name application" of literary theories to African American literature and to illuminate the larger contours of "Hurstonism" (Morrison 1989, 9; duCille 1993, 69, 80–85). I argue that the branding of Hurston as ideally, and sometimes exceptionally, theoretical, both within and outside of critical African American and feminist contexts, buttressed her entry into the literary canon.

While some scholars mined *Their Eyes Were Watching God* as the emblematic Black text for discussions of authentic Black or female voice, identity, textuality, and linguistic structures, other scholars, particularly scholars of Black women's literature, questioned the mass attention given to Zora Neale Hurston. Chapter 3, "Deconstructing an Icon: Tradition and Authority," examines selected critical responses to Hurston's central position within constructions of Black feminist literary traditions. Black feminist literary critics worked to enlarge discussions of tradition and expand literary histories by looking back to the nineteenth century and early twentieth century to include Black women writers that preceded Hurston and her contemporaries, including non-Black contemporaries. They also challenged and debated the terms of tradition itself to include experiences beyond the U.S. South and experiences beyond conventional constructions of authentic blackness, both terms so central in early constructions of Hurston's place within Black women's literary tradition. Finally, using Cheryl Wall's concept of "worrying the line," I explore how writers Michele Wallace and Heidi Durrow respond to constructions of Black feminist literary traditions when their "genealogical search is frustrated by gaps in written history and knowledge" (Wall 2005, 8). I also explore how constructions of Hurston's training and anthropological fieldwork support Hurston's authority and sustain new readings of her classic work *Their Eyes Were Watching God*.

The attention given to Hurston as a Southern writer is often reinforced by references to her anthropological studies, given her commitment to representing Southern Black folklore in her literature. Yet, while these references confer scientific authority on her fictional works, they offer limited explanatory contexts for understanding her anthropological works. These trends in reading and writing Hurston are ironic, given the omission of folklore theory from evaluations of her centrality to African American literature and given folklore's own complicated location between the disciplines of English and anthropology. Most important, references to Hurston's anthropological authority within literary studies beg the question of her actual marginalization within anthropology. Chapter 4, "Ain't I an Anthropologist?" considers how critical

trends in the 1990s effectively restricted a consideration of Hurston's conceptual contributions to anthropology. Through a critical invocation of Sojourner
Truth's mythic speech, and in a nod to Nell Painter's study of Sojourner Truth's
iconography in *Sojourner Truth: A Life, a Symbol* (1996), I imagine Hurston asking, "Ain't I an anthropologist?" I examine how Hurston's popular iconography,
which was largely constructed by biographical and literary assessments of her
life and work, as well as the commercial and rhetorical impact of the Walker
effect, discursively transferred across disciplinary boundaries to the field of
anthropology. As in literary studies, the recent reconsideration of Hurston
coincided with the prominence of poststructuralist and postmodernist perspectives within anthropology, as well as the inclusion of critical perspectives
from women and men of color and white women who were then entering
the field in larger numbers. Discourses concerning native, Black feminist, and
feminist anthropology shaped critical debates concerning the politics of race,
class, gender, and sexuality within the academy and the discipline, and these
discourses shaped the terms through which Hurston's work was read as that
of an experimental ethnographer. This chapter offers a detailed and cohesive
explication of the contexts of Hurston's reception within feminist anthropology
and the larger discipline, which have not been discussed in critical treatments
of Hurston's two ethnographies *Mules and Men* and *Tell My Horse*.

Chapter 5, "*Mules and Men*: 'Negro Folklore . . . Is Still in the Making,'" shows
that Hurston presented African American folk culture as dynamic and involving
both intra-group conflict and consensus in making cultural meaning. This was
an important conceptual contribution to anthropology during the 1930s, given
the static portrayals of Black culture and character that stereotyped Black life.
Contemporary critical readings have situated Hurston's ethnographies within
current anthropological frameworks but have not extensively explored her work
in relation to other scholarship on African American culture during the 1930s. I
demonstrate that Hurston's studies were part of a larger trend in ethnographic
experimentalism concerned with documenting and analyzing Black culture in
the United States during that period.

In discussing Hurston's experimental modes, her ethnographic authority,
and her contributions to anthropology, I compare *Mules and Men* with Charles
Johnson's *Shadow of the Plantation* (1934) and Hortense Powdermaker's *After
Freedom: A Cultural Study in the Deep South* (1939). All three authors were
part of a dynamic social-scientific community committed to the study of race
relations in the U.S. South. Each employed innovative approaches and represented a different disciplinary perspective, and they held divergent views
about the legacy of history in African American culture. My analysis highlights
Hurston's interest in documenting the dynamic production of folklore and

her distinctive contribution to critical debates concerning African American acculturation.

Chapter 6, "'Burning Spots': Reading *Tell My Horse*" addresses critical silences concerning her chronicling of the folk beliefs, rituals, and secular practices of people of the African diaspora within the field of anthropology. *Tell My Horse* is often praised as a travel narrative or, alternatively, deplored as an intrinsically flawed ethnography. Hurston's reputation as a literary celebrity and her self-reflexive narrative style inscribe her loyalties to literature and confirm her "undisciplined" status within anthropology. Critics also argue that her views on race, culture, and politics in Haiti and Jamaica reveal her cultural bias and her ethnocentric, even imperialist, assessments of U.S. policies. These designations limit receptions of *Tell My Horse* as a sociocultural study of religious beliefs and social life in these Afro-Caribbean societies. While acknowledging Hurston's narrative style, I argue that her ethnography pays systematic and rigorous attention to local cultural beliefs and practices and situates them within broader institutional and historical contexts. In addition, I discuss Hurston's methodology for the study of folk religion and describe her commitment to challenging stereotypical views of Vodou.

Within a Black feminist praxis perspective, I am concerned with chronicling the contributions of Black women writers and intellectuals to the production of knowledge. My interdisciplinary approach to reading Hurston provides a distinctive context for evaluating her work as a writer and anthropologist. Hurston's differing receptions across disciplinary boundaries prescribe a move against feminist icon and canon making because they privilege a special and individualized status of the works of a few token writers or works over a more inclusive and fluid set of works for critical engagement. I not only consider whether, when, and where constructions of feminist icons and imagined communities remain important as rhetorical and pragmatic strategies within academic discourse, but I also emphasize the importance of historical contextualization for producing transformative ways of reading individual and collective contributions to knowledge production within the academy. The implications of this perspective for Black feminist studies (particularly for literary scholars and anthropologists who perhaps find themselves strange bedfellows vis-à-vis the work of Zora Neale Hurston) are significant as the field moves forward in its efforts to transform the academy within and across disciplinary divides and beyond.

1

On Firsts, Foremothers, and the "Walker Effect"

The dominant narrative of Hurston's reemergence as a major literary figure often includes Hurston's "discovery" by Alice Walker. Celebrated author of *The Color Purple* (1982), Walker was the first African American woman to win a Pulitzer Prize for Literature and the first to win the National Book Award for Fiction. The author of several acclaimed novels and collections of poetry, she is also a noted civil and human rights activist, with her writings lauded for both their literary strengths as well as their distinctive and often groundbreaking representations of the pernicious influence of racism and sexism on the interior lives of Black people.[1] During the 1970s, Walker's critical and popular endorsement of Hurston, reinforced by her own growing literary import, significantly influenced receptions of Hurston's writing. The rhetorical descriptions of Hurston in several of Walker's essays define a number of tropes and motifs that were repeated in subsequent discussions of her work in both literary studies and anthropology. In particular, Walker represents Hurston's literary and ethnographic work as affirmative and authentic Black cultural works and, at times, defines Hurston's life as representative of *the* Black woman's experience. Her writings about Hurston significantly influenced Hurston's reputation as a model of Black womanhood and a literary foremother.

Walker's "foremother" archetype revised persistent references to forefathers as the theoretical and institutional founders of disciplines. Her assertion of Hurston as her literary foremother occurred within a larger context of women activists' efforts to question structures of patriarchy and define alternatives to patrilineal descent that structured knowledge production, institutions, and social relationships. Feminist scholars, informed by their experiences in consciousness-raising groups in the women's liberation movement, were raising questions about the sources of women's oppression. If a source was the patriarchal family, as many argued, then how might mothers and the experience of motherhood be considered and defined? Across many fields and disciplines, they defined and imagined maternal intellectual genealogies as untapped sources of knowledge, sources that they and their daughters might draw from to confirm their shared experience of oppression and to empower collective action against that oppression.[2] Many of these intellectual genealogies, however, included only white women, leaving Black women scholar-activists and other women of color to define and defend their own genealogies and "her-stories."

While Alice Walker is often cited as having discovered Zora Neale Hurston, earlier essays by scholars Mary Helen Washington, June Jordan, and Elleease Southerland, published in *Black World*, began a reclamation and evaluation of Hurston's literary work during the early 1970s in terms of Black consciousness and women's empowerment.[3] *Black World*, previously known as *Negro Digest*, was a leading periodical for a largely Black audience, which published critical scholarship on Black art, politics, and letters since its founding in 1942. Altogether the essays of Washington, Jordan, and Southerland established a Black woman's literary space within the periodical. Within a larger context of the civil rights movement and Black Arts era, their essays also signal an emerging contemporary Black feminist activism and criticism in the late 1960s and early 1970s. Their essays and discussions reflect an affirmative re-visioning of the Black experience through literature and reveal a concern with shaping a racial and gendered consciousness regarding the experiences of Black Americans through readings of Hurston's work.[4]

Mary Helen Washington's "The Black Woman's Search for Identity" argues that Janie's search for identity is a search for Black identity, rooted in the "Black" experience of the folk (1972, 71–74) and in terms that reinforce Black love and community. Washington describes *Their Eyes Were Watching God* as having captured the "miracle of Black love" that has survived "despite the inhuman definitions of man-hood and womanhood that have been forced upon us" (69). She describes Janie's quest for identity as "her search for Blackness" that evolves over the course of her three marriages and culminates with her marriage to Tea Cake. Theirs is a relationship that symbolizes a "centered[ness] in the Black community" as they work "down on the muck" alongside other workers (74).

Washington's discussion of Hurston's novel as an affirming text also defines "Blackness" as a singular and un-diversified experience.[5] Within her essay, main characters of *Their Eyes* fall into two categories: those who are alienated from the Black community because they aspire to "standards dictated by white society" (Nanny, Jody Starks, and Mrs. Turner) and those who are the Black community (Tea Cake and the workers on the muck) (71). Given the particular political and economic assault on Black communities and families in the early 1970s and the momentum of Black activist and cultural movements committed to resisting anti-Black prejudice and violence, this assessment resonated with contemporary Black audiences. *Their Eyes* certainly denotes Black communities with complex characterizations that represent varied racial politics and sociocultural experiences and customs. In addition, feminist critics have since provided readings of Janie and Tea Cake that complicate, for example, Janie and Tea Cake's relationship. The novel, of course, reveals that Tea Cake, the otherwise romanticized hero, beats Janie and justifies his abuse of her as his way of showing Mrs. Turner (and the community) that he has power and controls their relationship. Mrs. Turner, who covets Janie's European features and despises darker Black people, befriends Janie because they are both white in appearance. She speaks ill of Tea Cake and suggests that Janie should meet her brother, boasting that he has straight hair and that he publicly disparages Booker T. Washington. Tea Cake overhears their conversation and later decides to beat a silenced Janie in front of Mrs. Turner and her brother "tuh show dem Turners who is boss" (Hurston [1937] 1998, 147–48). The circumstances that prefigure Tea Cake's violence against Janie reveal a complex politics of color, class, and gender within the novel's Black communities that critics have argued make a romantic reading of *Their Eyes* as a "miracle of Black love" difficult (Washington 1987).

Washington would revisit the novel and Janie's place within the Black folk community within a later essay titled "'I Love the Way Janie Crawford Left Her Husbands': Emergent Female Hero," originally published in her work *Invented Lives: Narratives of Black Women 1860–1960*. She rightly complicates feminist readings of Janie as essentially empowered in a reading of the novel that underscores Janie's silent response to Tea Cake's beating (Washington [1987] 1993, 102). However, I would argue that the sole focus on Janie's voice tempers our understanding of how community voices figure in Hurston's work in this case to reveal a community's problematic romanticization of domestic violence. The community of the muck view Janie's and Tea Cake's highly emotional and public displays of silent despair (Janie) and audible regret (Tea Cake) romantically. While critics note that we don't hear Janie's voice (Washington [1987] 1993,

102; duCille 1993, 123), we are told that the "women see visions" and the "men dream dreams" when Teacake and Janie display a honeymoon phase immediately following the incident (Hurston [1937] 1998, 147). The community's response suggests that the domestic violence that occurs on the muck happens often enough and with some common patterns that distinguish Janie's and Tea Cake's versions as "romantic" by comparison. For one, women on the muck may raise their voices and fight back. As Sop-de-Bottom complains, "Mah woman would spread her lungs all over Palm Beach County, let alone knock out mah jaw teeth" (148). In response, Tea Cake explains to Sop-de-Bottom that Janie is "uh high time woman and uster things," wrongly implying that Janie's wealthy class status shapes her "respectable" silent response to domestic assault (148). The complicated politics of race, class, color, and gender hierarchies within these varied exchanges (between Tea Cake, Janie, Mrs. Turner, Sop-de-Bottom, and the men and women on the muck) illustrate how Hurston offers a less than idyllic and complex representation of Black life and love in *Their Eyes*. Hurston effectively centers the problem and prevalence of domestic assault in her novel, and Janie's silence strategically increases the narrative suspense. Near the novel's end, readers might wonder whether she will be able to defend herself against a rabies-maddened Tea Cake when his latent jealous streak fatefully remerges.

Again, Mary Helen Washington's early work on Hurston published in *Black World* lay a critical foundation for an even more focused assessment of her contributions to Black literature. Two years later, the August 1974 issue of *Black World* featured an image of Zora Neale Hurston on its front cover with the caption "Black Women Image Makers."[6] Two articles concerning Hurston's life and work are included within this issue: June Jordan's "Notes toward a Balancing of Love and Hatred" and Ellease Southerland's "The Novelist-Anthropologist's Life/Works." Jordan describes Hurston's *Their Eyes* as "the prototypical novel of affirmation," which, in contrast to Richard Wright's *Native Son* (1940), emanates from Hurston's experiences within a "supportive, nourishing" environment (Jordan 1974, 6). Noting that Richard Wright "has been presented as a solitary figure on the literary landscape of his period," Jordan describes how Hurston's erasure comes from readings that ignore her focus on Black love, perhaps viewing it as a less important aspect of Black life (5). Jordan calls for readings of both *Native Son* and *Their Eyes* to provide a more balanced discussion of their literary import: "But rightly we should not choose between Bigger Thomas and Janie Starks; our lives are as big and as manifold and as pained and as happy as the two of them put together" (7). Jordan further offers a cautionary statement that would prove prophetic in terms of Hurston's later reception: "We should absolutely resist the superstar, one-at-a-time mentality that threatens the varied and resilient, flexible wealth of our Black future, even as it shrinks and obliterates incalculable segments of our history" (9). In advancing Hurston's *Their Eyes* as an alternative literary representation of Black life and culture, Jordan warns against an iconizing impulse in the reception of Black literary works and argues that the "one-at-a-time mentality" originates with the "glare of white, mass-media manipulation" that chooses one Black literary "star" (4). Her appeal, directed to an audience of *Black World*, encouraged general readers and scholars to resist the mass media in its efforts to focus primarily on the merits of one Black author. One wonders if Jordan ever imagined that Hurston might succeed Wright as a literary "superstar" and that she would become such a central literary figure that years later critics such as Hazel Carby, Ann duCille, and Michelle Wallace would begin to question the inordinate attention given to her work.

Ellease Southerland's "The Novelist-Anthropologist's Life/Works" (1974) provides a biographical summary of Hurston's life and includes a discussion of her anthropological training and folklore research. She also provides summaries of some of Hurston's major works: *Jonah's Gourd Vine* (1934), *Mules and Men* (1935), *Their Eyes Were Watching God* (1937), *Tell My Horse* (1938), *Moses, Man of the Mountain* (1939), and a brief reference to *Seraph on the Suwanee* (1948).[7] In addition to Southerland's and Jordan's articles, the main section of the periodical features Mary Helen Washington's "Black Women Image Makers" and Alvin Ramsey's "Through a Glass Whitely: The Televised Rape of *Miss Jane Pittman*."[8] Washington's article describes how Black women authors Maya Angelou, Alice Walker, Gwendolyn Brooks, Paule Marshall, and Toni Cade Bambara use literature to revise negative stereotypes of Black women, while Ramsey challenges the "distortion" of Ernest J. Gaines's *The Autobiography of Miss Jane Pittman* in the televised version of the novel (Ramsey 1974, 31). The focus on gender and race in these four articles, along with Hurston's front cover image, give this issue of *Black World* a decidedly Black woman's focus, with Hurston as the framing icon. The "Black Women Image Makers" issue stands as a record of a larger reassessment of Hurston's life and work within Black studies.

The publication of this issue came during an era of increased publication of writings by and about Black women. A number of heralded collections of Black women's critical literature, essays, and creative writings emerged during the late 1960s and early 1970s as the U.S. feminist movement, civil rights movement, and Black Arts era overlapped in their interests in Black women's issues and political empowerment.[9] Alice Walker, now known as a celebrated Black feminist/womanist poet, essayist, lecturer, activist, and short story author, began her literary career during this period.[10] Among her many writings, between 1974 and 1979 Walker published essays and a public lecture that high-lighted the life and work of Zora Neale Hurston: "In Search of Our Mothers' Gardens: The Creativity of Black Women in the South" (1974), "In Search of Zora Neale Hurston" (later titled "Looking for Zora") (1975), "Saving the Life That Is Your Own" (1975), "Zora Neale Hurston: A Cautionary Tale and a Partisan View" (1977), and "On Refusing to Be Humbled by Second Place in a Contest You Did Not Design" (1979). These essays were published and republished in several widely circulated sources, including *Ms.* magazine, the first nationally circulated feminist magazine in the United States.

Walker's early Hurston essays are very persuasive and had a collective influ-ence on critical and popular readers, prompting a national and international audience beyond U.S. Black feminist circles and allies to begin consuming Hurston's works. The ways in which Walker's essays are read, consumed, and remain in demand were and are in many aspects beyond Walker's individual or ultimate control. The Walker and Hurston association depends on Walker's rhetorical skills, audience demand, and powerful institutional (academic and publishing) support. Moreover, audiences are captivated by her powerful poetic voice that has remained true to a communal and political ethos alongside sig-nificant shifts in Hurston's reception within the critical literature.

Although Walker has been credited with discovering Hurston, the five essays listed above, taken together, reveal that Hurston's work, although out of print, was in circulation among writers and teachers like herself. Walker's rhetorical construction of Hurston's "discovery" popularized Hurston to a broader audi-ence while calling for greater awareness and support of many Black women writers.[11] However, her expression of great veneration for the work of Zora Neale Hurston was not lost on multiple audiences, including civil rights and feminist audiences, with an ever-increasing interest in reading literature by Black women. In claiming Hurston as her literary foremother, Walker's own growing literary status as a writer propelled the mass interest in Hurston's personal-ity and in her literary and ethnographic productions. Significantly, Walker's essays were often paired with readings of Hurston's fiction, most often *Their Eyes Were Watching God*, in both literature and women's studies classrooms.[12] Articles in *Black World* reintroduced Hurston to a largely Black audience, but Alice Walker's crossover appeal ensured that a much larger and diverse popular audience would readily read Hurston's work.

Almost fifty years later, Walker is often credited with placing Hurston at the forefront of the Black female literary tradition and with introducing Hurston and her work to American popular culture and to the American literary canon. However, scholars have questioned how Hurston became an icon and how her work—in particular, *Their Eyes Were Watching God*—reached canonical status.[13] How was Zora Neale Hurston represented in these early essays so that she garnered a unique critical and popular attention apart from other Black women writers who are comparatively given less critical attention? Some scholars and critics, noting Hurston's massive popularity, have employed spiritual metaphors to describe the kind of attention given to Zora Neale Hurston and her most popular work, *Their Eyes Were Watching God*. As early as 1978, an article in the *Washington Post* described the beginning of the resurgent interest in Hurston as cult-like.[14] Literary critic Hortense Spillers describes spiritual, mythic, and mysterious aspects in Hurston's reception: "Talking about Zora Neale Hurston is like approaching the Sphinx—so much riddle, so many faces, and all of it occurring on fairly high holy ground since Alice Walker's remarkable discovery a couple of decades ago" (2004, 94).[15] Literary scholar Ann duCille, also employing spiritual or mythic metaphors, has referenced the unprecedented accord and canonical consumption of her work as "Hurstonism": "The legend of Zora is of biblical proportions: what once was lost now is found" (2005, 2).[16] In fact, many of Alice Walker's early essays employ a "what once was lost now is found" motif that, in part, illustrates and celebrates her "discovery" of Hurston. The essays' rhetorical arguments greatly shaped how some critical and popular readers of Hurston's work would understand and represent Zora Neale Hurston's life and literary contributions.[17]

The first of these essays, "In Search of Our Mothers' Gardens: The Creativity of Black Women in the South," was published by *Ms.* in May 1974 and is perhaps Walker's best-known essay.[18] Despite brief references to Hurston, it is significant as a "lost and found" Hurston story because a part of its title and its general sentiment is repeated in "In Search of Zora Neale Hurston," which was published the following year. It is also a foundational Walker effect essay in its focus on themes that would shape how Walker subsequently wrote about Hurston's life and influence, including themes of foremothering, references to authentic Black experience, and overcoming racial and gender oppression. Walker argues that Black women should look for the "genius" of their mothers', grandmothers', and great-grandmothers' creativity in the "low" or everyday arts such as quilting, gardening, and storytelling. For Walker, Black women were without "a room of their own," and despite the constraints of racism, sexism, and economic poverty, they created artistic genius in practical everyday forms.[19] In the essay, Walker mentions Phillis Wheatley along with Nella Larsen and Zora Neale Hurston as having created literary works despite their "contrary instincts." Walker says, "For when we read the poetry of Phillis Wheatley—as when we read the novels of Nella Larsen or the oddly false sounding autobiography of the freest of all black women writers, Zora Hurston—evidence of 'contrary instincts' is everywhere. Her loyalties were completely divided, as was, without question, her mind" ([1974] 1983, 236).[20]

At the time of Walker's essay, proponents of the Black Arts movement criticized Wheatley's work for its lack of a Black racial aesthetic. Walker defends Wheatley by explaining that references to "white" themes existed because of the conditions of her enslavement, and she argues that instead of ridiculing her themes and form, readers should celebrate Wheatley for creating art against seemingly insurmountable odds (237).[21] The conclusion of Walker's essay places more emphasis on Phillis Wheatley's life and accomplishments than on those of Zora Neale Hurston. However, Walker focused more centrally on Hurston in subsequent essays as she worked to make sense of the "contrary instincts" that, she argued, defined Hurston's sensibility as a writer. In essays, public lectures, and in the subject matter of her novels, she more pointedly defined an affinity for Hurston's life story, cultural background, and fictional themes. When Hurston is briefly noted in "In Search of Our Mothers' Gardens," she is not only mentioned in terms of "contrary instincts" but also as being the "freest of all black women writers" (236). The former representation later emerged in the criticisms of scholars, including anthropologists, as they worked to explain the experimental forms of Hurston's ethnographies. The latter reference revealed how Walker would single out Hurston's literary contributions in future essays in exceptional terms.

"In Search of Zora Neale Hurston" is Walker's first essay that significantly addresses Hurston. Because it was published just ten months later in the same national feminist magazine, readers might surmise by its title that Walker's "mothers' gardens" originated with the work of Zora Neale Hurston rather than in Phillis Wheatley.[22] In this essay Walker again employs a lost-and-found motif as she recounts her first trip to Hurston's "birthplace," Eatonville, Florida, where readers learn the many ways that Hurston is "lost" not only to Walker as a literary foremother but also to Hurston's hometown and larger Black community. However, with the essay's publication in *Ms.*, the "lost" Hurston would be found by a diverse feminist national reading audience who were also eager to address the invisibility of women of color in the literary arts.

Walker's essay begins with a quotation from Robert Hemenway's "Zora Hurston and the Eatonville Anthropology" (1972) that foreshadows the essay's tone and setting. Hemenway writes, "Zora Neale Hurston died without funds to provide for her burial, a resident of the St. Lucie County, Florida, Welfare Home.[23] She lies today in an unmarked grave. . . . Zora Neale Hurston is one of the most significant unread authors in America, the author of two minor classics and four other major books" (Walker 1975, 74). Walker's use of Hemenway's opening quotation frames a persuasive narrative that critiques the American literary society's ignorance of Hurston and recounts Walker's search for biographical information about Hurston. Walker poses as Hurston's niece in order to more easily gain information concerning Hurston's later life, and although there are flashes of Hurstonesque humor in Walker's narrative, her search for "Zora" becomes a somber search for Hurston's missing grave.[24] When she finds the gravesite, Walker, still posing as Hurston's niece, purchases a marker for the site in honor of Hurston's legacy.

Funeral rituals are symbolic and material demonstrations of cultural beliefs about family obligation and honor. The gesture of putting a marker on Hurston's grave has a powerful symbolic and real effect. The monument that Walker placed at Hurston's unmarked grave reads "Zora Neale Hurston, 'A Genius of the South,' Novelist, Folklorist, Anthropologist, 1901–1960" (Walker [1975] 1983a, 107). With the ritual act of placing a headstone on Hurston's lost and neglected gravesite, Walker inscribes Hurston into a place of honor and confirms her kinship with Hurston as she transforms it from fabled to fictive kin. The story of Walker's trip to Eatonville eventually framed Hurston's inscription into the literary canon, as subsequent popular and critical essays regarding Hurston's work often begin or end by recounting Walker's placement of a headstone on Hurston's abandoned gravesite.[25] These acknowledgments to Walker happen so frequently in the critical and popular literature that they have become their own rhetorical ritual.[26]

Of course, Walker's essay works to persuade readers that more than Hurston's physical body has been lost to readers: her corpus deserves more critical exploration. Walker's essay reinforces this point by interweaving the narrative of her search for Hurston's grave with italicized commentary that illustrates that Hurston was unfairly criticized by critics of the era, that she is sorely unrecognized by the town she grew up in, and that biographical details of her intriguing life story remain incomplete. For example, in addition to Hemenway's opening quote, commentary from Hurston contemporaries Arna Bontemps and Langston Hughes are juxtaposed by comments from anonymous readers (a librarian and students from Wellesley College and Yale University), all complicating the mystery of Hurston's life story and compelling readers to go on their own search for Hurston. One such quote, attributed to "Student, Special Collections Room, Beinecke Library, Yale University," reads, "You have to read the chapters Zora *left out* of her autobiography" (Walker 1975, 86). Alongside the narrative suspense of the search for Hurston's grave and the great pathos that Walker's prose invokes, I imagine the essay created a bandwagon effect for audiences, leaving readers to question, "Why don't *I* know more about Zora Neale Hurston?" and even convinced of their duty to learn more about her and to do so with great reverence.[27]

The third of Walker's Hurston essays, "Saving the Life That Is Your Own: The Importance of Models in the Artist's Life," was delivered as a public lecture in December 1975 at a meeting of the Modern Language Association (MLA) in San Francisco. Walker's central thesis is that artists need models in order to sustain their lives, both figuratively and literally. Walker begins the essay with the example of Vincent Van Gogh, whom she describes as a prolific artist who sold only one painting during his lifetime and whose life tragically ended in suicide. She notes that Van Gogh discussed that he had a lack of models for his work in a letter written shortly before his death.

Using the word "models" metaphorically, Walker describes her critical impressions of *Their Eyes Were Watching God* and *The Awakening* by Kate Chopin (1899) as examples of differences in plot resolutions in novels written by Black and white authors, respectively. Walker especially bemoans how students have not been taught *Their Eyes* because "it was written by a black woman." She says, "Loving both these books, knowing each to be indispensable to my own growth, my own life, I choose the model, the example of Janie Crawford. And yet this book, as necessary to me and to other women as air and water, is again out of print" (Walker [1975] 1983b, 7). Walker again describes how she "discovered" Hurston as she gathered research for a short story. Walker wanted the short story to involve aspects of "Voodoo" as a central plot element. However, as Walker researches for data, she continuously encounters racist descriptions (written by white researchers of "Voodoo"):[28]

> Well, I thought, where are the *black* collectors of folklore? Where is the *black* anthropologist? Where is the *black* person who took the time to travel the back roads of the South and collect the information I need: how to cure heart trouble, treat dropsy, hex somebody to death, lock bowels, cause joints to swell, eyes to fall out, and so on. Where was this black person? (11; Walker's emphases)[29]

Walker recounts that she eventually finds Hurston within a footnote to the "white voices of authority" (11). She then provides a brief biographical description of Hurston. She begins four of the paragraphs' sentences with "Zora" and twice repeats "*That Zora*" (12; Walker's emphasis). The aural effect of this intonation elevates Hurston's significance. It is also noteworthy that she uses Hurston's first name so that Hurston is at once elevated and made familiar. Walker later states that had Hurston's work been "lost," then Walker's own "mother's story would have had no historical underpinning, none I could trust, anyway." Walker also mentions that the short story she wrote drawing on Hurston's work is listed as "one of the *Best Short Stories of 1974*." Walker suggests that she owes this achievement to Hurston, asserting that she would not have written the story "had I not known that Zora had already done a thorough job of preparing the ground over which I was then moving" (13).

Walker's lecture underscores the lack of access to books written by Black women, and its tone resonates with the discourse of the Black Cultural Arts movement that espoused a politicized perspective on the production of Black arts and letters.[30] In addition, the essay particularly encourages the audience/ reader to consider that Walker's success is directly related to the influence of Hurston's work. She briefly mentions other literary "models"; however, the effect of the entire essay firmly ties Hurston to Walker, one of the central figures of a new generation of circa 1970s Black writers.[31] The significance of genealogies is reinforced via Walker's discussion of how the acclaimed short story is inspired by her biological mother and Zora Neale Hurston, whom she claims as her literary foremother. Furthermore, beyond the reference to Van Gogh's suicide, the essay's argument (that models are needed to save one's life) is an urgent appeal. It may not have been lost to listeners—and, later, readers—of the lecture that Walker considered suicide when faced with no options for a safe abortion as a young woman, an event that her first published book of poetry, *Once* (1968), openly chronicled (White 2004, 114–18). Walker makes a feminist and fearless admission in this literary work, especially given that abortion was illegal at the time. The same themes of Black female oppression, vulnerability, creativity, and strength would be taken up in Ntozake Shange's acclaimed choreopoem, *For Colored Girls Who Have Considered Suicide/When the Rainbow Is Enuf*, originally produced on Broadway in 1975 and later published in 1976. The importance of psychologically complex and fully human and political representations of Black women in the arts and popular media were beginning to resonate with U.S. audiences and certainly charged the reception of Walker's lecture.

Walker's address came at a time that marked the beginning of an increase in literary publications of contemporary Black women writers (Walker among them) by mainstream publishers, and Hurston's works were included in this wave because of Walker's essays and lectures. An excerpt from Mary Helen Washington's foreword to the 1990 and 1998 reprints of *Their Eyes* describes the context of Walker's lecture and subsequent responses:

> By 1975, *Their Eyes*, again out of print, was in such demand that a petition was circulated at the December 1975 convention of the Modern Language

Association (MLA) to get the novel back into print. In that same year a conference on minority literature held at Yale and directed by Michael Cooke, the few copies of *Their Eyes* that were available were circulated for two hours at a time to conference participants, many of whom were reading the novel for the first time. In March of 1977, when the MLA Commission on Minority Groups and the study of Language and Literature published its first list of out of print books most in demand at a national level, the program coordinator, Dexter Fisher, wrote: "*Their Eyes Were Watching God* is unanimously at the top of the list." (Washington [1990] 1998, xii–xiii)

In 1977, Walker's "Zora Neale Hurston: A Cautionary Tale and a Partisan View," was published as the foreword (dated December 1976) in Robert E. Hemenway's *Zora Neale Hurston: A Literary Biography* (1977).[32] In this essay, Walker again describes how she found Hurston. However, Walker revises her earlier "lost and found" story of finding Hurston as she prepared to write a short story that involved Vodou. She explains that she had heard of Hurston for the first time while auditing a Black literature course taught by Margaret Walker:[33]

> The reason this fact later slipped my mind was that Zora's name and accomplishments came and went so fast. The class was studying the usual "giants" of black literature: Chesnutt, Toomer, Hughes, Wright, Ellison, and Baldwin, with the hope of reaching LeRoi Jones very soon. Jesse Fauset, Nella Larsen, Ann Petry, Paule Marshall (unequaled in intelligence, vision, [and] craft by anyone of her generation, to put her contributions to our literature modestly) and Zora Neale Hurston were names appended, like verbal footnotes, to the illustrious all-male list that paralleled them." (Walker 1977, xi)

Walker's point, of course, is that Black women writers were often cursorily overlooked, even in academic courses expressly committed to Black literature. Notably, Hurston is but one of many Black women "lost" to the Black literature course, which Walker carefully notes, while even emphasizing the contribution of writer Paule Marshall. Larsen, Fauset, Petry, and Marshall were all Northern-born, but, as Walker later explains, her particular interest in rural Southern customs and her interest in Vodou as contexts for her short story led her to develop a keen interest in Hurston. Walker, a Black woman Southern writer, felt that she was without the literary models she needed to fictionalize the stories of Southern African Americans that resisted stereotypes of Southern Black folkways through dimensional and nuanced characterizations. Notably, she draws inspiration from Hurston's ethnography *Mules and Men*, which she calls "perfection." She praises *Mules and Men* and notes its appeal to her Southern relatives, many of whom were living in the North. The book reminded them of stories and customs from their Southern past. Because of the affirming effect that *Mules and Men* had on her Northern urban relatives with Southern roots, Walker asserts, "This was the first indication of the quality I feel is most characteristic of Zora's work: racial health, a sense of black people as complete, complex, *undiminished* human beings, *a sense that is lacking in so much black writing and literature*" (emphasis mine). Walker later contends that Hurston's "racial health" is defined by her attention to diasporic issues, attributed to her having grown up in a community of Black people: "In her easy self-acceptance, Zora was more like an uncolonized African than she was like her contemporary American blacks, most of whom believed, at least during their formative years, that their blackness was something wrong with them" (Walker 1977, 86). Walker says that if she were condemned on a desert island and allowed only two books, they would be Hurston's *Mules and Men* and *Their Eyes Were Watching God*, about which she states, "*There is no book more important to me than this one*" (86; Walker's emphasis).

Walker's affinity for Hurston is undeniable, and the distinctions she gives to Hurston's ethnography and writing elevate Hurston's work as distinctive in its ability to describe Black people's lives as complex. More pointedly, Walker's assessment reveals a Black Arts aesthetic mandate that Black art should represent Black people in ways that support "racial health" vis-à-vis an "uncolonized" African consciousness. Although not characteristic of all Black Arts or Black aesthetic productions, some of the early influential theorists of these movements during the late 1960s and early 1970s defined "Black Art" through a rejection of European influences and middle-class values (D. Smith 1991, 94). Critics like LeRoi Jones (Amiri Baraka), Larry Neal, and Addison Gayle produced anthologies of poetry and political essays that defined a variety of Black aesthetic interests but that sometimes assumed an authentic and singular blackness (D. Smith 1991, 94, 95–98). Collectively, their goals were to establish an autonomous and community-based art form in response to heightened political unrest and sustained racial oppression against African Americans. Artists and writers created productions to serve and uplift African Americans through the promotion of cultural practices not often dramatized or expressed in Western arts. These included embracing a range of social practices as distinctively Black and linked to African traditions. The Black experience was defined through the celebration and practice of African-inspired performativity in dance, song, attire, hairstyles, music, and poetry and in the production of literature that sought to represent this experience. Black women decisively shaped these literary efforts, including the works of Mari Evans, Audre Lorde,

Sonia Sanchez, Nikki Giovanni, June Jordan, Gwendolyn Brooks, and Alice Walker, which often displayed a revolutionary tenor in their portrayal of the experiences of Black women.

Within this context, Walker's judgment of other Black literature as "lacking" in comparison to Hurston's body of work is an ironic "cautionary tale." In the 1930s and '40s, Hurston failed to meet the standards of "the race" and was therefore marginalized as a writer, and by the 1970s her work is represented by Walker as the standard of "racial health" by which all other Black literature might be compared.[34] The title of Walker's 1977 essay declares her "partisan view" of Hurston, and her distinctive attention to Hurston (as opposed to the other footnoted Black women writers) is explained within the context of her own valid interests as a Southern writer. By 1977 Walker had published several collections of poetry and two novels. Her singular statement about *Their Eyes Were Watching God* (*"There is no book more important to me than this one"*) signaled the Walker effect to come. The persuasive statement was among the blurbs used to promote the first reissue of the novel in 1978 by University of Illinois Press.[35]

In 1979 Alice Walker edited a collection of Hurston's work titled, *I Love Myself When I Am Laughing . . . and Then Again When I Am Looking Mean and Impressive.*[36] The edited volume includes excerpts from Hurston's autobiography, *Dust Tracks on a Road*; excerpts from *Mules and Men* and *Tell My Horse*; selected short stories; excerpts from selected fiction; and selected essays and articles. Walker wrote its dedication, "On Refusing to Be Humbled by Second Place in a Contest You Did Not Design" (1979b). Like the previous essays discussed, this essay strongly asserted Hurston's artistry and genius, her particular ability to overcome the overwhelming odds of her race and gender, and her commitment to "the folk." Again, the folk are generally regarded as Southern, country, rural people whom Hurston represents. In addition, Walker underscores the limitations on Hurston's work because of the constraints of material poverty and patron dependency:

> Financial dependency is the thread that sewed a cloud over Hurston's life, from the time she left home to work as a maid at fourteen to the day of her death. It is ironic that *this* woman, who many claimed sold her soul to record the sources of authentic, black American folk art (whereas it is apparently cool to sell your soul for a university job, say, or a new car) and who has made of some of the universe's most naturally free stuff (one would be hard pressed to find a more nonmaterialistic person), was denied even a steady pittance, free from strings, that would have kept her secure enough to do her best work. (3–4)

In 1983 Harcourt Brace Jovanovich and The Women's Press, a feminist press based in London, published four of the five essays discussed here in a collection of Alice Walker's essays, lectures, and letters titled *In Search of Our Mothers' Gardens: Womanist Prose.*[37] Together the collected essays presented both Walker and Hurston to national and international popular audiences. Their combined effect underscores Hurston's significance as a writer and extends their mutual influence. Each essay chronicles, with variations, the search for and finding of Hurston. They also represent the end of Hurston's life as tragic. By emphasizing the material conditions of her life, both Walker's construction of Hurston's legacy and her claim as heir to the inheritance of that legacy become more apparent. Walker's critical acclaim is deeply interwoven with the reclamation of Hurston, and her rhetorical construction of Hurston significantly shaped Hurston's subsequent popular and critical reception.

Of course, Walker was not alone in recuperating Hurston's legacy through narratives of gratifying discovery. Both Sherley Anne Williams and Mary Helen Washington wrote forewords to editions of *Their Eyes Were Watching God* (1978 and [1990] 1998), respectively) in which each described encountering Hurston's most celebrated text for the first time. However, this fact is often lost in popular narratives of Hurston's legacy, rendering invisible the work of these scholars. Additionally, the individual narratives of discovery created a meta-narrative of *the* Black feminist literary tradition with Hurston at its center. For example, Washington provides a description of her "own discovery" of *Their Eyes* at a local Detroit Black book store in 1968 ([1990] 1998, x). She draws attention to the illustrated jacket cover that graphically figures Janie with "long hair cascading down her back, her head turning just slightly in his direction with the look of longing and expectancy" (xi). After this description, Washington writes:

> What I loved immediately about this novel besides its high poetry and its female hero was its investment in black folk traditions. Here, finally, was a woman on a quest for her own identity and, unlike so many other questing figures in black literature, her journey would take her, not away from, but deeper and deeper into blackness, the descent into the Everglades with its rich black soil, wild cane, and communal life representing immersion into black traditions. (xi)

This passage is noteworthy for its exotic representation of blackness; defined by a tropical geography that is figured to signify an essential blackness that one (by way of Hurston's Janie) descends into.

In addition, Washington's reference to jacket covers requires consideration of its jacket copy given the critical authority of those who endorsed Hurston's work. The 1998 Perennial Classics edition of *Their Eyes*, critically framed by Washington's foreword and an afterword by Henry Louis Gates Jr., included blurbs from Alice Walker, the *Saturday Review*, and scholar/poet June Jordan. Walker's quote *"There is no book more important to me than this one"* is taken from Walker's 1977 essay "Zora Neale Hurston: A Cautionary Tale and a Partisan View."[38] The blurb from the *Saturday Review* (a well-known critical magazine with a national and international audience) situates *Their Eyes* within the white male American literary canon: *"Their Eyes* belongs in the same category— with that of William Faulkner, F. Scott Fitzgerald, and Ernest Hemingway—of enduring American Literature" (Stevens 1937). Jordan's blurb, excerpted from *Black World*, reads, "The prototypical Black novel of affirmation: it is the most successful, convincing, and exemplary novel of Blackness that we have. Period" (Hurston [1937] 1998).[39] In short, the jacket promotional copy appealed to the tastes and political leanings of a diverse audience: Alice Walker's as well as those of *Saturday Review* and *Black World*. The text's popularity is appealed to, Hurston's place in a white male American canon is confirmed, and the text is cited as a source of authentic "Blackness."

As mentioned previously, in addition to Black aesthetic themes of race pride and cultural tradition, Walker also referenced themes of motherhood, family, and kinship. In the essay "In Search of Zora Neale Hurston" ([1975a] 1983), Walker describes how she posed as Hurston's niece so that she could gather information about Hurston's life; locate Hurston's unmarked grave in Fort Pierce, Florida; and arrange to have a headstone placed there. She explains, "Besides, as far as I'm concerned, she is my aunt—and that of all black people as well" (102). Years later, Walker's appeal for a cultural, if fictive, kinship continues. For example, during a 2004 National Public Radio (NPR) interview with reporter Vertamae Grosvenor to promote her novel *Now Is the Time to Open Your Heart* (2004), Walker reads from Hurston's *Their Eyes Were Watching God* and comments on its significance, employing familial and kinship ties:

> MS. WALKER: It is the grandmother spirit, the strong grandmother, the cinder grandmother, the no-nonsense grandmother, that's what's missing in this culture. That's who should be speaking to us now in this hour.
> GROSVENOR: For Alice Walker, Zora Neale Hurston embodied the disciplined, loving authority of the grandmother spirit of the Earth. By holding firmly to the authentic inner life of the black rural South, Walker says Hurston provided cultural nourishment and spiritual food. (Grosvenor 2004)

Rather than a literary foremother, Hurston is represented here as "the grandmother spirit of the Earth." Later in the interview Walker says, "I felt—and

I still feel, I will always feel very daughterly, very niecely in relation to Zora. And I feel a responsibility to her." Again, Walker appeals to the audience via metaphors of familial obligation and responsibility, including the nurturing of extended familial relationships and claiming of fictive kin.[40]

This interview reinforces Walker's representation of Hurston as "lost and found" while also offering another telling of Walker's discovery of Hurston. Walker mentions that she likely encountered Hurston's work in a collection edited by Langston Hughes, *The Best Short Stories by Black Writers, 1899–1967* (1967), which included Walker's "To Hell with Dying" and Hurston's "The Gilded Six Bits," but that she most likely did not notice Hurston's work because she "read all the men" and because the narrative was "so familiar and so country . . . so much what I was used to in Georgia that I didn't pay much attention to it." Grosvenor adds that a neighbor loaned Walker a copy of *Their Eyes Were Watching God*, which led to Walker's research about Hurston's life and work, including her trip to Eatonville and Fort Pierce, Florida, which Walker, of course, recounts in her essay "In Search of Zora Neale Hurston."

The theme of lost and found was not lost to news writers or to their readership, including a news article titled "Lost and Found" that appeared on the first page of the "Dixie Living" section of the *Atlanta Journal-Constitution* on February 3, 1991. Staff writer Cynthia Tucker noted the "rise" in Hurston's "literary reputation" and described the "Zora" festival held amid what she described as Eatonville's "decline," which she suggests might reverse its course with renewing interest in Hurston's work. In addition, she reports Hurston's bio and recounts that, rejected by her Black peers and criticized for her use of Black idiomatic language and a lack of concern for the "Race Problem," Hurston's work fell out of vogue. Tucker highlights that Walker found Hurston's unmarked grave in Fort Pierce and bought a tombstone for it, noting the inscription, typeset to represent Hurston's tombstone on the page:

ZORA NEALE HURSTON

"A GENIUS OF THE SOUTH"

1901 — — — 1960

NOVELIST, FOLKLORIST

ANTHROPOLOGIST

In effect, the narrative of Hurston's rise and fall as lost and found, as discarded and reclaimed, circulates in radio, newsprint, academic publications, classrooms, informal circles, and in new forms of media and has its source in the strength of Walker's rhetoric, which appealed to reader's emotions, character, and reason.

Themes of poverty, tragedy, and creative, social, and real death are powerful. They only partially explain, however, the rhetorical strength of Walker's essays and Hurston's reclamation as a feminist foremother. In the 1980s the theme of motherhood was employed as an organizing principle in feminism, with literary criticisms directly connecting the work of Walker and Hurston and in some instances working to complicate their affinity.[41] For example, within the collection *Mothering the Mind*, Mary Helen Washington's "I Sign My Mother's Name: Alice Walker, Dorothy West, Paule Marshall" works to foreground the importance of Walker's biological mother in the development of Walker's early work (Washington 1984, 161).[42] Dianne F. Sadoff's "Black Matrilineage: The Case of Alice Walker and Zora Neale Hurston" addresses how Walker writes Hurston as her literary foremother in ways that reveal its construction while avoiding critical "anxieties" one might expect to occur within a genealogical narrative, real or imagined. Sadoff asserts, "Race and class oppression intensify the Black woman writer's need to discover an untroubled matrilineal heritage" (1985, 5). In 1993 *Alice Walker and Zora Neale Hurston: The Common Bond* was published. Edited by Lillie P. Howard,[43] this collection of essays explores the relationships between Walker and Hurston in terms of biography (as shared Southern experience) and comparative thematic treatments of their respective novels. The collection firmly links Hurston and Walker together as central to the Black women's literary tradition in twelve essays that either compare and contrast *Their Eyes Were Watching God* with Walker's *The Color Purple* or that more generally compare and contrast themes of folklore and spirituality in the works of both writers. In effect, criticisms highlight the construction and critical connections between the two literary figures, providing opportunities to further analyze and interrogate their literary bond.

Walker and Hurston are paired throughout a significant amount of the literary criticism during this time, forming their own critical trope that interrogates race, class, and gender while underscoring their literary similarities and reinforcing the idea of a linear African American literary tradition. Their critical kinship, which permeates the field far beyond the few pieces I've referenced here, is unprecedented in the Black feminist literary tradition, and it begins with Walker's early essays. Collectively, the rhetorical arguments of these motherhood essays and edited collections have elevated Hurston to the status of Black literary foremother. These treatments of the dynamics of mother-daughter relationship, in both creative and critical writings, underscore Walker's literary connection to Hurston via matrilineal themes.

The resurgence of Hurston's work, following Walker's promotion of her in mainstream publications, has in part paralleled the growth of Black feminist studies (duCille 2005).[44] Within the context of Walker's reclamation of Hurston, some scholars began to refer to either Hurston the author or Hurston's work (in particular, *Their Eyes Were Watching God*) as seminal to understanding the importance of Black women's literary tradition. I do not intend to imply a one-to-one causation between Walker's essays and critical commentaries regarding Hurston's work, but rather an association, as many commentaries echo Walker's representation of Hurston's contribution as a "first of its kind" (duCille 2005, 80–81) and "authentically black." For example, Cheryl A. Wall's "Zora Neale Hurston: Changing Her Own Words" gives "first" status to Hurston in terms of an authentic raced and gendered voice:

> The developing tradition of black women's writing nurtured now in the prose and poetry of such writers as Toni Morrison and Alice Walker began with the work of Zora Neale Hurston. Hurston was not the first Afro-American woman to publish a novel, but she was the first to create language and imagery that reflected the reality of black women's lives. Ignoring the stereotypes, social and literary, that her predecessors spent their energies rejecting, Hurston rooted her art in the cultural traditions of the black rural South.... Hers became *the first authentic black female voice in American literature*. (1982, 76; emphasis mine)

Likewise, Mae Gwendolyn Henderson, in "Speaking in Tongues: Dialogics, Dialectics, and the Black Woman Writer's Literary Tradition," describes Hurston's *Their Eyes* as *the* classic Black women's text. She writes, "The classic black women's text *Their Eyes Were Watching God*, charts the female protagonist's development from voicelessness to voice, from silence to tongues" (1989, 124).

In another example of Hurston's positioning at the center of *the* Black women's literary tradition, Henry Louis Gates begins his anthology of writings of the Black feminist literary tradition titled *Reading Black, Reading Feminist: A Critical Anthology* with Hurston's essay "Art and Such" under the subheading "Constructing a Tradition." Gates details the literary movement of Black women writers since 1970, observing that the output of Black women's literary productions is a "major international literary movement" (1990, 1–3). He also notes that "black female authors often claim descent from other black women literary ancestors, such as Zora Neale Hurston and Ann Petry" (4), and he lists a number of anthologies edited by Black women that have "played a pivotal role in the institutionalization of black women in literature in the university curriculum" (5). Observing that every anthology "defines a canon and thereby preserves a tradition in what is designated as its most representative parts," (5) Gates considers Mary Helen Washington's ideas concerning the "fiction of tradition." Here Washington critiques the marginalization of Black women's literary works from the American literary and African American literary canons (1987, xvii-xviii). Gates acknowledges the complicated politics of defining a tradition, including the possibilities of "reifying it," and describes *Reading Black* as but "one effort" (1990, 6). Gates organizes his collection in terms of "literary revision" wherein Black women writers converse in "formal echoes, recast metaphors, even in parody" (7). He asserts that his anthology begins with Hurston because her "work and career more than those of any other black woman writer, have become the symbols of a reclaimed literary tradition (9).[45]

Beyond the Walker effect, early defining statements of a Black women's literary and critical tradition often focus on questions of voice and language that supported claims of Hurston's centrality in the Black women's literary tradition. This focus within Black feminist literary criticism formally began with Barbara Smith's "Toward a Black Feminist Criticism," wherein she defines the "principles which I think a black feminist could use" in outlining a specific Black feminist literary tradition ([1977b] 2000, 137). In addition to arguing that it should be attuned to the politics of race, class, gender, and sexuality, Smith argues for Black feminist criticism to make thematic and conceptual connections between writers (137). She suggests as possible directions the connections among "Zora Neale Hurston, Margaret Walker, Toni Morrison and Alice Walker" because they include "the traditional Black female activities of rootworking, herbal medicine, conjure and midwifery" and because "their use of specifically Black female language to express their own and their characters' thoughts" is not accidental (137). Smith's focus on only twentieth-century writers and her drawing of themes from Walker's "In Search of Our Mothers Gardens" further illustrate the influence of Walker's reading of Hurston. Hurston's work is given a central place in marking the importance of Black female cultural practices and language as definitive of a Black feminist literary tradition. However, Smith's attention to language specifically reflects larger theoretical concerns in literary criticism during the period. As Black feminist critics delineated a tradition of Black feminist literature and criticism, they began to draw on feminist discussions concerning female language.[46] In response to Smith, Deborah McDowell, for example, calls for considerations of language by Black feminist literary critics across interdisciplinary boundaries and less attention to broad and specific cultural themes such as those addressed in Smith's argument. McDowell writes in "New Directions for Black Feminist Criticism," "Further, black feminist critics should not become obsessed with searching for common themes and images in black women's works. As I pointed out earlier, investigating the question of 'female' language is critical and may well be among the most challenging jobs awaiting the black feminist critic" ([1980] 1995, 14).[47] In effect, discussions of language and voice in early statements of black feminist literary tradition considered Hurston as central to that tradition. These discussions lay a foundation for and signaled the advent of theoretical considerations of language and voice in Hurston's work beyond those defined by black women literary scholars.

The construction of Hurston's distinctive place in Black women's literary tradition, influenced by the Walker effect, was occasioned by a larger commitment to addressing the erasures of Black women's writing in critical discussion. This larger commitment was shaped by critical trends such as establishing possible themes and methods for evaluating Black women's literature and validating the presence and agency of Black women as writers who crafted narratives that addressed and imagined life on their own terms. Themes related to motherhood (foremothers and mothering) and traditions reflected a period of earnest and ardent recuperation, given the critical vacuum and prejudiced disregard for the work of Black women writers. The early efforts by Black women literary scholars to define a Black feminist literary tradition were strategic, their rhetoric reflective of the historical moment and in service to the task ahead: to establish the presence of an identifiable body of literature and, indeed, a community of readers, scholars, and activists who were wholly invested in the restoration and preservation of literature by and about Black women. In addition to Alice Walker, Barbara Smith, and Mary Helen Washington, other scholars such as Beverly Guy-Sheftall, Patricia Bell-Scott, Gloria Wade-Gayles, and many, many others established a body of sustained scholarship, reading lists and syllabi, dedicated courses, and centers and programs devoted to Black women's studies, including Black women's literary studies.[48] Without their works, as the larger record shows, generations of readers, writers, and scholar-activists in higher and secondary education might indeed be without the many literary models that, as Alice Walker asserted, were so necessary for their survival.

2

Signifying "Texts"
The Race for Hurston

But, unfortunately, it is difficult to ignore this new takeover, because theory has become a commodity that helps determine whether we are hired or promoted in academic institutions—worse, whether we are heard at all. Due to this new orientation, works (a word that evokes labor) have become texts.

—Barbara Christian, "The Race for Theory"

A literary work does not become part of the literary canon simply because it receives significant critical attention, notwithstanding the important and influential endorsement of Alice Walker. Hurston's work was either understudied or evaluated in terms that largely focused on *Their Eyes Were Watching God* (Corse and Griffin 1997), and Black women writers and literary critics, such as Mary Helen Washington, Sherley Ann Williams, Ellease Southerland, June Jordan, Alice Walker, Barbara Smith, Cheryl Wall, and others, reintroduced Hurston as a significant writer of the early twentieth century. Collectively, their work brought Zora Neale Hurston to the center of scholarship aimed at defining a Black feminist literary tradition. They also brought Hurston to the forefront of debates about tradition and Black women writers' authority within African American literature. Their role as scholars and writers was essential to Hurston's reemergence as an author deemed worthy of sustained critical attention, but the correlation between their significant literary criticism and Hurston's eventual canonicity is neither a direct one nor is it largely acknowledged. What were the greater conditions that eventually determined Zora Neale Hurston's canonization within American literature? Black women writers and literary scholars were growing in their appeal to a wider readership and in their receipt of major literary awards. They were breaking new ground within the academy in their pursuit of graduate degrees and the development of syllabi and courses that focused on the works and experiences of women and men of color. They were founding small presses and journals. They were defining critical approaches to reading the literary and cultural productions of African Americans, including defining a Black women's literary tradition. However, they did not have the widespread institutional power that could propel Hurston's body of work to levels of widespread national recognition and literary prominence. The growth of larger publishing houses with more integrated editorial divisions created opportunities to define Black culture and history for a national audience. For example, the groundbreaking archival project *The Black Book*, was edited by Toni Morrison and published by Random House in 1974. Expressly marketed to a Black audience (Morrison 2009), *The Black Book* helped to redefine attitudes among major trade book publishing companies about the profitability of publishing Black subject matter. Of course, there was also the relative success of publications by small presses for Black studies audiences, like Haki Madhubuti's Third World Press, founded in 1964, and for diverse feminist audiences, like the Feminist Press, founded in 1970. For Black feminist audiences, the Kitchen Table: Women of Color Press, founded in 1980, and *SAGE: A Scholarly Journal on Black Women*, founded in 1984, provided access to Black feminist perspectives on scholarship by and about Black women.[1] All told, institutions and publishing initiatives provided greater access to works published for a more diverse reading audience and, in some cases, proved their profitability. This diverse audience included a generation of students educated in historically Black colleges and universities and more inclusive predominantly white universities that were now supporting pedagogies for teaching race, class, sexuality, and gender consciousness. The subsequent emergence of analytical frameworks that considered race, class, gender, and sexuality as overlapping, interdependent, and simultaneous phenomena meant that readers and critics were receptive to ways of reading works by Black women authors, including the work of Zora Neale Hurston.[2]

Significantly, changes in literary theory exerted their own powerful influence on the reception of Hurston's work. Her work was prominently featured in some critical discussions as an ideal example of a kind of theoretical syncretism, one that merged poststructuralist theories with African American literary and cultural practices.[3] By the mid-1980s in the United States, parallel, and sometimes competing, trends within the larger academy included reevaluations and applications of the works of several widely celebrated theorists used in deconstructionist and poststructuralist forms of literary criticism. These included the works of Mikhail Bakhtin, Roland Barthes, and Jacques Derrida, among others. As this chapter's epigraph from Barbara Christian suggests, the rise of critical theory within literary studies intensified, if not created, a Marxian alienation from the expressed goals of many literary scholars who viewed their scholarship as a vocation and form of activism in redressing the omission and misinformation regarding Black intellectual histories and literary and cultural works. The growing popularity of this conceptual trend accompanied, if not directly minted, Hurston's canonization within American literary studies. There would seem to be an inverse relationship between these two trajectories when in fact the terms of Hurston's canonical ascension prove, ironically, a kind of logic of late(nt) racialized cultural and theoretical bias: even as Hurston's work rose in literary authority toward canonization, it was also alienated from extended close readings of its subject matter and historical contexts as the basis for its interpretation. As the commodification and demand for theoretical readings intensified, literary critics "raced" to write about Hurston in poststructuralist theoretical terms. During this era, and compared to the work of other Black women writers, Hurston's work is imbued with an unprecedented literary authority.

Critics have noted that scholars in African American literary studies found in the works of some literary scholars, like Mikhail Bakhtin, the theoretical authority to explain and emphasize that throughout history Black authors have employed various rhetorical strategies to speak to multiple, diverse, and adverse audiences and to reflect shifting experiences of racial identity. For example, Bakhtin's concept of "double voiced" is frequently read in terms that reference Du Bois's double consciousness within African American literature (Hale 1994, 446). Critical debates (or signifying texts) concerning the application of these bodies of theories reflect two primary concerns within the study of African American literature: (1) Should literary critics produce African American literary theories that could define a comprehensive cultural logic of African American literature? (2) What role, if any, should pervasive (or trending) theories, such as poststructuralism, have in defining the critical significance of African American literary works? These concerns are reflected within the impassioned debates between Henry Louis Gates, Joyce A. Joyce, and Houston Baker, among others, and they reveal some of the paradigmatic differences between scholars who argued either for or against the significance of new theoretical approaches to reading works produced by African American writers. Those advocating poststructuralists' and deconstructionists' theoretical approaches argue that they are useful tools toward defining and advancing an African American literary tradition, especially since their efforts ultimately advance readings of "Black" language and cultural expression. Those who reject this argument are not entirely against such theoretical approaches, but they are concerned that some of these approaches, aligned with white/European literary traditions, represent more powerful narrative standpoints and rhetorical authority in the academy. They argue that these approaches effectively decenter and marginalize other valid methods for analyzing and evaluating African American literature when applied to the literature en masse. Each side of the debate has its merits, but, more importantly for this study, the debates portend the ways that Hurston's work was increasingly read through the lens of critical theory or as theory itself.

Perhaps the most widely known statement regarding the demand for theory within the academy during this era is Barbara Christian's now-classic essay "The Race for Theory" (1987), from which the epigraph of this chapter is excerpted. Christian persuasively argues that the growing import of theory as a method for evaluating literary works exerted a hegemonic influence on the production of literary criticisms about African American literature. She compellingly argues that power dynamics and structural inequalities are embedded in the "wholesale" reception and application of poststructuralist theories to evaluate African American literary works, and she expresses concern about the demand these trends were making on her own work and on the work of her peers:

> There have been, in the last year, any number of occasions on which I had to convince literary critics who have pioneered entire new areas of critical inquiry that they did have something to say. Some of us are continually harassed to invent wholesale theories regardless of the complexity of the literature we study. I, for one, am tired of being asked to produce a black feminist literary theory as if I were a mechanical man. For I believe such theory is prescriptive—it ought to have some relationship to practice. Since I can count on one hand the number of people attempting to be black feminist literary critics, I consider it presumptuous of me to invent a theory of how we *ought* to read. Instead, I think we need to read the works of our writers in our various ways and remain open to the intricacies of language, class, race, and gender in the literature. And it would help if we share our process, that is, our practice, as much as possible since, finally, our work *is* a collective endeavor. (53)

Christian argues that managing the demand for theory as a commodity, in exchange for academic authority, ultimately constrains the recovery and analysis of works in African American literature. She warns, "If our emphasis on theoretical criticism continues, critics of the future may have to reclaim the writers we are now ignoring, that is, if they are even aware these artists exist" (58). Much is at stake in these exchanges of theoretical and literary authority, since, as Christian highlights, African American literature, the literature of women, and Black and female scholars themselves, only entered the academy in relatively greater numbers during the early 1970s (54–55). During this period, Black scholars were involved in the recuperation of African American literary works that were ignored, lost, or rendered invisible by American literary studies. In the case of Hurston, receptions of her ideas as theoretical in their representations and analysis of Black cultural practices created the right conditions for Hurston's works to be read in terms that would support her entry into the canon of American literature.

I argue that the "race for theory" that Christian describes also involved a concomitant "race for Hurston," as Hurston's work was either prominently featured or thematically alluded to in some of these discussions, often as ideal "texts" for the application of poststructuralist theory. Because Hurston's work was read as ideally poststructuralist for its use of Black language, for example, some audiences outside of the more marginalized fields of Black feminist studies and African American studies received her work as particularly significant. In addition, with the continued privileging of Hurston's work as theoretically significant, her import as central to Black literary and Black feminist literary tradition was further underscored. Hurston's *Their Eyes Were Watching God*, in particular, became a central text for new critical readings of voice, subjectivity, and questions of difference. How *Their Eyes* became a central text in Hurston's body of work and in the larger African American corpus (beyond its initial reception by Black feminist literary critics) involves a consideration of larger theoretical debates that framed Hurston's distinctive intellectual reception.

Signifying Debates

During the period that Hurston's *Their Eyes Were Watching God* gained access to the larger American literary canon, scholars were considering the powerful influence of poststructuralism on African American studies and Black feminist literary studies. A series of critical discussions and debates in 1987 and 1988 within African American studies foreshadowed the eventual consequences of the singular praise given to Hurston's work, in poststructuralist readings, as central to *the* Black feminist literary tradition and *Their Eyes* as a privileged African American text.[4] Some critics warned that African American literary productions might be tokenized because of a focus on extra-theoretical readings of African American literary productions. They also warned that the canonization of a few choice works would do little to change inequity in the larger academy. While the following discussions and debates do not discuss Hurston's work or her ideas explicitly, they do provide a larger critical context that frames her authority and canonization. In summary, they illustrate the privileging of works like Hurston's in poststructuralist readings of African American works as texts.

During the same year as Barbara Christian's "The Race for Theory," a series of articles was published in the journal *New Literary History* that further illuminated the critical tensions within African American studies concerning the impact of poststructuralism on its practical course.[5] Joyce A. Joyce argued against the effect of poststructuralism in shaping the Black canon in "The Black Canon: Reconstructing Black American Literary Criticism" (1987a). In particular, she critiqued the work of Henry Louis Gates Jr. and Houston A. Baker Jr., two prominent African American literary theorists, for what she argued was their obscuring or denial of the reality of racial politics in order to "play" race in their use of "European" literary criticism (341). According to Joyce, "The Black creative writer understands that it is not yet time—and it might not ever be possible—for a people with hundreds of years of disenfranchisement and who since slavery have venerated the intellect and the written word to view language as merely a system of codes or as mere play" (341). She further details Black literature's long tradition of producing works and criticism concerned with speaking to and elevating the condition of a Black audience, and she suggests that the advent of poststructuralist theories, and the Black critics who employed these theories, signals a considerable departure from that tradition.

Joyce's article was published alongside the invited responses of Gates and Baker. Each scholar responded in ways that are well documented in the critical literature of the period, including references to the "signifyin'" rhetoric that characterized their exchanges. Theodore Mason (1988), for example, refers to the particularly heightened exchanges between Henry Louis Gates, Joyce Joyce, and Houston Baker as "playing the dozens" in scholarship.[6] These "signifyin'" exchanges reveal racial and gendered politics and investments in critical theory and, in terms of Barbara Christian's critique, the authority given to critics who choose to speak the language of these new theories (Christian 1987, 52, 55). Yet even as these scholars debate the uses of theory, some reveal a theoretical bias toward literary works that represent prevailing ideas of authentic Black language and voice. For example, Gates, in part, responded:

> This is the challenge of the critic of black literature in the 1980s: not to shy away from literary theory; rather to translate it into black idiom, *renaming* principles of criticism where appropriate, but especially *naming* indigenous black principles of criticism and applying these to explicate our own texts. . . . For it is the language, the black language of black texts, which expresses the distinctive quality of our literary tradition. (1987b, 352)

Baker's response to Joyce, although conceptually different from that of Gates, also defines a critical need for poststructuralism in redefining representations of "black expressive culture." He rejects what he describes as Joyce's and others' "animosity" to poststructuralist theories:

> Their animosity springs from the fact that the new critical and theoretical modes marking investigations of black expressive culture so clearly escape the minstrel simplicity that Anglo-Americans have traditionally imagined and assigned (and that some Afro-Americans have willingly provided and accepted) as the farthest reaches of the black voice in the United States. (H. Baker 1987, 366)

Gates's privileging of "indigenous black principles" and Baker's call to revise "black expressive culture" in, arguably, more complicated terms via poststructuralist readings illustrate a potential bias toward works that reflect these "types" of Black culture. Hurston, lauded for her representations of folk culture in her literature and for her use of a rural Southern Black language, fits both mandates for African American critical theory. Poststructuralist readings of Hurston routinely praised her fiction for its Southern rural folklore content and its accurate representation of "Black" language and idiom.

While both Gates and Baker disagree with Joyce's critique, neither directly responds to Joyce's claim that poststructuralism privileges a consideration of some literary genres over others. Joyce noted:

> It is no accident that the Black poststructuralist methodology has so far been applied to fiction, the trickster tale, and the slave narrative. Black poetry— particularly that written during and after the 1960s—defies both linguistically and ideologically the "poststructuralist sensibility." According to Terry Eagleton, "most literary theories . . . unconsciously 'foreground' a particular literary genre, and derive their general pronouncements from this." ([Eagleton] 51) (Joyce 1987, 342)

Joyce's reference to Black poetry of the 1960s suggests that the application of poststructuralism to selected works within Black literature may ultimately avoid more contemporary political content. In addition, her argument that African Americanist poststructuralism privileged some genres and subject matter and excluded others highlights the contexts of the largely positive reception of Hurston's literary work. Given its focus on folklore and Black language, some of Hurston's work was prominently featured in particular discussions as an ideal example of a merging of poststructuralist theories with African American literary and cultural practices. For example, Hurston's *Their Eyes Were Watching God* garnered poststructuralist consideration because of her use of Black vernacular along with standard English (Peterson 1993, 767). Both feminist and African American scholars had already heralded Hurston's use of language as distinctive because she represented "authentic" racial and gendered voices. Gates, expressly, described Hurston as the "best" example of an African American vernacular tradition in literary form (1988, 170–216). Others, as I will discuss here, applied textual/linguistic theories to readings of Hurston's work in order to offer new critical discussions and advance Hurston's work as theoretical.

In "The Race for Theory," Barbara Christian refers to literary critical theory's "preoccupations with mechanical analyses of language; graphs" that seem to compete with literature's primacy (Christian ([1987] 2000, 281). Christian might have been thinking of Barbara Johnson's "Metaphor, Metonymy, and Voice in *Their Eyes Were Watching God*" (in Henry Louis Gates's 1984 edited collection *Black Literature and Literary Theory*) when she warned against this aspect of poststructuralism's influence. Johnson's article applies the ideas of Russian linguist Roman Jakobson concerning metaphor and metonymy to a reading of *Their Eyes Were Watching God*.[7] She challenges Jakobsonian assumptions concerning metaphor and metonymy as oppositional, and she argues that the relationship between the two tropes is more complex than Jakobson describes. Johnson asserts that at times it is difficult to determine the differences between the two tropes, and she finds it problematic that metaphor is more privileged as the trope that yields greater rhetorical or figurative meaning (B. Johnson ([1987] 1991, 157–58). Johnson also suggests that discussions of Jakobson's ideas should privilege neither metaphor nor metonymy toward understanding voice, and she uses Hurston's *Their Eyes Were Watching God* as the theoretical medium through which she examines a more complex interplay between these two tropes in order to test Jakobson's ideas. She privileges *Their Eyes* for her reading, which she refers to as Hurston's "best-known novel" because, she argues, its highly figurative use of language allows for an exploration of relationships between inside/outside, silence/voice, and metaphor/

metonymy (160–64). Johnson also cites Hurston's studies in anthropology as indicators of Hurston's insider/outsider experience, and these references authorize her use of Hurston's "best-known" literary work (158–60). She determines that Janie's movement toward voice comes not out of a unified identity but out of Janie's division into inside and outside at critical moments in the novel. Her close reading of select passages from *Their Eyes* reveals Hurston's fluid use of both metaphorical and metonymical narrative allusions to describe Janie's "self-division," which propels her to voice (161–63).[8]

Within the latter part of the article, Johnson uses semantic graphs to illustrate that the Black woman is both a raced and gendered subject who cannot be rendered or described in "universal" or essentialized ways, which Hurston's work also underscores (170). These "tetrapolar structures" are used earlier in the article by Johnson to illustrate the complex relationship between metaphor and metonymy described by Jakobson. Later, in her discussion on Black female subjectivity, she provides a graph that forms an x and y axis where gender (female and male) is read (left to right) along the y axis and race (white and black) is read (top to bottom) along the x axis. Each quadrant (from I to IV) formed by the intersecting axes represents "complementarity," "universality," "otherness," and X. X, the unknown, is the fourth quadrant formed by the intersecting black and female axes (169, fig. 4). The use of graphs in this regard is indicative of Christian's assertion that African American literary works were subsumed by this mode of analysis (Christian 1987, 53). In contrast, a Black feminist approach to reading seeks to define and illustrate literary representations of experience beyond the mapping of structures on a page, "to have some relationship to practice" (53).[9] In effect, the use of poststructuralist graphs here seeks to address a poststructuralist audience rather than to elucidate new meanings about the work itself. In this way, Hurston's "work" becomes a "text" (53). In keeping with Christian's arguments in "The Race for Theory," one might ask, Why do we need a graph to illustrate what we can otherwise find with a close reading of Hurston's narrative? Furthermore, given Christian's arguments, the space on Johnson's page might be used to receive and engage the works of scholars who have long articulated the logics of objectification and essentialism of Black women through interdisciplinary and theoretical studies including literary criticisms of Hurston's work.[10] Johnson's essay ultimately states a concern with addressing the erasure of Black women and defining the complexity of Black women's experience (166–71), but there is no sustained engagement with the varied body of scholarship (largely authored by Black feminist critics) either regarding these larger problems and commitments or regarding Hurston or *Their Eyes*.

Johnson's article is not only noteworthy for its application of critical theory in the evaluation of Hurston's work. Significantly, its subsequent publication within a prominent literary series frames the larger political context of Hurston's canonical status. When republished in a 1986 edition of Harold Bloom's *Modern Critical Views*, which featured essays concerning Zora Neale Hurston, Johnson's essay signaled and underscored Hurston's entry into the American literary canon (Wallace [1988] 1990, 175). *Modern Critical Views*, in Bloom's estimation, traces the key pieces that reflect "the most useful criticism so far available on the work of Zora Neale Hurston." The collection is organized historically from Franz Boas's 1935 preface to *Mules and Men* to Barbara Johnson's 1984 essay "Metaphor, Metonymy, and Voice in *Their Eyes Were Watching God*" (Bloom 1986b, vii). As the final essay, Johnson's article serves as a historical place marker of Hurston's canonization, and it is significantly noted by Bloom as "the most advanced critical essay yet devoted to Hurston" (viii). Michele Wallace argues that the publication of Bloom's anthology of collected essays promoted Hurston as canonical at the price of dismissing the feminist and African Americanist readings of her work responsible for introducing Hurston to the canon ([1988] 1990, 175). She quotes Bloom on Hurston: "Her sense of power has nothing in common with the politics of any persuasion, with contemporary modes of feminism, or even with those questers who search for a black aesthetic" (175).[11] Bloom's distinguishing of Johnson's article as "the most advanced critical essay yet" coupled with his dismissal of feminist and Black aesthetic critical perspectives on Hurston illustrates that Hurston's entry into the canon was occasioned by the authority of poststructuralist readings of her work over and beyond Black feminist or African Americanist ways of reading her literature. With Bloom's pronouncement, it seems that the work of Mary Helen Washington, Ellease Southerland, June Jordan, Alice Walker, Cheryl Wall, and other scholars whose writings provided close readings toward revealing the complex historical and cultural contexts of Hurston's work was summarily dismissed. As Christian suggests, critical considerations of Black works as more or less important largely depended on the works' ability to meet the demand for new theoretical interpretations (1987, 52). Authority like Johnson's is conferred to the critic who speaks the language of these new theories.

Strategies of reading a text can either foreclose or reveal a text's meaning. Barbara Johnson's "Thresholds of Difference: Structures of Address in Zora Neale Hurston" ([1985] 1986), then, provides an example of ways of reading Hurston from the same literary critic but with results that are different from those found in her earlier article. This later essay of Johnson's centers Hurston and expands our understanding of her more marginalized works in ways that largely avoid

Christian's concern that the burgeoning recuperation of lost works by Black women is marginalized in and by the hegemonic race toward poststructuralism (Christian 1987, 57). Here Johnson argues that Hurston's work writes against binary oppositions of insider/outsider and racial identity (in terms of Black and white) via "discursive exchange(s)" that illustrate shifting meanings of race and other forms of identity. Johnson uses examples from Hurston's essay "How It Feels to Be Colored Me" (1928) and "What White Publishers Won't Print" (1950), and she briefly addresses *Mules and Men*. She explores how these works illustrate race as socially constructed and racial experience as dependent on social context: "What Hurston vigorously shows is that questions of difference are always a function of a specific interlocutionary situation—and the answers, matters of strategy rather than truth" (B. Johnson [1985] 1986, 324). Although Johnson finds ideas in line with critical theory and its concepts of subjectivity within Hurston's work, her essay does not directly center any contemporary poststructuralist theories. Instead she relies on a close reading of Hurston's own works (as theoretical and historically relevant sources) to illuminate and explore Hurston's conceptions of shifting subjectivities.

Johnson herself notes the distinctions in her two treatments of Hurston's work in the introduction to her collection of essays titled *A World of Difference* (1987): "In Chapter 14, Zora Neale Hurston's ways of articulating racial and sexual difference are analyzed in rhetorical terms, while in Chapter 15, what is analyzed is the rhetoric of her ways of *baffling* the desire for an answer to the question of difference" (B. Johnson [1987] 1991, 5; Johnson's emphasis). This passage reveals Johnson's take on the rhetorical differences in her two readings of Hurston's work. I assert, however, that each reading places Hurston's works at either the margin or the center (or as object and subject) of the discourse, respectively. What is central in the first essay ("Metaphor, Metonymy, and Voice") is a poststructuralist reading of a Black woman's text. Hurston's work, which is both popular and convenient, provides that Black woman's text. Put another way, Johnson could "theoretically" read, in this case, another Black woman's text (or simply another text) to evaluate and revise Jakobson's oppositional understanding of concepts of metaphor and metonymy.[12] However, Johnson selected *Their Eyes* for its use of figurative language and its "best-known" status and further supports her choices by referencing Hurston's experience as an anthropologist. That Hurston's *Their Eyes Were Watching God* was chosen for this reading, I suggest, was determined by the growing interest and accessibility of *Their Eyes* as *the* classic Black woman's work for discussions of Black female subjectivity. Its use provides a space for Johnson's discussion of *the* Black woman's subjectivity with a semantic graph and a deconstruction of that graph

(B. Johnson [1987] 1991, 169–70), but the play on theory toward understanding the fluid and deconstructed nature of "existence" problematically erases Black women's literary criticism. Whether Johnson provides an original reading of Hurston's novel is uncertain and inconsequential, since her focus is not to read Hurston but to revise or correct readings of Jakobson. Earlier critical assessments offered by Black feminist literary critics and other scholars are obscured here in a reading that privileges or centers the authority of poststructuralism. The graph as an exercise simply illustrates a relationship that earlier critics of Black women's literature have discussed, and yet they are not widely cited within her article. In remarkable contrast, Johnson's analysis of Hurston's rhetoric in "Thresholds of Difference" centers Hurston's own discourse and theoretical ideas and, in effect, describes Hurston's implicit theories of difference through a rhetorical analysis of her non-canonical essays and ethnography.

In 1987 Karla F. C. Holloway published *The Character of the Word: The Texts of Zora Neale Hurston*. Holloway's study signals a defining moment in critical approaches to Hurston with the merging of the Walker effect, Black feminist literary criticism, and new critical theory. Described in a foreword authored by Henry Louis Gates as "the most sophisticated analysis of Hurston's use of language to date," it offers a linguistic reading of Zora Neale Hurston's use of Black dialect within her fictional works (Gates 1987a, xi). Holloway asserts that when read and analyzed together, Hurston's *Jonah's Gourd Vine; Their Eyes Were Watching God; Moses, Man of the Mountain;* and *Seraph on the Suwanee* suggest a methodology of Hurston's narrative construction. She traces Hurston's use of Black dialectical forms and Standard English forms in her narratives and argues that Hurston shifts between the two to propel the narrative and the main protagonist toward increased self-awareness. More specifically, Holloway demonstrates that Hurston's novels follow a narrative pattern: as the novel's and the character's self-awareness progress, the narrative voice (in Standard English) and character voice (in dialect) gradually merge so that by the novel's denouement it becomes increasingly difficult to determine which voice is being used. She briefly extends her reading of dialect to *Mules and Men* and writes, "Hurston indicates through language and the storytellers' consciousness of language that they are the story as well as the tellers of story" (1987, 95). Holloway's discussion is distinctive because it treats Hurston's less popular fiction in addition to *Their Eyes*. Holloway explains her theoretical approach to Hurston's work:

> The development of black literary theory has made it important that the politics and the sociopolitical perspectives within this literature be brought together in an intense scrutiny of the text itself, as well as the external forces

that have affected its construction. Critical theory has examined this literature in terms of its various pronouncements regarding and documenting
black life. Such theory has established a firm foundation for the next level
of critical inquiry that must emerge from black literature. (11)

As previously discussed in chapter 1, the "Walker effect" describes the influence
of Alice Walker's rising and continued authority on Hurston's popular iconography and subsequent canonization. Holloway's work bears reference to the
continued effect of Walker in readings of Hurston, even as scholars began to
move Black literary theory to respond to more recent developments in critical discourse. Holloway cites Alice Walker's discovery of Hurston and frames
her first chapter with an excerpt from Walker's essay "In Search of Our Mothers' Gardens." Because of the ways that controversies regarding Hurston's life
shaped her receptions, Holloway describes her own "responsibility" to "set
the record straight" regarding Hurston's contributions to African American
and American literature. As mentioned previously, she also announces the
need for critical theory to be applied to African American literature and, in
particular, to Hurston's work.

The following year, Henry Louis Gates endorsed Hurston with a "first" status
for his discussion of a theory of "Signifyin(g)" and his concept of "the speakerly
text." In *The Signifying Monkey: A Theory of African American Criticism* (1988),
Gates defines his concept of "the speakerly text" as a "text whose rhetorical
strategy is designed to represent an oral literary tradition, designed 'to emulate
the phonetic, grammatical, and lexical patterns of actual speech and produce
the 'illusion of oral narration.'"[13] He writes:

> The speakerly text is that text in which all other structural elements seem to
> be devalued, as important as they remain to the telling of the tale, because
> the narrative strategy signals attention to its own importance, an importance
> which would seem to be the privileging of oral speech and its inherent lin-
> guistic features. (1988, 181)

Gates asserts that Hurston's *Their Eyes Were Watching God* "is the first example
in our (African American) tradition of the 'speakerly text'" that "cleared a rhetorical space for the narrative strategies that Ralph Ellison would render so
deftly in *Invisible Man*" (181). In general, Gates defines "Signifyin(g)" as the
tradition of revision and repetition that occurs in various modalities within
African American vernacular and literary tradition. He also asserts, "Hurston
seems to be not only the first scholar to have defined the trope of Signifyin(g)
but also the first to represent the ritual itself" (196).

In addition, Gates questions what factors created the unprecedented canonization of Hurston and offers a rationale for her status:

> Thirty years later, however, Zora Neale Hurston is the most widely taught black woman writer in the canon of American literature. Why is this so? While a significant portion of her leadership is sustained by her image as a questioning, independent, thoughtfully sensual woman, I believe that Hurston has such a strong claim on a new generation of reader—students and teachers alike—because of her command of a narrative voice that imitates the storytelling structures of the black vernacular tradition. Indeed, no writer in the African-American literary tradition has been more successful than Hurston in registering the range and timbres of spoken black voices in written form. (xii)

Gates's answer underscores his vernacular theory of "Signifyin(g)," which in turn draws significantly on Hurston's *Their Eyes Were Watching God* as well as *Mules and Men* for its argument. Gates's use of Hurston's text centrally situates her within new critical theory discussions in African American literature while also illuminating the popular appeal of her work. His arguments reveal the terms of the focus on Hurston's work in ways that privilege her transcriptions of Black (1920s U.S. Southern rural) vernacular voice. Furthermore, defining its contribution as a primarily "speakerly text," where all other "structural elements" are less important reduces, rather than expands, the contexts through which Hurston's work can be read and assigns intrinsic value to her use of "vernacular" voices.

An evaluation of Mae Gwendolyn Henderson's "Speaking in Tongues: Dialogics, Dialectics, and the Black Woman Writer's Literary Tradition" (1989) provides an example of how Black aesthetic/cultural readings merged with poststructuralism in defining *the* Black woman's literary tradition via Hurston's novel *Their Eyes Were Watching God*. Henderson defines the Black feminist literary tradition through a consideration of themes and concepts in *Their Eyes*, using Mikhail Bakhtin's theoretical ideas (concerning dialogism, consciousness, and heteroglossia) and glossolalia (the religious practices of speaking in tongues). Henderson reads *Their Eyes* for the ways that Janie, its main protagonist, expresses "the dialectics/dialogics of black and female subjectivity [that] structure black women's discourse," and she describes the novel as "the classic black women's text" (Henderson 1989, 121–24).[14] Specifically, Henderson applies a poststructuralist concept to define Janie's voice as reflective of a "plurality of voices" and a "multiplicity of discourses," which she paradoxically defines in narrow terms:

> Like Janie, Black women must speak in a plurality of voices as well as in a multiplicity of discourses. This discursive diversity, or simultaneity of discourse, I

call "speaking in tongues." Significantly, glossolalia, or speaking in tongues, is a practice associated with Black women in the Pentecostal Holiness church. . . . As a trope it is also intended to remind us of Alice Walker's characterization of Black women as artists, as "Creators," intensely rich in that spirituality which Walker sees as "the basis of Art." (122)

Having further defined her concept of speaking in tongues (which she says is "her trope for both glossolalia and heteroglossia") in its application to "the classic black women's text," Henderson applies the concept to her reading of Sherley Anne Williams's *Dessa Rose* (1944) and Toni Morrison's *Sula* in order to illustrate Black women as both silenced and resisting silence (Henderson 1989, 123).[15] She rightly asserts that the Black woman writer's literary tradition should be understood in terms of multiple voices: "As gendered and racial subjects, black women speak/write in multiple voices—not all simultaneously or with equal weight, but with various and changing degrees of intensity, privileging one parole and then another" (137). Henderson intends her poststructuralist reading of Hurston's text to represent a shift away from readings that marginalize Black women's works as "token" texts, "subsumed under the category of woman in the feminist critique and the category of black in the racial critique" (117). Although her approach recommends a concept rooted in some Black cultural religious practices, for Henderson, "it is Mikhail Bakhtin's notion of dialogism and consciousness that provides the primary model for this approach" (118).

More specifically, there are a number of assertions within Henderson's article that reflect themes and patterns in Hurston's canonization within literary studies. First, Henderson's argument makes a rhetorical gesture toward Hurston's *Their Eyes Were Watching God* as the classic Black woman's text and Alice Walker's essay "In Search of Our Mothers' Gardens: The Creativity of Black Women in the South" as informing a particular kind of spirituality as art within Black women's experiences.[16] The use of glossolalia as a theoretical trope situates her reading within a tradition of Black women writers as rooted in the cultural practices of Black women. Its use is intriguing, as it offers a metaphorical example of "multiple voices" in culturally specific terms. However, Henderson assumes that the practice of glossolalia resonates with the experiences of all Black women and can be applied to all Black women's works. In addition, her reference to Walker's essay makes an allusion to the practice as particularly Southern, which further limits its application. Henderson also describes and applies the concept of multiple voices in both poststructuralist and Black culturalist terms. Bakhtin's "dialogism" informs her application of glossolalia and is privileged as "the primary model." In so doing, she elevates

Bakhtin's theoretical perspective above her own theoretical use of glossolalia. Henderson assumes that using a poststructuralist perspective will move critical considerations of Black women writers and their works beyond marginalized readings of "other" toward readings that allow for a more complex subjectivity (1989, 117). However, in the process she has paradoxically "subsumed" her own reading of a Black women's literary tradition as multivocal. Her theory of multivocality is othered when it is "subsumed" (as subject to Bakhtin's "dialogism") and when it is defined in essentialist or narrow cultural terms. Henderson's use of Bakhtin is not fundamentally problematic. It may, in fact, provide Henderson with a theoretical construct that reveals that Black women are diverse in their subjectivity, that they do not share the same experiences, and that they may be vocal or silent in opposition to oppression as represented in several literary works. However, these aspects of Black women's diversity could be argued without referencing Bakhtin as "the primary model" of her approach.

The movement toward a feminist poststructuralist reading of Black women's literary traditions promotes poststructuralism as particularly theoretical. It also signals the power invested in its use and its potential currency within the larger academy. In *Reading Black, Reading Feminist*, an anthology that features Henderson's article, editor Henry Louis Gates Jr. describes her argument as "a truly critical stance that would resist all monisms of all sorts, and that insists on plural subject-positions, and on a dialogic subjectivity that is radical to both race and gender" (1990, 11).[17] The assumption embedded within Henderson's treatment and Gates's subsequent praise is that "race" and "gender" cannot be or have not been radically conceived as plural constructs without Bakhtin's notion of dialogism. These statements suggest the relinquishment of analytic authority by Black feminist literary critics and African American critics to more institutionally powerful critical trends within the academy. Like Gates's treatment of Hurston in *The Signifying Monkey*, Henderson's article is evidence of the shifts and tensions between Black aesthetic cultural readings and poststructuralist readings occurring during this time. Hurston's work is a central figure in these discursive exchanges, as it is commonly found at the nexus that joins these distinctive and overlapping discourses.

I have discussed how poststructuralist scholars who read Hurston's work through these "new" theoretical lenses underscored her "foremother" status and how these new readings occasioned Hurston's entry into the canon. Some critics, however, perceived her entry into the canon as due to an essential quality of her works. For example, I have mentioned previously Gates's privileging of Hurston's "command of a narrative voice that imitates the storytelling structures of the Black vernacular tradition" (Gates 1993, xii). Gates also marked Hurston's place in the canon in *The Signifying Monkey*:

> For Hurston is now a cardinal figure in the African American canon, the feminist canon, and the canon of American fiction, especially as our readings become increasingly close readings, which Hurston's texts sustain delightfully. The curious aspect of the widespread critical attention being shown to Hurston's texts is that so many critics embracing such a diversity of theoretical approaches seem to find something new at which to marvel on her texts. (1998, 180)

Gates argues, in effect, that what makes Hurston's work so distinctive is its ability to sustain close readings. However, as Christian warns and Johnson's reading demonstrates, rather than significantly new statements about the import of Hurston's work, new critical theories work (or practice or play or exercise) *on* them. We, as readers, don't necessarily learn new ways of interpreting Hurston's text so much as we learn how Hurston bears, like the mule trope she invokes in her own work, the theoretical overtures of her current receptions. In Gates's assessment, Hurston's works are uncharacteristically passive in their response to "so many new critics." She "delightfully sustains" their close readings, as they "marvel" at her limitless potential (180).

It is useful here to consider Toni Morrison's "Unspeakable Things Unspoken: The Afro-American Presence in American Literature," which enlarges these debates beyond the African American literary canon to discuss canon formation in European and American contexts. She describes the universality of rhetorical movements/postures in articulating hegemonic canonical positions, suggesting that current canon debates follow a predictable form. Arguing that canon formations are about "vested" politics, Morrison suggests that recent debates have made the topic of race "speakable" (1989, 1–9). She claims, "Finding or imposing Western influences in/on Afro-American literature has value, but when its sole purpose is to *place* value only where that influence is located it is pernicious" (10). She goes on to describe the subsequent effect:

> My unease stems from the possible, probable consequences these approaches may have upon the work itself. They can lead to an incipient orphanization of the work in order to issue its adoption papers. They can confine the discourse to the advocacy of diversification within the canon and/or a kind of benign co-existence near or within the reach of already sacred texts. Either of these two positions can quickly become another kind of silencing if permitted to ignore the indigenous created qualities of the writing. (10)

By "indigenous" Morrison does not mean native or authentic qualities that when applied to the value or authority of the tradition of African American literature evoke problematic critical referents and that are a common way of evaluating African American literature: "When African American art is worthy, it is because it is 'raw' and 'rich,' like ore, and like ore needs refining by Western intelligences" (10). Instead, by "indigenous" she means original, as in emanating from the author's creative and imaginative process. To illustrate, she provides a brief discussion of the "indigenous" process involved in constructing meaning in her own novels. Morrison explicates the first lines in each of her novels and reveals a fluid and complex interplay between historical contexts, cultural specificities and allusions, word choice (for their alliteration, assonance, rhythm, and tone), tonal and aural imagery, character development, and solid plot development. She enacts what Christian refers to as "practice" in her attention to "the intricacies of the intersection of language, class, race, and gender in the literature" and in the sharing of "process" (Christian 1987, 53).

Morrison's explications are exciting for the way they reveal how her decisions as author are made or originate from an anticipation or relation to reader reception. She illustrates how African American culture is crafted and represented in her works in ways that require no authenticating stamp of Western or Eurocentric discourse to determine its meanings or values. Her discussion suggests that the same process of "choices" is true in the works of other African American writers who can also be explicated in the same manner: "We are not, in fact, 'other.' We are choices" (Morrison 1989, 9). In summary, Morrison argues against the use of hegemonic references, such as poststructuralism, to place value on African American literature. She illustrates how meaning and literary merit can be derived through a close reading of works that considers their own cultural referents to evaluate the meanings of those texts. When African American works are read in ways that suggest that their literary value comes only in relation to more hegemonic works, they are orphaned, othered, and tokenized (10). The reception of Hurston's *Their Eyes Were Watching God* as discussed is an example of this dynamic. It is sometimes orphaned from preceding literary works or contemporary works with shared historical contexts that may shed light on its available meanings. Thus separated from its contexts, *Their Eyes* is easily tokenized and ossified in static readings of its meanings.

Hazel Carby offers a response to Morrison's article published in the same issue of the *Michigan Quarterly Review*. Titled "The Canon: Civil War and Reconstruction," Carby's response speaks to the broader political and cultural contexts of canon formation that Morrison references in her address. Carby argues that the canon wars are about dominance and "complex modes of inequality" within the academy and society at large: "Focusing on books and authors means that we are not directly addressing the ways in which our society is structured in dominance" (1989, 37). She challenges the assumptions that the inclusion of works by women of color will result in an equality of the works and the groups they represent (36–37). Carby gives the example of how within some English departments "courses on culturally marginalized literatures are not part of the requirements," and therefore they have an "exotic relation" to the central literature, in which "students occupy the position of tourist" (38). Even if "marginal" works are included within academic courses, systems of inequality that structure the academy ensure that these works will not be centrally considered.

In addition, Carby notes that the European or American canon "depend(s) upon the idea of a pure and authentic culture that can be embodied in a careful selection of texts. However, in Afro-American studies we too have been searching for a pure and authentic culture" (41). Here Carby addresses the issue of canon formation in terms of its insistence on a "folk" sensibility that connects works from the slave narrative to the present day into a falsely "authentic" and "pure" cultural "unity" (41). She writes, "I would suggest that instead of searching for cultural purity we acknowledge cultural complexity" (42). Carby's essay, like Morrison's, underscores the broader contexts of Hurston's authority within the American literary canon, given its regard as a classic and "authentic" Black text. Her argument, in relation to this project, further suggests that Hurston's token presence in the canon will not fundamentally alter the structural inequalities of the academy. In addition to cultural complexity, community matters in Black feminist critical projects.

Returning to my discussion of the "Walker effect," when writer Alice Walker calls for our consideration of our mothers' gardens as a metaphor for a serious consideration of the significance of Black women's literary work, she references Hurston, Phillis Wheatley, and Nella Larsen. For Walker, these diverse women writers, whose works span across centuries of Black women's literary production, were marginalized as a community from critical consideration and were a model for writers like herself. Although June Jordan presciently warned against adopting a "superstar, one-at-a-time mentality" in Black World (1974, 7), subsequent considerations of Hurston's work by some Black feminist literary critics and African American literary critics set the stage for her token inclusion within the academy. Thereafter, when Hurston was read in ways that privileged poststructuralist readings of her work as more authoritative, her own literary authority was disassociated from several communities: from communities of scholars who chose to read her work outside of new commodified theories, and from critics who chose to focus on other Black women writers. Hurston's work enters the canon, while her contemporaries, predecessors, and the Black feminist scholars who focus on their work remain marginalized (Wallace [1988] 1990, 175). As Carby says, "The mere presence of marginalized cultures in the curriculum changes very little" (1989, 38).

Deborah McDowell, in "Transferences: Black Feminist Thinking: The 'Practice' of 'Theory'," charts how poststructuralism, with its tendency to challenge authority, objectivity, subjectivity, and positionality, emerged just as Black feminist criticism began to be authoritatively defined (1995b, 168). McDowell responds to arguments that Black feminists question the usefulness of critical theory because they are not only ideologically conservative but also ignorant or fearful of critical theory. Like Christian and Joyce before her (Christian 1987, 57; Joyce 1987b, 381–82), McDowell takes no issue with the use of new theories, nor does she argue for a split between theory and practice. Instead, her concern is with their institutional power to disrupt the work and broad commitments of Black feminist literary criticism. For example, she lists five institutional dynamics of the relationship between poststructuralism and the Black feminist critical project. Briefly and generally paraphrased here, she maintains that particular forms of poststructuralism worked to displace Black feminist efforts to assert "the significance of black women's experience" (168), to fully interpret the works of Black women writers, to center an analysis of any work within relevant historical contexts, to acknowledge the agency of authors in the production of their works, and to work to both define and debate the usefulness of literary tradition and canons in terms that center Black women writers (168–69).

Notwithstanding the influence of new critical theories on Black feminist and African Americanist literary criticisms, canons, and traditions, Hurston's work technically "survived" literary poststructuralist theoretical scrutiny as texts. For the most part, within literary studies, neither her work nor discussions of her life were marginalized when interest in her work expanded beyond the discourses of Black feminist criticism.[18] More specifically, in the case of Hurston's canonical status, her representations of Black language in her work, concurrent with her popularity as a Black feminist foremother in Black feminist literary criticism, made her work a convenient (as well as highly marketable) object for the application of new critical theories.[19] As the demand for Hurston's works increased, some readings of her narrowed in their critical scope. At times she is reduced to an essentialized raced and gendered object and becomes the embodiment/vehicle of the integration of Black feminist and African American literary theory with critical theory. She is, as Morrison suggests, orphaned,

70

silenced, and silencing of divergent readings of her work or the works of others within the tradition (Morrison 1989, 10). Ironically, or perhaps inevitably, the silencing of these divergent readings occurs because they are drowned out by critical treatments that privilege Hurston's Black (vernacular and objectified) voice (duCille 1993, 69).[20]

Concerning the canonization of *Their Eyes*, Corse and Griffin write, "The environment within which *Their Eyes Were Watching God* and its peer texts were reevaluated was profoundly different than earlier environments because of the availability of new critical perspectives that radically challenged the ability of academia to deny the validity of African-American literary scholars claim for inclusion" (1997, 195). However, their analysis of the social contexts of critical theory does not consider the role of "social actors" in the process of rhetorically elevating Hurston's *Their Eyes*, the contested debates about new critical perspectives, as well as representations of Hurston the author, in the process of canonization. Within the aforementioned readings, Hurston is distinguished and elevated into the American literary canon because her body of work is proven capable of carrying theory. Ironically, given the symbolism of mules in Hurston's *Their Eyes* and in *Mules and Men*, her work becomes a "theoretical mule." Not only is Hurston "a convenient figure to study" (West 2005, 251), but any cursory theoretical treatment of her work is also convenient.

McDowell writes about how within the system/institution of the academy, with its own contexts of racism and sexism, Black women are either invisible and ignored or rendered as "other." Sojourner Truth's "Ain't I a Woman" is appropriated to represent a Black female politics rather than a Black feminist theory. She does not embody both (McDowell 1995b, 158–63):

> But the repetition of Sojourner Truth's name makes no *real* difference. In dominant discourses it is a symbolic gesture masking the face of power and its operations in the present academic context. As a figure in remove, summoned from the seemingly safe and comfortable distance of a historical past, "Sojourner Truth" can thus act symbolically to absorb, defuse, and deflect a variety of conflicts and anxieties over race in present academic contexts. (162)

Hurston represents another occurrence of this symbolic process. In addition, as I show in the following chapters, literary critics in the late 1980s acknowledge Hurston as a Black female theorist, even as their criticisms work to define and deconstruct the effects of Hurston's iconography and the terms of a Black women's literary tradition, a project that worked to create and preserve a critical space for the works of many Black women writers, including Black women writers from the nineteenth century.[21] In some instances, Hurston's training as an anthropologist and her theorizing about culture are commonly referenced within evaluations of her literary work, which lend anthropological authority to her literary authority. Altogether, critical assessments reveal how the "repetition" or exchange of Zora Neale Hurston's name "makes no *real* difference" when it narrows a broader way of reading and understanding her many works (and the works of other Black women writers) and when it curtails an expansive understanding of literary and anthropological histories beyond her popular legacy.

3

Deconstructing an Icon
Tradition and Authority

While some scholars mined *Their Eyes Were Watching God* as the emblematic Black text for discussions of authentic Black or female voice, identity, textuality, and linguistic structures, other scholars, particularly scholars of Black women's literature, questioned the mass attention given to Zora Neale Hurston. How did some Black women writers and critics respond to concerns about Hurstonism during this early period of Hurston's canonization from the 1980s to 1990s? They worked to enlarge discussions of tradition and expand literary histories by looking back to the nineteenth century and early twentieth century to include Black women writers that preceded Hurston and her contemporaries, including non-Black contemporaries.[1] They also challenged and debated the terms of tradition itself to include experiences beyond the U.S. South and beyond conventional constructions of authentic blackness, both terms so central in early constructions of Hurston's place within Black women's literary tradition. They also, I argue, troubled notions of genealogy in constructions of Black women's literature, "worrying the line," which Cheryl Wall describes as occurring "at those moments in literary texts when the genealogical search is frustrated by gaps in written history and knowledge" (2005b, 8). In this way, Hurston's central and iconic position was revised, even as references to her anthropological training and research, beginning with Robert Hemenway's literary biography of Hurston ([1977] 1980) remained significant in establishing her literary authority.

Beginning in the mid-1980s, the latter period of Hurston's establishment within the American literary canon, Black women literary critics such as Deborah E. McDowell, Hazel Carby, Michele Wallace, Nellie McKay, Ann duCille, bell hooks, Hortense Spillers, and Carol Boyce Davies, among others, directly addressed Hurston's central place in Black women's literary history. Some questioned Hurston's critical positioning as the foremother of a Black feminist literary tradition, citing the erasure of other Black women writers who preceded her. Others asserted that the terms of Hurston's canonical rise effectively displaced critical assessments of other Black women writers both prior to and since the period commonly referred to as the Harlem Renaissance. Altogether, their criticisms challenged scholarly projects that defined Black feminist literary traditions in limited terms, terms that might exclude the influence of male writers, non-Black writers, Black mixed-raced writers, and Black writers of the African diaspora beyond the U.S. South. In some assessments, critics troubled tradition making, as they read early calls for and claims made about Black feminist literary traditions as ahistorical. They defined Black women writers as a complex and identifiable community of critics and authors and revisited how a Black women writer's literary production both drew from and addressed diverse audiences, sources of inspiration, and scholarship. Ever sharpening and expanding critical frameworks and contexts for their work, assessments and reassessments of Black women's literary histories emerged. The following reading provides a frame for evaluating some of the ways that critics and authors worked against the influence of "Hurstonism" (duCille 1993, 69).

Deborah E. McDowell's "The Changing Same: Generational Connections and Black Women Novelists—*Iola Leroy* and *The Color Purple*" ([1984] 1995) stands out for how it resists conventional comparisons between Walker and Hurston and traces the Black women's literary tradition prior to the twentieth century. McDowell considers how Alice Walker's own literary influences might be read beyond Hurston to include writers of the late nineteenth century:

> For Walker, as for so many woman writers, the process of that discovery [of voice] begins with thinking back through and reclaiming her female ancestors. While much has been made (with Walker's encouragement) of Walker's obvious debt to Zora Neale Hurston, there has been virtually no acknowledgement that she owes an equal, though different debt to Black women writers before Hurston. ([1984] 1995, 46)

McDowell links Alice Walker's *The Color Purple* to Frances E. W. Harper's *Iola Leroy* (1892). She shows how Walker's characterization of Celie and Nettie's sisterhood within *The Color Purple* revises and situates Harper's representation of Black womanhood. Harper's characterization of Iola Leroy as an "exemplary image" of true womanhood, a mulatta committed to racial uplift, was carefully crafted to challenge received racist notions of Black women as essentially licentious. Walker's characterization of this sisterhood within *The Color Purple* revises and situates Harper's representation. Nettie's letters to Celie reveal a commitment to racial uplift and the cult of true womanhood, which readers read alongside a more modern (and folksy) evocation of a Black woman's (Celie's) emerging erotic, spiritual, and epistolary authority (McDowell [1984] 1995, 43–51). Their letters to each other (and the novel itself) are a metaphorical bridge between Black women writers of the nineteenth and twentieth centuries, across different registers (language, audience, and reception) of public and private narratives. Walker, McDowell asserts, refuses intertextual "adversarial and parodic" revision (of either characters) in service to an intertextuality that ultimately works to uplift diverse Black women as sisters, bonding as readers and writers (48).

Hortense Spillers in "Afterword: Cross-Currents, Discontinuities: Black Women's Fiction," in *Conjuring: Black Women, Fiction, and Literary Tradition*, writes, "Traditions are not born. They are made" (1985, 250), in effect challenging prior constructions of tradition in genealogical terms. She further asserts, "Reading against the canon, intruding into it a configuration of symbolic values with which the critics and audiences must contend, the work of black women's writing community not only redefines tradition but also disarms it by suggesting that the term is a critical fable intended to encode and circumscribe an inner and licit circle of empowered texts" (251). Hurston's Janie, then, is read by Spillers as a break from the traditions of representations of "passing," with Janie's characterization reflecting "*inner*-directed" agency (and perhaps conflicts) in comparison to "Larsen's and Fauset's agents," whose conflicts are apprehended by Spillers as "imposed by an outer means or force" (252–53). Regarding Hurston's literary community with Nella Larsen and Jessie Fauset, Spillers states, "It is as though Hurston never heard of either, let alone read and studied their work" (252). As will be discussed later, P. Gabrielle Foreman offers a reading that counters Spillers's assessment of Hurston's connection with both Larsen and Fauset (Foreman 1990, 655). However, Spillers's larger argument here is to complicate the terms of tradition, to illustrate how "'tradition' for [the] black women's writing community is a matrix of literary discontinuities that partially articulate various periods of consciousness in the history of African-American people" (251).[2]

Hazel Carby looked to Hurston's contemporaries to enlarge and critique the inordinate focus on Hurston in discussions of Black women's literary history and tradition. In *Reconstructing Womanhood: The Emergence of the Afro-American Woman Novelist* (1987b), Carby addresses the writings and work of nineteenth- and early twentieth-century Black women toward defining and assessing a history of Black women novelists. Her essay "The Quicksand of Representation: Rethinking Black Cultural Politics" (1987a) argues that receptions of the Harlem Renaissance and the concept of the "New Negro" largely ignore the "economic radicalism" that characterized the period. For Carby, receptions of Hurston "epitomized the intellectual who represented 'the people' through a reconstruction of 'the folk' and avoided the class conflict of the Northern cities" (1987a, 166).[3] Carby argues that an inordinate attention to Hurston sidelines authors like Nella Larsen (1891–1964) and Jesse Fauset (1882–1961), two Black women writers whose works "responded to an emerging black urban working class" (166–67). In addition to looking back to the nineteenth and early twentieth centuries, Carby also addresses the impact of narrow constructions of tradition for Black women writers in the mid- to late twentieth century:

> In the search for a tradition of black women writers of fiction, a pattern has been established from Alice Walker back through Zora Neale Hurston, which represents the rural folk as bearers of Afro-American history and preservers of Afro-American culture. This construction of a tradition of black women writing has effectively marginalized the fictional urban confrontation of race, class, and sexuality that was to follow *Quicksand*: Ann Petry's *The Street* (1946); Dorothy West's *The Living is Easy* (1948); Gwendolyn Brooks' *Maud Martha* (1951); and the work of Toni Morrison. (175)

Carby is critical of tradition making and overstates that Hurston's work does not attend to class dynamics;[4] however, her central argument rightly works to address the omission of other Black women writers, given the focus on Hurston within early Black women's literary tradition making.

Nellie McKay's "'Crayon Enlargements of Life': Zora Neale Hurston's *Their Eyes Were Watching God* as Autobiography" (1990) expands ways of reading Hurston and Black women's literary tradition making beyond the genre of the novel. McKay links Hurston's most celebrated text to the personal/auto-biographical/travel/slave narratives of Black women of the late 1800s to the early 1900s. She notes that *Their Eyes Were Watching God* is often heralded for its fictional representation of the archetypal Black woman's identity and self-actualization as embodied in Janie Crawford, with critics and biographers routinely noting how Hurston's own romance with a younger man (as described in her autobiography) influenced her narration of Janie's romance with Tea Cake, a man ten years younger. McKay's sustained reading of *Their Eyes* describes how themes of community, travel, self-development, and positive racial consciousness come together in Janie's life story that, while different in form, leave readers with a strong autobiographical impression. McKay addresses how Hurston's *Their Eyes*, then, meets conventions of autobiography when compared to autobiographical narratives of an earlier era by authors such as Nancy Prince (1799–1856) and Mary Church Terrell (1863–1954) (McKay 1990, 58). As in *Their Eyes*, the works of Prince and Terrell were concerned with "the tradition of Black women celebrating themselves" toward an autonomous and empowered self (68).

P. Gabrielle Foreman's "Looking Back from Zora, or Talking Out Both Sides My Mouth for Those Who Have Two Ears" (1990) offers ways of reading Hurston's work that revise her place within a Black feminist literary tradition while also reasserting the importance of critical projects to define such traditions. Foreman considers tradition as neither solely dependent on essentialist arguments of identity nor neatly bound to writers as projects of revision and signification. Tradition exists as a shared experience: "Our writers often, though by no means always, share (if not as lived experience then as awareness of the 'race's' positioning) a cultural, religious fabric and/or socio-political positionality. This broader text, this often overdetermining 'influence' may suggest the echoes, signifying strategies, and historical continuities that frame a tradition which embraces no easy linear fallout, no uncomplicated trajectory of similarities" (650). Noting the works and writings of authors and critics such as Barbara Smith, Barbara Christian, and June Jordan, Foreman addresses the significant omission and unavailability of the work of Black women writers, including Hurston. Foreman asserts, "There is strength in numbers, in communities, in traditions. Just as it is dangerous to adopt the convenient bracketing off of 'race' at a time when it is no longer expedient for a power structure which has insisted on race's existence to maintain its hegemony, it is dangerous to dismiss Black women's literary traditions" (662).

Foreman's work ultimately illustrates how Hurston's work is in conversation with other works by and about Black women of the nineteenth and early twentieth centuries. For example, she argues that, like Hurston's *Their Eyes*, earlier works veiled and subverted literary meaning and also subverted stereotypical representations of the tragic mulatto. Foreman illustrates that Frances E. Harper's *Iola Leroy* (1892) and Jessie Fauset's *Plum Bun* (1929) move beyond characterizations of sentimental and romanticized heroines typical of the era, and their narratives reveal how power dynamics are skillfully embedded to subvert expectations of the genre. Each novel challenges constructions of traditional black womanhood, not unlike Hurston's Janie in *Their Eyes Were*

Watching God (Foreman 1990, 655). Harper's Iola Leroy may profess the part of a "weak, innocent, and defenseless" woman, but she enacts "a strong, independent character, hardly in need of protection" (Foreman 1990, 652). Fauset's Angela Murray (the main character of *Plum Bun*) is a resourceful woman who cogently describes a strategic desire for power as she contemplates passing for white and marrying a white man. In addition, Foreman argues that Harper, Fauset, and Hurston used "literary veiling" to push beyond the expectations of "race women" of the era and the expectations and control of the publishing industry and of both mainstream and Black elite literary audiences (655–57). Hurston revised but did not erase traditions/tropes/forms in African American literature that preceded her own work. Foreman's assessment suggests that writers, readers, and critics create a tradition in order to preserve works that would otherwise be marginalized: "The lack of a discernible tradition has been a silencing agent in the history of Blacks, of women, of Black women, of indeed many marginalized groupings. Without a 'tradition' into which to fit us, we have been misunderstood, misinterpreted, and finally, and often quickly, dismissed—thus the tone of urgency, the tone of survival that often resonates in our work" (662).

Notwithstanding the critical work to build community, the critical and popular receptions of Walker's essays, as well as Hurston's received authority and literary legacy, meant that some contemporary readers and writers did not see themselves reflected within constructions of a Black women's literary tradition. Some produced creative works and criticisms that challenged the terms of tradition itself to include experiences beyond the U.S. South and to confront received notions of racialized kinship within the tradition. Michele Wallace, for example, worked to expand Black women's literary tradition in terms beyond the U.S. South. Her essay "Variations on Negation and the Heresy of Black Feminist Creativity" (1989) offers a tangential critique of the singular critical attention given to Hurston via a discussion of Wallace's reception of "In Search of Our Mothers' Gardens." Wallace describes the constraints imposed upon Black women writers by the various institutions and group affiliations that mediate their literary productions.

Her own monograph, *Black Macho and the Myth of the Superwoman* (1979), received criticism for suggesting that Black women writers did not question stereotypes of Black women. In her own defense, she writes, "It was my view that Black women writers were verifying 'the myth of the superwoman' by creating perverse characterizations, which displayed inordinate strengths and abilities as the inevitable booby prize of a romanticized marginality" (1989, 61). Wallace explains that although she was aware of the works of many Black women writers, *Black Macho* was, in part, a response to sentimental representations of Black women writers:

> It was around this time that I read Walker's first book of short stories, *In Love and Trouble*, as well as the essay "In Search of Our Mothers' Gardens," which immediately became essential reading for Black feminists, but which struck me then as afflicted by the same nostalgia for and valorization of the rural and the anonymity of the unlettered that I considered so problematic in the work of Black women novelists. In particular, the premise of the article—that Black women writers should speak for generations of silenced Black women—posed certain conceptual difficulties for me. First, no one can speak *for* anybody else. Inevitably, we silence others that we may speak at all. This is particularly true of "speaking" in print. Second, there was an implicit denial of the necessity for generation conflict and critical dialectic, which I found totally paralyzing. Anyhow, my mother was a prominent artist, well educated and active in the Women's Movement. So how could I pursue Walker's proposal? Moreover, didn't it imply that Black women writers would always "speak" from the platform of a silenced past? (1989, 59)

Wallace's essay, then, works to revise her own project regarding the myth of the superwoman and to contextualize her reading of Black women writers during the era of its production. When Wallace describes Walker's work as "essential reading for Black feminists," she suggests the significant influence of Walker's popularity apart from Walker's own careful and persuasive rhetoric. In light of subsequent criticism, including criticism from Alice Walker, Wallace admits that at the time *Black Macho* was published, she was aware of a number of Black women novelists who challenged stereotypes and other problematic representations of Black women characters and communities, including subsequent Black feminist critical readings of *Their Eyes*, which had broadened her view (1989, 57–60).[5] However, "as a young Black woman who was in search of feminist solidarity *and* a writing career, I wanted something very specific from the Black women writers I read" (58).

A year before her reconsideration of receptions of her own work and that of Walker's, Wallace provided a pointed assessment of the critical and uncritical consumption of Hurston during the emergence of poststructuralist readings of Hurston's work. Wallace's article "Who Owns Zora Neale Hurston? Critics Carve Up the Legend," originally published in the *Village Voice Literary Supplement* for a popular audience, presents Hurston, in summary, as the Black/female/object worshipped in fanatical fashion, her body of work consumed irreverently, her true contributions shrouded by the very discourses (poststructuralist) that seek to resurrect her ([1988] 1990, 175).[6] In addition, Wallace asserts that there exists a critical distance between the work of Black feminist criticism and the works of contemporary Black women writers:

> Forceful Black feminist critical voices are needed to verify the crucial assault on the logic of binary oppositions of race, class, and sex already launched by contemporary Black women novelists, poets, and playwrights. Scrutiny of Hurston's nonfiction writing could inspire us to take on this task. Instead, the thrust of Black feminist writing on Hurston implicitly proposes her life and work as a role model for contemporary Black female scholarship, intellectual curiosity, and literary production. The model is too narrow. (181)

As Wallace assesses the critical limits of receptions of Hurston in defining a Black women's literary tradition, she notes that Black women writers have themselves worked to critique stereotypical characterizations of "race, class, and sex" in their works. The treatment of race, in particular, within constructions of early Black feminist criticism about tradition (notwithstanding the critical attention given to "passing" and the trope of the tragic mulatto) provides an opportunity to consider further the model and effect that Wallace critiques. Wallace suggests that her own mother's education, activism, and success as a professional artist meant she could not realize Walker's model for Black women writers.[7] Beyond education and professional status, how might race, as a construct, complicate claims to Black feminist literary tradition (and communities) for budding writers in search of Black women's literary gardens? In a contemporary context, as multiracial identities are further defined, references to Black foremothers frustrate claims to Black feminist literary traditions and community for some African American multiracial women.

For example, Heidi Durrow, author of *The Girl Who Fell from the Sky* (2010) and daughter of a white Danish mother and African American father, found Alice Walker's genealogical references constraining. In the critical essay "Dear Ms. Larsen, There's a Mirror Looking Back" (2008), Durrow signifies on constructions of race in Walker's essays "In Search of Zora Neale Hurston" ("Looking for Zora") and "In Search of Our Mothers' Gardens." Durrow raises and answers the question of whether a Black woman with a white mother can inherit a Black woman's literary tradition vis-à-vis Black maternal genealogies (Freeman Marshall 2013, 27–35). Durrow's essay, an obvious homage to Walker's classic essays, describes her own search to find the gravesite of Nella Larsen, author of *Quicksand* (1928), *Passing* (1929), and several essays, who Durrow adopts as her own Black multiracial literary foremother of Danish descent. Durrow's essay revises Walker's proposal, defining Larsen's influence with direct references and allusions to Walker's search for Hurston, and Durrow details her own and Larsen's search for racial identity as she works to center Larsen's literary authority (Durrow 2008, 107). Durrow asserts that the work and legacy of Nella Larsen frees her from the writer's block that plagued her as she "struggled to write the stories that she thought a black woman writer *should* write" (105). In a gesture that evokes Walker's memorial to Hurston, Durrow places a headstone on Larsen's unmarked grave. The ritual act signifies the rhetorical strength and enduring influence of Walker's "In Search of Zora Neale Hurston" even as it challenges Walker's conventional framing of a Black women's literary tradition and ultimately honors Larsen's contribution to that tradition (Freeman Marshall 2013, 31).

Durrow's essay offers a revisionist critique of Black feminist literary tradition making, and in doing so, it fulfills Hazel Carby's call for Black feminist criticism to be "regarded critically as a problem, not a solution, as a sign that should be interrogated, a locus of contradictions" (Carby 1987b, 15). However, the essay does not completely reject the import of tradition and related constructs as encountered in Walker's essays. As critic and author, Durrow takes up the contradictions she encounters in Walker's essays as problem, solution, and sign, writing "herself" within a Black women's literary tradition with the publication of *The Girl Who Fell from the Sky*. With allusions to Larsen's *Passing* and Toni Morrison's *The Bluest Eye* (1970) and *Beloved* (1987), Durrow works to revise and expand select representations of multiracial identity and experience. In "Dear Ms. Larsen, There's a Mirror Looking Back," vis-à-vis her reading of Morrison's *The Bluest Eye*, Durrow describes her difficulty in locating her own multiracial experience within contemporary Black women's novels. She observes, "Not once, *not ever* in repeated adolescent or college-age readings of the book did it occur to me that I was Pecola's mirror opposite. I was the little black girl with blue eyes who yearned for my difference to disappear" (2008, 104). Two years later, her debut novel offers additional allusions to Larsen's *Passing* and Morrison's *The Bluest Eye*. More specifically, Durrow's characterization of Rachel, a Black "new girl," born with blue eyes of a white Danish mother and Black father, "worries" genealogical representations of racial identity in Black women's literature via allusions to Morrison's characterization of Maureen Peal (Morrison 1970, 62–75; Wall 2005b, 8).

In Morrison's novel, Maureen, the "new girl" in a community in Lorain, Ohio, is Pecola's foil. Her interactions with Claudia, Frieda, and Pecola, young Black girls with neither color nor class privilege, highlight the intricacies and internalizing of systemic racism, which they navigate largely on their own. An escalating exchange between the four girls reveals Claudia's anger and jealousy at Maureen's light skin and beauty, privilege, and wealth and unveils Maureen's colorism. Morrison's novel makes possible a reading of the influence of white beauty standards and systemic racism on the psyches of young Black girls, but the larger social contexts of Maureen's particular experience are left unexplored. Therefore, Durrow's *The Girl Who Fell from the Sky* offers readers "new girl" Rachel, who navigates her newfound Black family and larger community as a Black multiracial girl with blue eyes. Despite assumptions of a totalizing privilege, Rachel's reception by this community presents her experience of multiracial privilege as situational, contextual, and complicated by her working-class status. In addition, Durrow is "worrying the line" between the histories and social contexts that inform Larsen's *Passing* and Morrison's *Beloved* when Rachel's white mother, Nella, jumps from a roof with her Black mixed-race children (Wall 2005b, 8). Nella, originally from Denmark, is distraught by the growing realization of her own unwitting racism when it is revealed to her that "jigaboo," a term she has used endearingly to refer to her children, is considered a synonym for the word "nigger" (Durrow 2010, 155).[8] Along with the unrelenting stress of poverty, addiction, and intimate partner violence at the hand of her racist white boyfriend, she is unable to reconcile her children's multiracial genealogy with the reality of the anti-Black racism they will undoubtedly experience. In part, Nella commits suicide and filicide because she realizes that she is unable to keep her children "safe" (Durrow 2010, 104, 154, 157, 247), all allusions to Morrison's *Beloved*.

Within *Beloved*, the word "safe" is a refrain, a repetend, in the mind and mouth of Sethe. Her escape from Sweet Home, School Teacher, and slavery is motivated by her desire to keep her children both free and safe from School Teacher's racist and calculated cruelty. Upon School Teacher's attempt to arrest and return Sethe and her children to slavery, Sethe attempts to kill them all. Only Beloved, the infant, dies, her ghost haunting Sethe and the novel's narrative. So Sethe, clearly traumatized, repeats and rationalizes her motive (Morrison [1987] 2004, 192, 193, 231, 254). For example, Sethe tells a stunned Paul D, "I stopped him. . . . I took and put my babies where they'd be safe" (231). Durrow's novel, in effect, revises this central internal conflict in *Beloved* as *The Girl* imagines how a white mother who bore Black multiracial children experiences and tragically responds to racism (Durrow 2010, 153–57; Freeman Marshall 2013, 27–35). In this way, Durrow, as reader and author, moves beyond the influence of Walker's "In Search of Our Mothers' Gardens" and Morrison's *Bluest Eye*. "Frustrated by the gaps," Durrow "worries the line" of genealogies in Walker's essay and other notable works (Wall 2005b, 8). She draws inspiration from a literary foremother other than Hurston, inscribes her literary lineage to Nella Larsen, and revises a matrilineal genealogy (within a Black women's literary tradition) to include a white mother and her surviving mixed-race daughter.

As illustrated in this reading of Durrow's work, Cheryl Wall's *Worrying the Line: Black Women Writers, Lineage, and Literary Tradition* provides a conceptual framework for exploring how Black women writers reconstruct family history "within texts" (2005, 13), including ways their protagonists "manage to close the gaps between the available written knowledge and the connections to the past they seek (17).[9] Wall is among the literary critics who accorded Hurston central status in early critical assessments of Black women's literary traditions (Wall 1982, 76). However, her work also situated Hurston within a larger community of Black women writers, especially within the context of duCille's and other critical efforts to define and revise "Hurstonism." Significantly, Wall's work simultaneously codified and expanded Hurston's legacy beyond her classic novel *Their Eyes Were Watching God*. For example, among Wall's many works, her edited volumes *Zora Neale Hurston: Novels and Short Stories* (1995c) and *Zora Neale Hurston: Folklore, Memoirs, and Other Writings* (1995b), both published with the Library of America, gather Hurston's extant writings into two collections that preserve Hurston's contributions to literature, folklore studies, and anthropology. In addition, Wall's *Women of the Harlem Renaissance*, published the same year, supports a consideration of Hurston's work within a community of her contemporaries Jessie Redmon Fauset (1882–1961) and Nella Larsen (1891–1964).[10] Wall states:

> Hurston's recuperation intensifies the need to examine the lives and works of her female contemporaries: to identify common themes and metaphors in their writings, to determine who they were and where and how they lived, and to study the level of interaction among them. Hurston's achievement in *Their Eyes Were Watching God* and other books was the end result of a struggle enjoined by a generation of literary women to depict the lives of Black people generally and of Black women in particular, honestly and artfully. (1995a, 9)

As literary critics like Wall and others focused on revising and expanding the critical attention given to Hurston and other Black women writers within the United States, Carol Boyce Davies and Molara Ogundipe-Leslie's *Moving beyond Boundaries*: Vol. 2, *Black Women's Diasporas* (1995) gathers the critical and creative works from Black women writers throughout the African diaspora and encourages critical readers to consider how the "popular recognition" afforded Hurston and other U.S. writers either excludes or marginalizes Black women writers beyond the States. Boyce Davies's introduction to this work considers the project of canon making within the United States, which, she argues, creates an inordinate focus not only on Zora Neale Hurston but also on Toni Morrison, Alice Walker, Gwendolyn Brooks, and Maya Angelou, with Hurston as a "classic case of exclusion and recanonization" (1995, 7–12).[11] In addition, Boyce Davies asks readers to consider the ways that Hurston might be compared to writers beyond the United States: "What does it mean, therefore, to the larger understanding of Black women's writing transnationally when Hurston's work is interpreted, particularly within a narrow North American focus?" (8). Included in the collection is bell hooks's "Zora Neale Hurston: A Subversive Reading" (1995), which asks readers to consider the books that Hurston read in their assessments of her work. hooks comparatively considers Virginia Woolf's "A Room of One's Own" alongside *Their Eyes Were Watching God* for the ways it informs Hurston's treatment of "the construction of 'female imagination' and the formation of a critical space where woman's creativity can be nurtured and sustained" (245). Both Boyce Davies and hooks, then, subversively move against Hurstonism by encouraging readings of Black women's writings that expand rather than contract ways of reading and writing about their works.

Altogether, the works of black feminist literary critics connected Hurston to her contemporaries and to writers of the nineteenth century, and encouraged assessments of works by Black women writers beyond the rural U.S. South and, indeed, beyond the United States. They continued to trouble the terms of tradition for literary criticism, including "worrying the lines" of genealogies that might limit the works and representations of those within the field. Even with their deconstructions of Hurston as iconic or central, what remains distinctive in some of their descriptions of Hurston's literary authority was the import of her training and anthropological fieldwork. Ironically, this context framed Alice Walker's initial interest in Hurston's work as an authoritative source for her own creative and critical writing. Beyond Hurston's complex and contested literary authority, informed as they were by receptions of Walker's work, within literary studies, readings of Hurston's anthropological authority also helped to sustain new readings of Hurston's work.

Zora Neale Hurston: Artifact and Theory

Some literary scholars take note of Hurston's training as an anthropologist and consider how her anthropological scholarship and training impacted the content and form of her literary works. In this way, Hurston's anthropological data is mined for its cultural artifacts; these artifacts lend both a material reality as well as theoretical authority to culturalist readings of her work. Hortense

Spillers describes Hurston as "one of the major theoreticians of Black culture" and cites Hurston's "Characteristics of Negro Expression" (1934) in particular as a "systematic statement on Black culture" (Spillers 2004, 94n4). As mentioned previously, Henry Louis Gates's theory of "Signifyin(g)" draws on Hurston's illustration and definition of "signifyin'" in *Mules and Men* as well as in *Their Eyes Were Watching God* for its theoretical authority. These and other scholars read her work (fictional, autobiographical, and ethnographic) as authoritative productions of her anthropological inquiry and as cultural and historical artifacts that provide both the theory and data needed to evaluate and analyze Hurston as a literary writer.[12]

As an example, Hurston's literary biographer Robert Hemenway published "Zora Hurston and the Eatonville Anthropology" in *The Harlem Renaissance Remembered* (1972).[13] This essay discusses the impact of Hurston's anthropological education on her literary work. Hemenway defines Hurston's authority as a fiction writer in terms of her personal folk experience and her study of folk culture. He describes Hurston's unpublished novel "Herod the Great" as "a straightforward, Standard English, historical narrative of the ruler of Galilee," and he argues that it fails because "it illustrates how far Hurston had retreated from the unique sources of her aesthetic: the music and speech, energy and wisdom, dignity and humor, of the Black rural South. Her achievements increase or diminish in direct proportion to her use of the folk environment which she had grown up in and would later return to analyze" (192). Hemenway, writing in the early 1970s during a heightened period of the Black Arts movement, provides a reading of Hurston's life that he admits is intended to generate more interest in her work. He self-reflexively takes care to note in the prefatory statement of his essay that he is a white male offering a "reconstruction of the intellectual process in a Black woman's mind," and later expounds, "All men possess an anthropology which is less their own creation than a special burden of value and idea culturally imposed" (190). Sensitive, then, to his own possible critical bias, he argues against those who believe in the "mythical 'objectivity' of criticism and the presumed 'universality' of literature" (190). He says, "This leaves the critic in the same tentative position as the artist: he creates offerings. That is all the following essay presumes to be" (191). Hemenway's apology frames his treatment of Hurston's life as a "personal tragedy" (191). He describes how, despite her education and her body of work, she is reduced to having to "seek a publisher by unsolicited mail" (192). Markedly, Alice Walker would excerpt and assume Hemenway's tragic tone in her recuperation of Hurston's work.

Hemenway is also concerned with addressing the impact of Hurston's anthropological studies on her literature, which, he notes, "is seldom discussed when dealing with Hurston, but I believe it is central to understanding her role in the Renaissance and her subsequent career" (196). He concludes that Hurston's anthropological experience created "intellectual tensions" that thwarted her work. Her turn to writing literary works that treated subject matter other than Black Southern folk (*Seraph on the Suwanee* [1948], "Herod the Great," and her research in Central America) is interpreted as Hurston's "final retreat" from a "dual consciousness" and "the rejection of her folklore value" (198–99). Hemenway then turns his discussion to Hurston's use of data from her hometown of Eatonville in her literary work: "Not all of Hurston's writing during the Renaissance years deals with Eatonville, but certainly the best of it does" (202). Cheryl Wall would echo a similar criticism of Hurston's *Seraph on the Suwanee*, often regarded as Hurston's least successful novel: "From any vantage point, however, it represents an artistic decline. Hurston was at her best when she drew material directly from Black folk culture; it was the source of her creative power" (1982, 96). These judgments reflect or determine a general trend in Hurston's literary reception: *Seraph on the Suwanee*, for example, received little critical attention as compared to the critical attention given to her more canonical works (duCille 1993, 123).

Hemenway's comments mark a very early example of how Hurston's research experience in anthropology is detailed as central to understanding her literature and in defining her authority. As mentioned in chapter 1, Ellease Southerland's "The Novelist-Anthropologist's Life/Works" (1974) provides a biographical summary of Hurston's life and includes a discussion of her anthropological training and folklore research, and Alice Walker framed her early interest in Hurston's anthropology to aid her in her own creative writing (Walker 1975b, 11). In addition, Southerland's 1979 essay "The Influence of Voodoo on the Fiction of Zora Neale Hurston" (1979), in *Sturdy Black Bridges: Visions of Black Women in Literature*, reads Hurston's *Their Eyes*; *Moses, Man of the Mountain*; *Jonah's Gourd Vine*; and *Spunk* alongside *Mules and Men* and *Tell My Horse* in order to illustrate how Hurston's fictions drew from the data she collected in her anthropological studies (172–83).

However, with poststructuralist conversations in anthropology, considerations of Hurston's anthropological contributions expanded to include discussions of self-reflexive ethnography in order to describe her play on positionality in her literary and autobiographical work. In some instances, these discussions focused on redefining the authority of Hurston's less successful or authoritative works. For example, Francoise Lionnet's "Autoethnography: The An-Archic Style of *Dust Tracks on a Road*" ([1989] 1990) considers Hurston's autobiography *Dust Tracks on a Road* (1942) in light of negative reviews that criticize it for the ways it fails to conform to a conventional autobiographical model. Rather than writing a conventional autobiography that defines the historical facts and events of her life, Hurston illustrates in *Dust Tracks* "how she has become what she is—an individual who ostensibly values her independence more than any kind of political commitment to a cause" (Lionnet [1989] 1990, 383).[14] Lionnet proposes that Hurston's autobiography be considered an auto-ethnography: "the defining of one's subjective ethnicity as mediated through language, history, and ethnographical analysis" (383). She suggests that Hurston's autobiography mirrors the form of ethnography and reveals Hurston's "skepticism about the writing of culture" formed by the problematics of writing about culture from a "position of fundamental liminality—being at once a participant in and observer of her culture" (384). To argue for a rereading of Hurston's autobiography, Lionnet cites a passage in which Hurston challenges the idea of truth as "a matter of degree" that is informed and defined by the relationship between rhetorical "form and content, style and message" (386). Lionnet questions why Hurston's ideas concerning truth can't be applied to a reading of her autobiography: "Couldn't we see in this passage Hurston's own implicit theory of reading and thus use it to derive our own interpretive practice from the text itself, instead of judging the work according to Procrustean notions of autobiographical form?" (386). Lionnet's discussion provides a compelling argument for the consideration of Hurston's autobiography in terms that allow for its assumed "inconsistencies" of form to be reconsidered in light of Hurston's body of work.

I mention the above-referenced articles to underscore the consideration of Hurston's anthropological experience as lending authority to her literary projects. More broadly, I want to consider here the inequality of disciplinary authorities within the academy. While Hurston's anthropological authority is questioned by some within the field of anthropology because of its literary aspects (as I address more fully in chapter 4), her cultural theorizing is clearly considered authoritative in considerations of her literary work. Questions concerning the nature of truth and fiction as well as science and art are central to these discussions of authority. Hurston's literary work is at times represented as more realistic, reliable, and successful when it relies on data gleaned from her anthropological experience. In contrast, her anthropological work is deemed less authoritative because of its use of literary conventions that have led some to question whether Hurston's anthropologies are in fact fictions.

Hurston represents a rare as well as problematic occurrence within Black feminist literary criticism. In light of Deborah McDowell's discussion regarding the tendency to relegate the intellectual work of Black women as political and not theoretical (1995b, 161–67), Hurston's theoretical ascension is unique. Within the literary field, her work may have a theoretical authority that the works of many other Black women (as writers and critics) do not, despite their engaged discussions concerning the processes and politics of sociocultural dynamics in literature and in the world at large. Literary critics within the larger American literary canon often acknowledge Hurston as a Black woman theorizing in terms of her training as an anthropologist. In these instances, then, the incursion of hegemonic or more powerful theoretical discourses elevates Hurston to "theory" through references to its more "scientific" attributes. Anthropology as a discipline, in part, claims its scientific authority through its four fields approach, which combines physical anthropology, archaeology, linguistic anthropology, and cultural anthropology. During the height of poststructuralist debates, when cultural anthropology and its method of ethnography were critically challenged for their claims to scientific authority, literary criticisms referenced Hurston's anthropological experiences and data and, in the process, discursively transferred her anthropological authority to their considerations of her work.

However, as noted, Hurston's anthropological research is a vital source for understanding her literary productions. When studies consider the direct influence of her anthropological research on her literature through close readings of her ethnographies, they produce readings that expand our understanding of Hurston's use of plot and characterization, among other literary elements, within her narratives. *Their Eyes Were Watching God*, for example, maintains its universal appeal, for both critical and popular readers, because of its elegant portrayal of Janie's resistance to chauvinism and sexual and gender-based violence in her pursuit of love and erotic passion. These themes, especially within the context of the women's movement, attract new waves of readers to the book's narrative. However, many early critical readings assumed that the novel, set in Central Florida and the Everglades, featured only Southern customs and vernacular. When these readings consider her anthropology, many assume that Hurston drew only from her experience as a native Southerner and her anthropological research as published in *Mules and Men* and "Hoodoo in America" (1931) to craft the largely fictional narrative. However, Hurston used her findings from her anthropological research in Haiti and Jamaica to craft a culturally syncretic novel. Considering Hurston's studies of Vodou cosmology, in particular, provides new insights into her characterization of Janie, the novel's celebrated heroine.

Since the 1990s, a number of readings have reconsidered *Their Eyes Were Watching God* in light of the transnational contexts of its production in Haiti and, specifically, in terms of Hurston's research about Vodou cosmology and Janie's characterization.[15] Derek Collins's "The Myth and Ritual of Ezili Freda in Hurston's *Their Eyes Were Watching God*" (1996) convincingly argues that Janie's characterization includes significant allusions to Ezili Freda, with some minor references to Ezili Dantor.[16] In particular, Collins notes the striking similarities between Ezili Freda and Janie: "The love goddess Ezili Freda, unmistakably parallels Janie with regard to her physical beauty, her barrenness, her focus on erotic love, and the lack of permanence in her relationship with men" (140). For Collins, ignoring Hurston's folklore means that literary criticisms of her work will ultimately fail to render its complexity: "No longer can the novel be read exclusively or even primarily within the context of American racial and gender politics (as in Walker, 1979), because it undeniably contains a Haitian dimension" (150).

Three years later, Daphne Lamothe, in "Vodou Imagery, African American Tradition, and Cultural Transformation in Zora Neale Hurston's *Their Eyes Were Watching God*," similarly assesses the import of Hurston's anthropology for understanding the, by then, classic novel. Like Collins, Lamothe reads Janie as two aspects of Erzulie: Janie's physical beauty parallels Erzulie Freda, and Erzulie Dantor parallels Janie's eventual association with a working-class folk identity within the muck of the Everglades (1999, 162, 164). In addition to Janie's characterization, Lamothe reads Hurston's use of Vodou imagery as enabling her to address "migration, culture, and identity," all themes of modernity, which other writers of Hurston's era also address (157–58).

The figure of Erzulie, like the other *loas* (Haitian Vodou gods) that Hurston describes in *Tell My Horse*, is a dynamic and significant one in Haitian Vodun. Noting the long lists of variations on the major loa, Hurston describes Erzulie Freida as the goddess of love personified as a mulatto with "firm full breasts and other perfect attributes" (Hurston ([1938b] 1990, 122). She also briefly describes Erzulie, *ge-rouge* (the red-eyed), as another "aspect" or expression of Erzulie, who religious scholars note is often confused for Erzulie Dantor (122). Anthropologist Karen McCarthy Brown, in *Mama Lola: A Vodou Priestess in Brooklyn*, defines three aspects of Erzulie (Freda, Danto, and Lasyrenn) as figuring a trinity representation of female subjectivity within Vodun and as "the most important" of the "Ezili" group, with each "more understandable in relation to the others" ([1991] 2010, 220). With this in mind, and given that earlier readings by Collins and Lamothe read Janie as Erzulie Freda and Erzulie Dantor, I consider Janie in *Their Eyes* as also significantly personifying Erzulie-Lasyrenn, a Haitian loa or spirit who is also associated with love, marriage, and self-possession and who likely shaped Hurston's characterization of Janie.

Remarkably, there is no direct reference to Lasyrenn in *Tell My Horse*. Hurston notes that each loa is infinitely complex and that Erzulie is the most popular of them all, and she provides a detailed description of only "Erzulie Freida" within *Tell My Horse*. However, a single photographic image of Lasyrenn is included within the ethnography following the discussion of Erzulie Freida (fig. 10). Often figured as a beautiful mulatto (a trait she shares with Erzulie Frieda), Lasyrenn is commonly represented as a mermaid in Haitian art. The image, the icon, painted on a door, is of a fish-tailed, bare-breasted woman adorned with a necklace of beads, and an image, perhaps a single fish, appears to float above her in midair. The photo has a simple caption: "Door of the room to Erzulie" (Hurston ([1938b] 1990, 117). Its inclusion demonstrates that Hurston was aware of Lasyrenn as an aspect of Erzulie, even though there is no other commentary on this visual representation or specific conceptual understanding of Lasyrenn within the ethnography's narrative. Erzulie-Lasyrenn has syncretic connections to other water goddesses throughout the African diaspora (including Mammy Water, or Mama Wati). These are generally regarded as *lwa*, or loa (primary spirits) of the ocean, whose "names are regularly invoked to maintain, refresh, and strengthen the spirit needed to endure the hardships and challenges of lives scattered and shattered by the avarice, arrogance, and brutality of those who would enslave others for their own benefit" (Drewal 2008, 78).

Brown describes Erzulie-Lasyrenn as follows:

> Lasyrenn is connected to Mammy Water, whose shrines are found throughout West Africa. Some suggest that the mermaid persona, also common for Mammy Water, was derived from the carved figures on the bows of the ships of European traders and slavers. Thus the Vodou *lwa* Lasyrenn may have roots that connect, like nerves, to the deepest and most painful parts of the loss of homeland and the trauma of slavery. It is therefore fitting that she also reconnects people to Africa and its wisdom. In many stories, people are captured by Lasyrenn and pulled under the water, down to Ginen. Sometimes these stories are descriptions of tragic drownings or of suicides. But as often as not such tales are strategies used by the poor and otherwise disenfranchised to gain access to the prestigious role of healer. (K. Brown [1991] 2010, 223–24)

More specifically, aspects of Lasyrenn's personality and mythology provide evidence that Janie is the personification of this central Vodun loa/lwa. Loas require a special ceremony or "marriage" that ties the practitioner to their loa (K. Brown [1991] 2010, 10, 57, 139). Following this "marriage," the person's loa offers support, protection, and advice in exchange for their favorite foods and other earthly items and rites. However, Lasyrenn is distinctive from other loas,

FIGURE 10. "Door of the room to Erzulie." The image, the icon, painted on a door is of a fish-tailed, bare-breasted woman adorned with a necklace of beads, and a single fish appears to float above her in midair. Its inclusion in *Tell My Horse* demonstrates that Hurston documented the loa Erzulie-Lasyrenn, the mermaid who heals. In Zora Neale Hurston, *Tell My Horse* ([1938] 1990). New York: Harper and Row.

as her initiates require no outside ritual to confirm their "head." An allusion to Janie's "marriage" to or personification of Lasyrenn is revealed when one considers Brown's description of those who form a marriage with the mermaid loa:

> The stories have a common pattern. A person, usually a woman, disappears for a time—three days, three months, three years. When she returns, she is a changed person. Her skin has become fairer, her hair longer and straighter. Most important, she has gained sacred knowledge. Immediately after her

return, she is disoriented, does not talk, and does not remember what happened to her. But gradually a story emerges, a story of living for a time "below the water," where the spirits instructed her in the arts of diagnosis and healing. (224)

The novel's initial framing includes Janie's remarkably silent return after her near drowning in a flood and an extended and exaggerated description of her voluptuous physical appearance, including her "firm buttocks" and "pugnacious breasts" and her "great rope of black hair swinging to her waist and unraveling in the wind like a plume" (Hurston ([1937] 1998, 2). The characterization offers a remarkable parallel with the mermaid imagery of the loa/lwa. Pheoby also brings food to Janie to greet her when she returns from "the dead" (from the flooding following a hurricane) and before hearing about and learning from Janie's life-altering and cathartic story. But why figure Janie in terms of a mythical Lasyrenn? As a figure within the larger Erzulie family, those "married" to Lasyrenn are provided with a distinctive opportunity for self-reflection: "Gazing at her is like gazing at your own reflection. It is seductive because she gives you a deeper and truer picture of self than is likely to be found in the mirrors of everyday life" (K. Brown [1991] 2010, 223).

Janie's journey is one of self-reflection, as readers (and Pheoby) are invited to follow her meditations on love through her three marriages. By the novel's end, Janie is self-possessed as Lasyrenn the healer, a fitting allusion given Janie's survival of the hurricane and subsequent flood as well as her "otherwise disenfranchised" status within her community (K. Brown [1991] 2010, 223–24). Janie offers her healing story of a journey of self-love along with the instruction that "love is different with every shore" (Hurston [1937] 1998, 191). The message has the potential to resolve the community's concerns about Janie's choices in love and life and to encourage them not to limit their potential for "self-revelation" by insisting on relationships that meet "traditional" mandates that ultimately promote unequal power dynamics between partners. More immediately, Pheoby experiences Janie's story as encouraging her personal development, as when she states that she has "growed ten feet higher" (192). The story also empowers her to actively transform her marriage beyond the usual limits of social constructions of gender, since she intends to "make" her husband take her *fishing*, an allusion to Lasyrenn's iconic image (192).

Janie, separated from her lover by death, is grief stricken for a narrative moment, but she resists misery in favor of her memories of Tea Cake. The final sentence visualizes a larger-than-life Janie with a "fish-net" horizon draped over her shoulder, magnificently laden with "life." Janie's figuration is mythically rendered as Hurston draws a direct parallel to Erzulie-Lasyrenn within the final sentences of the novel:

> The day of the gun, and the bloody body, and the courthouse came and commenced to sing a sobbing sigh out of every corner in the room; out of each and every chair and thing. Commenced to sing, commenced to sob and sing, singing and sobbing. Then Tea Cake came prancing around her where she was and the song of the sigh flew out of the window and lit in the top of the pine trees. Tea Cake, with the sun for a shawl. Of course he wasn't dead. He could never be until she herself had finished feeling and thinking. The kiss of his memory made pictures of love and light against the wall. Here was peace. She pulled in her horizon like a great fish-net. Pulled it from around the waist of the world and draped it over her shoulder. So much of life in its meshes! She called in her soul to come and see. (193)

Finally revealed as an incarnation of Lasyrenn within the final passage of the novel, she ultimately "called in her soul to come and see," which suggests an altered state or trance possession (171). Michael Awkward, in *Inspiriting Influences*, apprehends this aspect of the novel's end when he suggests that Janie is "able to conflate physical and spiritual into one, interactive, interdependent system and, thus, to resolve a double consciousness into a unified, Black sensibility" (1991, 56). That "Black sensibility," however, is not only defined in racial terms but is also quite literally an invocation of cultural meaning associated with Erzulie-Lasyrenn, a Haitian feminine deity linked closely to Mama Wati, whose initiates require no outside ritual to confirm their "head" and are instead ultimately self-possessed through their survival of a traumatic event (K. Brown [1991] 2010, 224). Unlike Erzulie Freida and Erzulie Dantor, only Erzulie-Lasyrenn is closely tied with the silent ritual of return from a near drowning and related fish imagery. Unlike the imagery of Erzulie Freida, who represents an unending sadness due to childlessness and an unending succession of failed relationships, Erzulie-Lasyrenn offers a self-possession whose healing is of her own creation.

4

"Ain't I an Anthropologist?"

Sometimes, I feel discriminated against, but it does not make me angry.
It merely astonishes me. How *can* any deny themselves the pleasure of
my company? It's beyond me.
—Zora Neale Hurston, "How It Feels to Be Colored Me"

Hurston's anthropological work has not been more fully recognized within
the field of anthropology in part due to the marginalization of American folklore and, in particular, African American folklore within the discipline. The
long history of the relationship between folklore studies and anthropology
includes the overlapping and competing interests and perspectives of literary
folklorists and anthropological folklorists at the turn of the nineteenth century.
For example, each field worked to standardize their respective methods and
professionalize their approaches as distinctive fields through the granting of
graduate degrees. In the simplest sense, "the literary folklorists were usually
located in departments of literature, and the anthropological folklorists in the
departments of anthropology" (Zumwalt 1988, 9). As a matter of method, literary folklorists traditionally treated folklore apart from its social contexts, while
early anthropological folklorists, largely under the direction of anthropologist
Franz Boas, emphasized folklore research as significant to the study of culture
and the lives of the people being studied (Zumwalt 1988, 10). Hurston studied
the theoretical and methodological perspectives that defined anthropological

folklore, including the gathering of cultural data within its social contexts and with specific attention to cultural relativity, historical particularism, and cultural change.

Anthropologist Lee D. Baker's history of the construction of race in anthropology illustrates that in the 1920s many Black scholars, like Hurston, were attracted to anthropology—and, in particular, the study of folklore—because of the opportunities its methods provided for "documenting and celebrating their African heritage" (1988, 143). Noting the proliferation of monographs and articles, including those published in the *Journal of American Folklore* (JAFL)— more than fourteen issues during a twenty-year period—Baker addresses how the production and publication of scholarship regarding African American culture seemingly thrived, largely under the direction of Franz Boas, as a vital part of the discipline (144–48). As one of the editors of the journal, which was the publishing arm of the American Folklore Society (AFLS), Boas routinely encouraged his students to publish their research within the journal and to reinforce the synergy between anthropology and folklore studies (L. Baker 1998; Zumwalt 1988, 69). Hurston's article "Hoodoo in America," for example, was published in the journal in 1931. However, by the 1940s, the study of African American folklore within the discipline of anthropology began to wane due, in part, to lack of institutional and financial support (L. Baker 1998, 164). Later, the institutionalization of folklore as a distinctive professionalized discipline began with the founding of the first PhD program in folklore at Indiana University in 1949 (Zumwalt 1988, 7).

Significantly, "the Negro folklore promoted by the AFLS has been virtually erased by historians of anthropology and locked out of the anthropological canon" (L. Baker 1998, 164–65). However, beginning in the late 1980s and early 1990s, when feminist anthropologists engaged in debates concerning the politics that inform the writing of ethnography, some began to pay significantly more attention to Hurston's ethnographies. Nonetheless, with the exception of references by Black feminist anthropologists within the field, in many cases the title of "anthropologist" or even "anthropological folklorist" is rarely given to Hurston, with some anthropological scholars preferring to refer to her as a folklorist in literary terms and to her works as either collections of folklore or travel narratives.[1] These designations define Hurston's contributions as more literary than anthropological and inform receptions of her work as non-authoritative ethnographic productions. For example, instead of sustained close and contextual readings of Hurston's ethnographic work as an anthropological folklorist, Hurston is read in poststructuralist terms. These readings occasion Hurston's entry into the feminist anthropological canon as a textual innovator. As such, she is considered as either a highly experimental and problematic ethnographer or as extraordinary in her experimental approach to ethnography. However, a narrow focus on Hurston's works as "texts" elides a consideration of the conceptual contributions of her anthropology and the research she advanced as a scholar who studied the theoretical and methodological perspectives that informed anthropological folklore. In addition, these assessments set her apart from a community of African Americanist scholars that also experimented with ethnographic form.[2]

I explore the reception of Hurston by feminist anthropologists during the same period that established her literary authority and entry into the American literary canon in order to elucidate the rhetoric and politics that inform her marginalization. The critical context of Hurston's reception as an anthropologist leads me to ironically invoke "Ain't I an Anthropologist?" as a signification on Hurston's place in anthropology, even as the question nods to the myth of Sojourner Truth's utterance "Ain't I a Woman?" (Painter 1997, 258–80). Despite the phrase's complicated construction and broad reception as a symbol of Truth's life and work (McDowell 1995b, 161–63), its currency as a metonym for Black feminist scholar-activist interventions should signal, as McDowell advances, resistance to the erasure of Black women's thinking as both poetics and politics (159–61). Given this erasure, I consider how historical contexts are often too easily ignored in the recuperation of Hurston's work and thereby enable its narrow reception and her problematic representation and transfer as an iconic token. The discussion that follows lays a foundation for reading Hurston as not just a transferable symbol of Black feminist inclusion but also as an anthropological scholar with intellectual agency (172). My use of the phrase "Ain't I an Anthropologist?" as a title for this discussion encourages a questioning about receptions of Hurston's professional subjectivity and historical erasure, voiced in a Black folk speech that she studied and carefully represented, a voice that marvels at its own erasure from a discipline that she, too, worked to shape. I also consider a series of questions about the role of Hurston as an icon in academe and anthropology. To echo McDowell, Is there any *real power* in Hurston's token use in the academy: in the uncomplicated repetition of her name? (McDowell 1995b, 162; emphasis mine). Did the repetition of Zora Neale Hurston's name in African American, feminist, and American literary spheres make a difference to feminist anthropologists? If so, how? Given Hurston's canonized status among literary scholars and the repeated references to her anthropological training, why has Hurston not achieved sustained consideration by feminist anthropologists beyond a reading of her work as innovatively and problematically textual?

Anthropologists who examine Hurston's work have mostly done so in the context of describing the nature and scope of women's past contributions to

ethnography and evaluating the conditions of ethnographic authority in ethnographies written by women. This interest in Hurston's anthropology marked
a relative resurgence in references to and publications about her ethnographies
that was occasioned by an emergent interest in defining and defending a politics
of ethnographic authority. Critical discussions within feminist anthropology in
the 1980s and '90s mainly address *Mules and Men* and *Tell My Horse* in terms of
their narrative structures. Critics describe her works as innovative and experimental in their use of literary strategies and reflexive positionality, in which
Hurston's presence and voice as a researcher are figured within her works. Some
represent them as complicated by discourses of the Harlem Renaissance, early
American anthropology, and by competing demands of individuals on her work
(Mikell 1983, 27; Gordon 1990, 146–62; Hernández 1995, 148–65). As mentioned
previously, these individuals primarily include Franz Boas, her anthropology
professor and mentor; Charlotte Osgood Mason, her patron; and Alain Locke,
Black scholar and intellectual and editor of *The New Negro* (1925), who are
sometimes described as collectively exerting a "triple pressure" on Hurston's
anthropological productions. This latter argument in particular suggests that
these competing forces, combined with poverty, racial oppression, and gender
oppression, manifest as a lack of structure and narrative cohesion within her
works. These receptions delimit the ways in which her works can be read as
contributions to understanding culture and cultural processes and investigated
as cultural artifacts of particular historical moments. They also delimit or elide
an understanding of an African American literary and cultural tradition in which
literature functions as social science and sociopolitical revision and in which
social-science productions employ literary elements to influence popular audiences. Finally, these readings miss that, rather than defining authority in terms
of a distanced and objective researcher, Hurston's first-person narrative directly
enacts the authority of a "You are there, because I was there" mode.[3]

A relatively small number of articles have defined Hurston's ethnographic
authority within the field of anthropology during this period. Deborah Gordon's "The Politics of Ethnographic Authority: Race and Writing in the Ethnography of Margaret Mead and Zora Neale Hurston," published in *Modernist
Anthropology: From Fieldwork to Text*, is a definitive critical essay within the
field of anthropology regarding Hurston's ethnographic authority. While the
article's title references "the politics of ethnographic authority," Gordon's essay
is marked by a bias toward the authoritative conventions of professional ethnography (1990, 147). In comparing two ethnographies with decidedly different
contexts of production against a defined although contestable standard, this
bias leads to a slanted reading of "authority" and "professional" in Gordon's
evaluation of Margaret Mead's *Coming of Age in Samoa* (1928) and Hurston's

Tell My Horse (1938). Gordon writes, "I propose to contrast Mead's ethnographic textual practice with that of Hurston in order to show the connections between disciplinization, style, and race and gender in the making of professional anthropology" (1990, 150). She defines Mead's *Coming of Age in Samoa* as successful in conveying professional authority and in achieving the rhetorical effect of what it is: an "ethnographic monograph" (150). Hurston's *Tell My Horse* fails by comparison against a professional standard that it never sought to imitate (Kaplan 2002, 389). Instead, I argue that, notwithstanding contemporaneous receptions of her work, Hurston's ethnography is self-consciously both professional and "popular" in its attention to cultural issues and content. In addition, Hurston's experimental form of ethnography was distinctive but not unusual. Other social scientists also experimented with ethnographic form. Some, wanting to reach a broader audience, responded to demands for literary realist works in varying degrees and thereby expected to change public opinions regarding their own and other cultures.[4]

Gordon reviews the institutional and historical contexts of each ethnographer's productions, but her treatment of each is uneven and frames Hurston as Mead's anthropological foil. In her discussion of Mead, Gordon notes how institutional sexism limited her access to an academic position, and she concludes that her class and racial privilege, nonetheless, "permitted a writing style that has a circuitous relationship to the professionalization and disciplinization of anthropology" (1990, 162). In contrast to her discussion of Mead, Gordon's treatment of Hurston includes a sustained discussion of Hurston's mentors and patrons (Franz Boas, Alain Locke, Charlotte Osgood Mason) and how they influenced the heterogeneity of *Tell My Horse*. She argues that Hurston's mentors/patrons held conflicting ideas concerning the uses of folklore and that these conflicts, in addition to reflecting Hurston's varied interests, constrained Hurston's ability to produce a standard or "traditional" modern ethnography (1990, 158–62).

Gordon also notes Hurston's use of culturally marked "figures of speech" and her representations of her conflicts with government officials, which reveal dynamic fieldwork interactions, including the impact of the fieldworker on the cultural setting (Hurston [1938b] 1990, 36, 45). However, Gordon's argument ultimately qualifies these interactions as evidence of Hurston's "undisciplined" ethnography. Thus, she concludes, Hurston was "never allowed the status of 'anthropologist'" (1990, 162). An excerpt from Gordon's final paragraph reads: "Mead's ethnographic authority, an effect of both textual and social production, was built on a sense of identity that was not fragmented by the interfacing of racial and literary politics. The authority of Hurston's text was dispersed, fragmented, and excessive rather than whole and tempered by the careful restraining of competing discourses" (162).

Because Gordon links Mead's authority and Hurston's supposed failures of professional anthropological authority to a discussion of their identities, descriptions of Hurston's *Tell My Horse* signify as descriptors of Hurston's identity and require further scrutiny. In contrast to Mead's "sense of identity," Gordon represents Hurston's identity, as well as her text, as "fragmented," "dispersed," and "excessive." These descriptions of Hurston and her works are further accentuated when compared to Mead's "whole . . . tempered . . . careful . . . restrain[ed] discourse" (156, 157, 162). Gordon further describes Mead's rhetorical movements as "stylized," while Hurston's "style of generalization is excessive and blatant in its assertions about Jamaica and Haiti" (156). She claims that Hurston "fails to make certain rhetorical moves that signify the authority of the anthropological monograph that Mead wrote so effectively" (156). Hurston "violated ethnographic codes" (157), includes culturally marked "figures of speech" within her ethnography (155), and represents her conflicts and negotiations with government officials to provide resources for the local people (155). Notwithstanding Gordon's interest in addressing Hurston's subjective descriptions of Haiti, which scholars have addressed as a revision of Ruth Benedict's views on "culture and personality" in its cultural critique of the U.S. occupation of Haiti (Mikell 1982; Plant 2003; Duck 2004; Karem 2011; Mitchell 2013), Gordon's descriptions mirror constructions of whiteness as orderly and proper and blackness, especially Black womanhood, as disorderly and excessive.[5]

That Gordon offers a comparison of the two scholars on the basis of their race and class experiences further complicates her discussion of Mead's and Hurston's respective authorities. Gordon not only defines distinctions between the two authors' works, but she also defines their quality in terms of their identities. She conflates a discussion of class and race experiences (as essentialized identity) with equivocal descriptions of Hurston's work. The result is an implied binary opposition between the two ethnographies, the two women, and their class and race identities. Gordon's project to compare the two works for how they differ in terms of the authors' racial and class identities and experience falls short of offering a balanced discussion of either Mead's or Hurston's ethnographic authority.

Mead's celebrated *Coming of Age in Samoa* attempted to revise American cultural attitudes concerning adolescence in the United States, and Gordon notes Mead's work as a model of cultural criticism. In contrast, Gordon reads Hurston's cultural criticism as an example of her "ethnocentric bias" (1990, 156). She particularly notes Hurston's "opinion that the American occupation of Haiti aided in the development of the country" (156). Hurston's supposed "ethnocentric bias" can also be framed as a complex cultural critique of Haiti, Jamaica, and American foreign interests. Scholars have explored how Hurston's narrative concerning Haitian politics and Vodou religious beliefs in *Tell My Horse* offered a subversive commentary on the impact of the American occupation of Haiti from 1915 to 1934 (Trefzer 2000, 299; Duck 2004, 136). American popular opinion supported the American occupation of Haiti for its geo-economic and political strategic interests through a rhetoric of Haiti's racial and cultural "primitiveness" (Plummer 1982, 130; Trefzer 2000, 300).

On one level, *Tell My Horse* appears to provide a narrative in keeping with that popular opinion, especially in Hurston's comments about improvements to Haiti's infrastructure left in the wake of the U.S. occupation: "The occupation is ended and Haiti is left with a stable currency, the beginnings of a system of transportation, a modern capitol, the nucleus of a modern army" (Hurston [1938b] 1990, 74). However, Hurston "carefully restricts her praise to its material accomplishments," leaving her commentary on the social and political impact of the U.S. occupation interwoven throughout the ethnography (Duck 2004, 136). She complicates her meta-narrative with commentaries that sarcastically reveal the limits of the benefits of North America's invasion for "democracy." For example, Hurston reports on the "black Marine" who served in the Garde d'Haiti, "which had been centralized and professionalized under the guidance of the U.S. Marines" (Hurston [1938b] 1990, 136–37; Duck 2004, 140). Hurston recounts how she overhears him cursing profusely, his blasphemous curses learned from American soldiers: "I kept hearing 'Jesus Christ!' and 'God Damn!' mixed up with whatever he was saying in Creole" ([1938b] 1990, 136). Upon meeting her, the "black Marine" offers to kill "something" for Hurston as proof of his Marine service:

> "But yes," he replied proudly, "I am a black Marine. I speak like one always. Perhaps you would like me to kill something for you. I kill that dog for you."
> It was a half starved dog that had taken to hanging around me. (137)

In this passage Hurston reveals a violent "legacy of the U.S. occupation" (Trefzer 2000, 305) in the person of a Garde d'Haiti imitating a U.S. Marine, and thereby "undercut[s] much of her nationalist rhetoric" (Duck 2004, 136). In addition, Hurston's blasphemous Marine signifies on American religious irreverence in a powerful—albeit veiled—critique, given America's interest in "saving" Haitian citizenry from "Voodoo" practices. Racist representations of Vodou as essentially profane and wicked helped to justify the American occupation, so Hurston's documentation of her exchanges with the "black Marine" as an effect of the U.S. occupation of Haiti likewise functions as a cultural critique.

CHAPTER 4

Gordon's critique of Hurston's *Tell My Horse* as simply "ethnocentric" misses the complexity of Hurston's rhetoric.

Gordon's decision to discuss Hurston's lack of authority (as read against a model of professional ethnography) is even more curious when one considers what Gordon omits in discussing Mead's professional authority. Gordon briefly notes the controversy surrounding Derek Freeman's *Margaret Mead and Samoa: The Making and Unmaking of an Anthropological Myth* (1983), which charged that Mead's research findings were false and methodologically flawed, but Gordon dismisses the controversy as having any bearing on Mead's authority. Gordon then leverages Mead's popularity, as compared to Hurston's, as evidence of Mead's authority:

> *Coming of Age in Samoa* still retains its status as a classic ethnography. The debates surrounding the 1983 publication of Derek Freeman's *Margaret Mead and Samoa: The Making and Unmaking of an Anthropological Myth* confirm the high degree of interest anthropologists still have in this account. Unlike Hurston's ethnographies, which went out of print, and have only recently been reedited and reprinted, Mead's book has gone through numerous reprintings with her updated introductions. It is, thus, worth looking at Mead's writing to discern textual practices of the ethnographic monograph. (1990, 150)

Gordon thus defends Mead's authority against would-be critics by comparing its historical and current popularity within anthropology to Hurston's recently recovered popularity. Similarly, Gordon cites Hurston's mixed reviews as reflective of her lack of professional authority but does not mention the negative reviews that greeted the publication of *Coming of Age in Samoa*, which would likewise complicate a discussion of Mead's professional authority.[6] For example, some reviewers doubted Mead's portrayal of an uncomplicated Samoan life (sans venereal diseases and mental disorders) and how she managed, with only a brief stay in the field and rudimentary knowledge of the language, to elicit the intimate details concerning adolescent sexuality from her respondents (Bernreuter 1929, 489; B. M. 1929, 226).

Other reviewers criticized *Coming of Age* for its popular appeal, describing it as "a scientific study published as a popular book" (B. M. 1929, 226), attenuating Gordon's claims that *Coming of Age* is an "ethnographic monograph."[7] Gordon acknowledges that Mead's work targets a lay audience, but she still strongly asserts the professional status of Mead's ethnography over and above Hurston's:

> Mead speaks in *Coming of Age in Samoa* as an anthropologist bringing knowledge of Samoa to a nonacademic audience. In this sense her authority enacts a complementary move in relationship to the constructions of past fieldworkers as amateurs. Both the move to cleanse anthropology of the impurities

of the nonscientific past and the move to claim to write without academic "jargon," as Mead refers to it, nonetheless assume a system of classification that separates "popular" knowledge from social science. Hurston's text does not acknowledge that separation. (1990, 157)

Hurston's work acknowledges that separation throughout *Tell My Horse*, as indicated, for example, by her detailed discussions and delineations of Vodou religious practices and beliefs in "Part III: Voodoo in Haiti" and in her appendix, which details at length (with musical notation) songs of worship and other miscellaneous songs (Hurston [1938b] 1990, 113–287). However, with the peculiar omissions of both historical and recent sources concerning Mead's professional authority, Gordon's use of Mead's continuing popularity as justification for her present-day authority, in comparison to the reporting of Hurston's mixed reception, is another inconsistency in the historical consideration of the authority of both ethnographies. Because of this temporal slippage, "contemporary" readers may analyze Gordon's "historical" critique of Hurston's professional authority as the current definitive statement of her anthropological authority.

Questions concerning objectivity and intellectual rigor often arise for scholars engaged in work where racial politics has influenced the aims of their scientific discovery. Franz Boas, mentor to both Hurston and Mead and the "father" of American anthropology, is known in part for his scholarship that challenged evolutionary sciences that promoted racist views of the biological inferiority of racial groups.[8] His legacy has been criticized for not developing a systematic theory or concept of culture and for being limited by his liberal project of "attacking the simple-minded, rigid, and ethnocentric evolutionary schemes to framing an accurate, flexible, and humanistic one" (Wax 1956, 65). In "The Limitations of Boas's Anthropology," Murray Wax argues that Boas's research and style of scientific reporting were constrained by "dominant convictions," including the focus on describing individual variations over systematically defining group characteristics, such that "he could not produce any positive, integrated work of significance, and his function became that of critic" (1956, 63, 69; Boas [1932] 1983, 611). Wax at times describes Boas's work in terms not unlike those used by Gordon in her critique of Hurston's *Tell My Horse*:

[Boas would] collect a considerable mass of data of the most objective kind—material object or text. He would describe these succinctly and with little or no interpretation. The data, so presented, would speak for themselves: they were an exception to the general hypothesis and it was therefore refuted. Then Boas would present his own point of view: the situation was a complex one; the refuted hypothesis had ignored the complexity; a full analysis, if humanly possible, would reveal many factors in operation. (1956, 63)

Wax would prefer for Boas to explicitly analyze the meanings or significance of cultural artifacts or practices. He concludes, "Boas's forte was criticism. . . . But cultural anthropology also required positive leadership, and here Boas failed" (74). Within anthropology, both Hurston and Boas are criticized for failing to meet standards of professional anthropology based on the form of their analysis. Boas's position in the canon as "father" remains firm despite these criticisms. With Gordon's critique, Hurston's marginal position is justified by her arguably unprofessional and unauthoritative ethnography.

Gordon provides an elaborated discussion of the patron/mentor contexts of Hurston's ethnographies in order to explain the contemporaneous mixed reception of *Tell My Horse*. However, a discussion of Hurston's ethnographic authority should consider the editing and marketing of her ethnographies by their publisher, Lippincott (West 2005, 9). Genevieve West has described the role that Lippincott played in sensationally editing and marketing *Tell My Horse* and argues that reviews of the book were influenced by its marketing (2005, 127–67). The book jacket copy "stresses Hurston's scientific credentials," noting her funding by the Guggenheim Foundation and her attention to scientific "facts" while also problematically using "stereotypes to attract nonscientific readers" to Hurston's work (133). By eliding the realities of the publishing industry and Hurston's lack of control over how her works were marketed and received, Gordon makes Hurston's lack of popular authority an essential quality of her scholarship rather than shaped by these larger forces.

In addition, with regard to Hurston's limited academic career (Gordon 1990, 148), Gordon does not consider the obvious institutional racism of the era and the lack of university positions available for Black intellectuals outside of historical Black colleges and universities, which led many Black intellectuals to pursue other graduate degree paths.[9] In addition, Black colleges and universities had few departments of anthropology, and therefore a career path in this field meant risking unemployment (Drake 1978, 94). Even in historically Black colleges and universities, significant institutional barriers persisted for women who attempted to enter the field of anthropology.

Furthermore, the attention to questions of textual authority in poststructuralist terms (via Hurston's professional biography) delimits a "rereading" of Hurston's ethnographic work in ways that Gordon acknowledges it is due (1990, 150). Hurston's ethnography should be evaluated against a different set of questions. For example, how does *Tell My Horse* (and *Mules and Men*) speak authoritatively to its various and diverse audiences, and how does Hurston describe her understanding of specific cultural concepts within regions within the U.S. South and Jamaica and Haiti?

Answers to these questions will be taken up across chapters 5 and 6. However, several essays by anthropologist Gwendolyn Mikell have the distinction of more fully introducing Hurston to the discipline through a series of essays and articles that consider her work within their immediate social and historical contexts. Taken together, Mikell's essays provide an overview of Hurston's ethnographic work and her anthropological biography, providing a significant foundation for considering Hurston's contributions to conceptual discussions within anthropology. The essays also reveal Mikell's arguments for the intellectual agency of Zora Neale Hurston both beyond and in light of the mentoring she received. As such, Mikell's works move us closer to a sustained treatment of the broader historical contexts of Hurston's work. Mikell's "When Horses Talk: Reflections on Zora Neale Hurston's Haitian Anthropology" (1982) offers a discussion of *Tell My Horse* as an ethnographic source in such terms. In contrast to Gordon, Mikell's discussion focuses less on Hurston's use of language and ethnographic authority. It instead reviews the cultural data Hurston presented and comments on the immediate social contexts of her works. For example, Mikell notes Hurston's attention to the import of colonialism on the Haitian "personality" (as an outsider) and her descriptions of Vodou practices (as an insider). Like Gordon, Mikell notes the influence of Hurston's mentors but cautions against overstating it. Ruth Benedict, for example, is noted as having influenced Hurston's attention to psychological descriptions of Jamaicans and Haitians as "personalities."[10] Boas influences Hurston's attention to describing cultural details and "facts" rather than presenting overt descriptions of grand theory. However, Mikell also considers Hurston's agency as an intellectual and argues that Hurston moved beyond both of her mentors in attending to cultural contradictions as historically situated. For example, she describes how Benedict's approach led Hurston to adopt a "psychologizing view of culture," which Hurston also largely revises by addressing the legacy of colonial rule in Haiti and its influence on cultural attitudes and beliefs (Mikell 1982, 221). She concludes, "Thus Hurston's work, while influenced, cannot be accurately described by the joint perspectives of her mentors" (222).

Mikell clearly asserts Hurston's intellectual agency and authority in "When Horses Talk," taking up questions regarding the influence of Hurston's mentors on Hurston's anthropology and evenly detailing Hurston's analysis of Haitian Vodou, and color, race, class, and sexual politics in both Jamaica and Haiti (222). Her next essay, "The Anthropological Imagination of Zora Neale Hurston" (1983), works to expand a discussion regarding the influence of Hurston's mentors on her work; it also expands her treatment of Hurston's anthropology to include *Mules and Men*. In order to understand Hurston's contributions to the field of anthropology, and unlike Gordon's treatment of Hurston's anthropological authority, Mikell's essay works to describe the particular intellectual traditions that inform Hurston's ethnographic content. She discusses both the historical and theoretical influences for both works as she makes a case for Hurston's conceptual contributions to anthropology. Mikell notes that Hurston's obscurity is not only caused by Hurston being "overshadowed by literary giants" (1983, 27) but that it was instead "the result of triple pressures related to her overt feminist stance, racism which encouraged artistic rather than academic endeavors, and the constraints imposed upon research funding agencies and donors during this period" (27).[11]

Moreover, Mikell describes how Hurston's intellectual experience is influenced by the dynamic worlds of Barnard College and Columbia University, where Boas's ideas, while influenced by evolutionary and diffusionist theories of culture, also "countered strict reliance on the evolutionary and diffusionist models as explanatory tools" (29).[12] Mikell mentions that *Mules and Men* was greatly influenced by Boas's training and that it was also a "unique contribution to the collection of folklore and mythology from the Native American cultures which the Columbia students produced." Mikell adds, "In all of these works, the people speak for themselves, outlining their understanding of the meaning of the cultures as it had been presented to them" (29). Mikell's addition of this description of *Mules and Men* suggests that Hurston's work, while unique for its form—although, I would add, not unique in its focus on Southern Black culture in the United States—was also not unusual in foregrounding the voices of "the people." In addition, Mikell again notes the influence of Benedict's psychological perspective in informing Hurston's descriptions of the culture and personality of *the* Haitian or Jamaican people. It is worth noting here that these "personality" passages are criticized for their essentialist qualities by contemporary critics of Hurston's *Tell My Horse*, including Gordon (Gordon 1990, 154).

However, Mikell again notes that Hurston, because of her firsthand experience with racial discrimination and the legacies of U.S. slavery, moves beyond descriptions of cultural personalities to provide a historicized context for understanding her "personality" descriptions. Following Mikell's argument, then, one might read Hurston's discussion of Haiti's colonial history and "mulatto/Black" political dynamics (Mikell 1983, 30) in a different light than the one Gordon offers.[13] For example, Hurston quotes extensively a conversation that she had with an unnamed but "well-known physician of Port-au-Prince":

> Our history has been unfortunate. First we were brought here to Haiti and enslaved. We suffered great cruelties under the French and even when they

had been driven out, they left here certain traits of government that have been unfortunate for us. Thus having been a nation continually disturbed by revolution and other features not helpful to advancement[,] we have not been able to develop economically and culturally as many of us have wished. These things being true, we have not been able to control certain bad elements because of a lack of a sufficient force. "But," I broke in, "with all the wealth of the United States and all the policing, we still have gangsters and the Ku Klux Klan. Older European nations still have their problems of crime." ([1938b] 1990, 207–8)

Within this passage, Hurston offers a pointed cultural critique of America by equating violence in Haiti with America's legacy of organized racial violence and organized crime. Readers of this exchange receive a brief glimpse of Haiti's colonial oppression, and they also come to understand that the critique they offer Haiti might well be critiques of their own nation. Hurston's culturally relativistic response resists a reading of her ethnographic perspective as imperialistic (Duck 2004; Karem 2011; Mitchell 2013).

In addition to addressing the broader intellectual traditions that influenced Hurston's work, Mikell also describes Hurston's "feminist awareness," something she shared with Margaret Mead, in her attention to gender and sex roles in both *Mules and Men* and *Tell My Horse*. One of Mikell's compelling arguments is that both works reveal the complexity of sex role socialization and maintenance: "In her anthropology as in her literature, Zora Neale Hurston offers us a view of Black culture in which women are willing, contributing partners, despite slavery, historical oppression, and the exploitation of colonialism" (1983, 27, 32). Here Mikell suggests that Hurston's ethnographies reveal the dynamics of women's oppression, through both their resistance to and collusion with gender oppression, as complicated by macro-historical and macro-economic processes. In addition, Mikell likens the more recent recuperation of Hurston's work to that of Ruth Benedict and Margaret Mead:

> It was the lay public's appreciation of *Patterns of Culture* and *Coming of Age in Samoa* which thrust Benedict and Mead upon the consciousness of the professional anthropological community. Similarly, it was Alice Walker's respect for her female ancestor [that] led her to restore and mark Hurston's grave, calling her "A Genius of the South." (1983, 33)

Mikell's observation challenges the assumption that Benedict's and Mead's authority and subsequent canonization result from their intrinsic professional authority as traditional scholars, as opposed to being greatly shaped by audience tastes and demands for their work.

In 1988 Mikell published a biographical entry on Hurston in *Women Anthropologists: A Biographical Dictionary*. Because this is a biographical essay, her analyses of Hurston's ethnographies are brief. Mikell offers no specific analysis regarding *Mules and Men*, but she does note that Boas wrote its introduction and that Hurston requested Ruth Benedict's comments on the text (1988, 161). Mikell discusses the mixed reception of Hurston's ethnographies by Black and white, popular and critical audiences, and offers an explanation that contrasts two perspectives on Black culture, by white and Black intellectuals, in broad historical terms:

> Whereas the Howard University and New York black intellectuals were concerned with overcoming the race issue and revealing the inherent dignity and originality in Afro-American culture, the white American intellectual community was searching for useful models for the representations of reality, and for ways in which fieldwork techniques might enhance an understanding of nonwhite cultures. Correspondence between Hurston and Locke during this period reveals that these black scholars were skeptical that whites were really open to the symbolic and ritual content of black folklore. (162)

The distinctions that Mikell makes here provides an opportunity to consider two discrete, but overlapping, intellectual concerns evident in Hurston's ethnographic work and to underscore Hurston's interests: challenging racist attitudes and realistically representing culture. However, these respective interests were not simply divided between African American scholars and white scholars. Both Black and white ethnographers were interested in how realistic portraitures of culture could both reveal cultural meaning and, in the process, revise racist attitudes concerning Black culture. Furthermore, Hurston was right to question whether white readers could overcome their cultural bias and conceive and imagine Black culture as complex and full of meaning. Hurston, aware of her multiple audiences, employed rhetorical strategies to present her research findings and negotiate their complex reception. Her claim to ethnographic authority within the discipline of anthropology should not be delimited by her commitments and her distinctive approach to confront white cultural bias in a 1930s audience, which Mikell's essays address.

Two years later Gwendolyn Mikell authored another brief intellectual biography, "Feminism and Black Culture in the Ethnography of Zora Neale Hurston" (1990), which also considers the personal and institutional contexts influencing Hurston's research perspectives in *Mules and Men* and *Tell My Horse*.[14] Mikell discusses the reception of Hurston's ethnographies and provides a general summary of the intellectual contributions of the two books. Her focus in *Tell My Horse* is "to examine Hurston's theoretical, methodological, and anthropological frameworks with respect to feminism and black women within black culture and to raise questions about the derivation of and change in these ideas" ([1990] 1999, 53–54).

One key argument in Mikell's critical biography is that Hurston's views concerning the gender and race content within *Tell My Horse* are more fully articulated than they are in *Mules and Men*. Despite her own evidence to the contrary, Mikell writes, "Except for portrayals through folklore and literature, Hurston is amazingly silent in her early work about her views on the condition of women in the United States" ([1990] 1999, 62). More specifically, it seems Mikell considers *Mules and Men* to be a collection of folklore rather than an ethnographic narrative of folklore practices. As such, she argues that it is not explicitly concerned with the conditions of American women. However, *Mules and Men* depicts men and women's social interactions as they tell folktales and otherwise interact with one another within varied contexts (Wall 1998). These illustrations, in the voices/dialogue of the respondents, overtly articulate their views about Black women and men and reveal sexism and resistance to sexism within the community. In addition, Hurston's selection of specific folktales about gender politics within "Part I" illustrate her concern with representing questions of race and gender (Wall 1998, 55–58; Hurston 1935 [1978], 33–34), and her interest in representing women's empowered leadership as hoodoo practitioners is represented within "Part II" (Wall 1998, 63–65).

Mikell also considers the lack of recognition that Hurston has received within anthropology. She considers several possible explanations, posed as a series of questions: Hurston did ethnography "in her own way," which limited her academic opportunities, so "Hurston was eventually viewed as, and began to conceive of herself as, more artistic than scholarly" ([1990] 1999, 53); she was "denied her full use of her own research materials" by patron Charlotte Osgood; her "framework" was "contextual, literal, creatively symbolic, and participatory" (53). However, while Hurston decided not to pursue a PhD in anthropology, there is no evidence that she perceived herself as less scholarly. Mikell's analysis imposes a binary division of Hurston's work that determines her artistic work as non-scholarly. Hurston's fiction and essays illustrated a concern with scholarly analysis even as she produced work "in her own way." In addition, Hurston's contractual relationship with Mason ended in 1933, prior to the publication of *Mules and Men* and *Tell My Horse* (Hernández 1995, 155). It is more likely that the impact of her publisher's editing and advertising of her ethnographies strongly influenced the final form, as well as the marketed representations, of Hurston's ethnographies (West 2005, 77–81, 177). In addition, Hurston's decision was determined not only by a lack of funding but also by the reality that there were few academic opportunities available to Black female anthropologists at either segregated Black or white colleges and universities during this period (Drake 1978, 85–109).

Mikell calls for a new reading of Hurston's ethnographies. She says, "Anthropologists need to view her work anew through the lenses provided by interpretive and feminist anthropologists as well as in light of the questions posed by world systems theorists and globalists" ([1990] 1999, 66). Mikell, herself, had begun just such a critical consideration eight years earlier in her 1982 article "When Horses Talk: Reflections on Zora Neale Hurston's Haitian Anthropology."[15] Mikell attends to Hurston's treatment of colonialism as a "causal factor" of a Haitian cultural "personality." She argues that Hurston's perspective extended Benedict's concern with personality as patterned to a consideration of the historical dynamics of culture and personality as situated within global contexts of colonial rule and postcolonialism (1982, 221). Using both an interpretive and feminist lens, Mikell also attends to Hurston's representations of color, class, race, and gender politics (222) and to Hurston's distinctive ethnographic approach in presenting her findings as insider and outsider (219–28).

While Mikell makes no direct comparisons between Hurston's work and that of other Black anthropologists, her article does note the controversial reception of Hurston's ethnographies by scientific communities, including Black intellectuals of the day. Many Black intellectuals took issue with Hurston's focus on "primitive" or "folk" representations of Black culture (Mikell [1990] 1999, 53). Racial political projects of the era were more concerned with contradicting these representations, and, for some, Hurston's representations seemed to reference stereotypes even as she worked to render Black folk life and culture in more complex ways. In addition, as West argues, the sensational marketing of Hurston's ethnographies may have compromised an unbiased or fresh reading of her work as an attempt to render folk culture in culturally relativistic terms (2005, 8–9).

Although Mikell's contributions were both biographical and critical in their form, more significance has been given to the biographical details of Hurston's life in subsequent literature. This focus on biography can be attributed to the fact that two of the essays were produced for publication in an edited biographical "dictionary" and in a collection of biographical/intellectual essays, respectively. This perhaps led to a predominance of biographical data (along with concurrent discussions of her life from biographical and literary sources) from which feminist anthropologists culled their critical ideas concerning the historical contexts of Hurston's ethnographic work. However, even in instances where "When Horses Talk" and "The Anthropological Imagination of Zora Neale Hurston" are cited, descriptions of Hurston's diverse experiences as a Harlem Renaissance writer and anthropologist are seen as delimiting her contributions to anthropology.[16] Mikell's concern that Hurston's ethnographies be considered for their import as theoretical, conceptual works went largely ignored, a function of a poststructuralist focus on experimental ethnography as problematic to feminist anthropology, which I discuss later in this chapter.

Following Mikell's and Gordon's discussions of Hurston's ethnographies, Graciela Hernández, in "Multiple Subjectivities and Strategic Positionality," published in *Women Writing Culture*, provides a treatment of Hurston's work "that recognizes the nexus of historical forces *circumscribing* her scholarship" (1995, 148; emphasis mine).[17] Although Hernández works to restore Hurston to anthropology, in effect, the essay focuses on Hurston as a subject of Hurston's ethnography rather than a sustained consideration of the larger content of her ethnography. She refers (in footnotes) to Alice Walker's "In Search of Our Mothers' Gardens" (1975) and Hazel Carby's "The Politics of Fiction, Anthropology, and the Folk: Zora Neale Hurston" (1990) and asserts that her own treatment "is an attempt to move beyond polar categorizations that either lionize or disparage her as a cultural figure" (Hernández 1995, 148). Therefore, Hernández provides an analysis of *Mules and Men* that primarily addresses the ways Hurston frames herself within the text as an ethnographer (158). First, however, she defines how Hurston's work is situated as experimental:

> I will argue that Hurston's ethnographies are experimental in the sense that they extend ethnographic conventions to what have been bracketed, until recently, as literary strategies. Furthermore, Hurston introduces an authorial presence into her work, eschewing the assumption that the ethnographer stands outside the social relations of the field and subsequent representations of fieldwork. The subjective accounts found in *Mules and Men* (1935) and *Tell My Horse* (1938), two of Hurston's ethnographies, anticipate current dilemmas and scholarly trajectories. The use of the subjective destabilizes Hurston's ethnographic authority, yet it also provides a vantage point from which to view her shifting allegiances. (151)

These shifting allegiances are discussed by Hernández under the subheading "Biographical and Historical Considerations," in which she summarizes parts of Robert Hemenway's biography of Hurston and notes her childhood and education, her involvement in the Harlem Renaissance, her mentor (Franz Boas) and patron relationships (Mrs. Rufus Osgood Mason), and Hurston's decision to pursue and then not to pursue a PhD in anthropology (151–53). Hernández then turns her attention to the work of Gwendolyn Mikell and Deborah Gordon. She credits Mikell with noting "three worlds" within which Hurston's work should be considered: her Southern and Black heritage, the Harlem Renaissance, and her education at Columbia. Hernández suggests that Gordon's article "flesh[es] out the demands" of these various settings and historical moments in Gordon's attention to Hurston's relationships with Alain Locke, Franz Boas, and Mrs. Rufus Osgood Mason (154–55).[18] She describes Hurston's ethnography in terms of "literary strategies" and "literary harmonics."[19] These not only describe a relationship between "subjective and objective voices" but also describe how "Hurston heavily implicates her audience in the creative act by calling on a reader's subjective interpretations of the text. Hurston seems to self-consciously realize that the creation of meaning is as much a matter of a reading strategy as it is about her own writing strategy" (156). Hernández does not sustain a close reading of any of the folktales in *Mules and Men*. Instead, she largely represents "Hurston's portrayal of herself," which, she says, "shifts as she narrates her movement from one setting to another" (158).

Hernández's main finding from her application of this approach is that Hurston's role as a female ethnographer doing field research within a mostly male community results in Hurston negotiating gender and class in ways that are more difficult as the narrative progresses.[20] In this regard, Hernández's central idea is that Hurston's "body" is on the line as she negotiates the attention she receives from men, as she deflects threats of violence against her from women in the field because of the male attention she receives, and as she participates in a hoodoo ritual in New Orleans that requires her to wear a snake's skin. Hernández references these instances as "sexual energy," "sexually charged," and "highly charged sexual imagery," and she offers little other analysis concerning the contexts or meanings of these exchanges within the text (158, 160). More specifically, it seems Hernández is concerned with the consequences of how Hurston represents herself (as either a daughter of the community or a potentially sexually [accessible] woman) in the communities she researches (158). Her reading of *Mules and Men* offers little analysis of the folklore or hoodoo content of the text, how Hurston's "literary harmonic" reveals its layered meanings to the reader, or how Hurston's representation of herself meaningfully frames the representation of the folktales and discussion of hoodoo rituals in the second half of the text.

Hernández does make a direct reference to a folkloric sermon, which she interprets as another example of charged male and female relationships, and notes that it reveals "deep-seated assumption[s]" of heterosexuality and "the limited number of social roles available to women" (159). She provides a brief analysis concerned with Hurston's raced and gendered body, and she does note that Hurston's text provides an example of "the socially constructed nature of race and gender . . . the different ways that race, class and gender manifest themselves in the South" (157). However, Hernández's focus on Hurston as the primary subject of Hurston's ethnography (as opposed to the numerous respondents figured in the work) highlights a critical tendency in feminist anthropological receptions of Hurston's work during this era. Instead, in order to define her contributions to the field of anthropology more broadly and feminist anthropology more specifically, anthropologists should consider her research subjects within *Mules and Men*: African American folklore and religious practices.

Hernández says that Hurston uses traditional ethnographic tropes to illustrate that her work is authoritative,[21] countering Gordon's assessment of Hurston's ethnographies as ignoring standard ethnographic tropes. However, Hernández echoes Gordon's conclusion when she finds that Hurston "debunks her own interpretive power" by illustrating that "the text cannot be separated from a complex web of social relationships" (1995, 160, 161). Shifting from a perspective that centers "text" instead of her "work," I propose instead that insofar as Hurston works to illustrate community in dialogue about a variety of topics, including her own negotiations within that community, Hurston intentionally represents her own authority as one among many within the field. Notwithstanding her own personal as well as learned knowledge about the subject in this field and location, she is there to gather the community's folktales. Furthermore, the individuals and communities within *Mules and Men* represent collaborative and competing authorities in their sharing of various folktales and other folklore and cultural knowledge.[22]

Rather than define authority in terms of the distanced and objective researcher, Hurston enacts another type of authority within this ethnography: the "You are there, because I was there" mode.[23] In fact, this mode is underscored by Hurston's realistic representation (via internal and external dialogue) of her presence in the work. It is also directly supported by Boas's endorsement of Hurston within the preface of the ethnography for offering the "intimate setting in the social life of the Negro" and "the Negroes['] reaction to everyday events" (Boas [1935] 1978, x). Notwithstanding poststructuralist concerns regarding the authority of the author (Hernández 1995, 161; McDowell 1995b, 168), Hurston's interpretive power is implied by her inclusion of specific dialogic scenes within the ethnography that document her collected data. Hernández does apprehend this complexity in Hurston's work when she references how *Mules and Men* represents a "a complex web of social relationship" and otherwise briefly credits Hurston's for the "important historical information" found in this work (161–62). However, the "poststructuralist turn" effectively erases the authority of Hurston as ethnographer when Hernández concludes that "Hurston casts doubt on the ethnographer's ability to adequately represent these different communities and criticizes a discipline that offers people up for view through the lenses of the spyglass" (161).[24]

Hernández's reading of Hurston's authority is largely informed by critical discussions within feminist anthropology in the 1980s and '90s, which also occasioned the rise of poststructuralism in literary studies and led scholars in anthropology to mainly address *Mules and Men* and *Tell My Horse* in terms of their narrative structures. These discussions generally take two positions. Critics describe Hurston's works as innovative and experimental in their use of literary strategies and reflexive positionality in which her presence and voice as a researcher are significantly figured within her works (Gordon 1990, 162; Hernández 1995, 151). They also represent these works as complicated (and in some cases limited) by discourses of the Harlem Renaissance, early American anthropology, and by competing demands of individuals on her work (Mikell 1983, 27; Gordon 1990, 146–62; Hernández 1995, 148–65).[25] At times this latter argument in particular suggests that these competing forces, combined with poverty and racial and gender oppression, manifest as a lack of structure and narrative cohesion, which are represented as the elements necessary to assert the ethnographic authority that more successful anthropologists command. Both critical poles delimit the ways in which these works can be read as contributions to understanding culture and cultural processes and investigated as cultural artifacts of particular historical moments. They also delimit or elide an understanding of an African American literary and cultural tradition in which literature functions as social science and sociopolitical revision and in which social-science productions employ literary elements to influence popular audiences.

Thus far, my discussions of these articles operate at the micro level of Hurston's anthropological reception. Beyond the individual choices made by individual scholars, there are also larger critical trends in the history of feminist anthropology that framed assessments of Hurston's work. As such, they define a zeitgeist that curtailed considerations of Hurston's ethnographies for their anthropological content.

"Partial Truths" and "Awkward," "Dangerous," "Cautious," "Dilemma[ed] Responses"

Feminist anthropology is ambivalent at best about the relationship between feminism, experimental anthropology, and the ethics of a feminist anthropological practice. In this section I examine the call-and-response between selected key articles and essays to illustrate how the prevalent perspective of postmodernism/poststructuralism shaped Hurston's reception by feminist anthropologists in primarily textual terms. In reclaiming Hurston (often as *the* only early example of a woman of color in anthropology), anthropologists have given little attention to her works' conceptual arguments about culture. Instead, Hurston as the subject/object of her ethnographies (in the position of narrating researcher) and ritualized tellings of her life as tragic inform most of the critical treatments of her work. Her celebrated reclamation as a literary artist, heightened during the advent of poststructuralism in both literature and anthropology, brings attention to her anthropological productions but also positions her ethnographic work as unusually and problematically textual for some feminist anthropologists. Most of the articles discussed in this section do not specifically refer to Hurston's work or to her ideas concerning culture but rather are concerned with broader feminist politics of ethnographic representation. However, the assumptions revealed in their arguments illustrate an influential context of Hurston's reception.

The advent of poststructuralism/postmodernism within the field of anthropology included an increased interest in the politics of text making in the production of ethnographic cultural representations. In response to poststructuralist literary theories, some scholars, most notably James Clifford and George Marcus, explored the application of these theories to anthropology. The two scholars organized a "seminar on the making of ethnographic texts" (Marcus and Clifford 1985, 267), which was attended by anthropologists, historians, and literary critics, and then published an edited collection of essays titled *Writing Culture: The Poetics and Politics of Ethnography* (Clifford and Marcus 1986).[26] This text shaped subsequent critical trends in feminist anthropology, including the production of scholarship that historicized and canonized women anthropologists in ethnographic terms. James Clifford's introduction to the collection, titled "Partial Truths" (1986), drew significant responses from feminist anthropologists.

"Partial Truths" asserts the primacy of writing to the production of ethnographic texts, which includes not only methodology of fieldwork and data collection but also creative constructions of a final written text that seeks to describe a culture. The final authoritative account, however, is embedded with "rhetoric and power" (11). Clifford writes:

> The notion that literary procedures pervade any work of cultural representation is a recent idea in the discipline. To a growing number, however, the "literariness" of anthropology—and especially of ethnography—appears as much more than a matter of good writing or distinctive style. Literary processes—metaphor, figuration, narrative—affect the ways cultural

phenomena are registered, from the first jotted "observations," to the completed book, to the ways these configurations "make sense" in determined acts of reading. (1986, 3–4)[27]

The essays in *Writing Culture* explore from a variety of perspectives what Clifford describes as not only a "post-anthropological" but also a "post-literary" period in anthropology (5).

Clifford's statement that "ethnographic truths are thus inherently partial—committed and incomplete" is commonly cited in the critical literature that responds to his work (7). However, in addition to discussions regarding the textuality of ethnography, feminist scholars note his cursory dismissal of feminist contributions to these new post-literary discussions. He explains why no feminists are included in the volume:

> Planning the seminar, we were confronted by what seemed to us an obvious—important and regrettable—fact. Feminism had not contributed much to the theoretical analysis of ethnographies as texts. . . . But feminist ethnography has focused either on setting the record straight about women or on revising anthropological categories (for example, the nature/culture opposition). It has not produced either unconventional forms of writing or a developed reflection on ethnographic textuality as such. (20–21)

In addition, Marcus and Clifford published a report of this seminar titled "The Making of Ethnographic Texts: A Preliminary Report," in which they write, "Historical and institutional constraints, the need of any new perspective to be authoritative in recognized ways, and patterns of tenure and recruitment may be largely responsible for the fact that the seminar was unable to draw on any developed debates generated by feminism on ethnographic textual practices" (1985, 268).

Feminist anthropologists and scholars of feminist anthropology and ethnography responded to the frank and sexist exclusion of feminism in this work with a series of articles in which they describe a feminist tradition of experimental ethnography, discuss the potential impact of poststructuralism on feminist anthropology, and compare and contrast the political aims of each perspective. Concerned with the ethics of the practice of experimental ethnography, and with defending their ability to evaluate women in "other" cultures without employing experimental modes, some argue that these modes may intensify inequities between researchers and their respondents (Strathern 1987; Stacey [1998] 1991, 113). In addition, as these approaches called for attention to the ethnographer's subjectivity, shifting rhetorical modes were received as examples of the limits of experimental anthropology (Gordon 1990; Hernández 1995, Mascia-Lees et al. 1989). Notwithstanding interest in recuperating Hurston's work to anthropological canons (Visweswaran 1988a), her ethnographic authority is influenced by the broad critical reception of poststructuralism within feminist anthropology.

Perhaps the earliest response to Clifford and Marcus's critique was offered by Marilyn Strathern in "An Awkward Relationship: The Case of Feminism and Anthropology" (1987). Strathern's response to the question of why there is an absence of feminist participation in poststructuralist conversations regarding ethnography suggests that the answer can be found by considering the different ways knowledge is produced in anthropology and feminist studies. Specifically, Strathern offers a discussion of the differences between anthropology and feminism in terms of their theoretical understandings of and relationship with the other:

> Feminist inquiry suggests that it is possible to discover the self by becoming conscious of oppression from the Other. Thus one may seek to regain a common past which is also one's own. Anthropology suggests that the self can be consciously used as a vehicle for representing an Other. But this is only possible if the self breaks from its own past. These thus emerge as two very different radicalisms. For all their parallel interests, the two practices are differently structured in the way they organize knowledge and draw boundaries, in short, in terms of the social relations that define their scholarly communities. (289)

Each community has its own worldview, and they are difficult to reconcile. These worldviews create two different sets of disciplinary questions and practices, each tightly bound to its perspective. Citing the assumptions that underlie experimental anthropology, Strathern argues that the goal to create symmetrical relations between ethnographer and "informant" in the form of collaborative ethnography is "from a feminist perspective . . . a delusion, overlooking the crucial dimension of different social interests" (290). Her descriptions of the feminist response to poststructuralist anthropology, when applied to Hurston's ethnographic practice, suggest that both Hurston's work and her very legitimacy as a researcher may be defined as a "delusion." Hurston represents herself within her works as both "informant" and anthropologist, self and other. Because these tensions (between self and other) run throughout her anthropological work, her identity as an anthropologist is potentially received as a fallacy or the work of good fiction.[28]

I have previously discussed how Graciela Hernández, in "Multiple Subjectivities and Strategic Positionality" (1995), describes Hurston's shifting positionality as destabilizing her ethnographic authority. Strathern's reading sheds some light on Hernández's reception of Hurston in poststructuralist terms. If self and other are mutually exclusive, then a reading of Hurston's ethnography through the feminist response to poststructuralism denies a consideration or interpretation of her authority as a "native researcher," where her self/other and researcher/"informant" are complexly implicated. However, given the widespread use of native respondents during Hurston's time to gather and interpret research by anthropologists, Hurston's authority should be hard to question. Discussions of her authority should bear in mind the importance of "native researchers" for both the collection and analysis of research data.

In addition to fulfilling the interests of Boas in the language of African Americans in the U.S. South, Hurston's narrative use of dialogue conveyed her authority as a native researcher despite concerns that her analysis was not objective enough—a common critique of native researchers that assumes there exists an essential and realizable objectivity. Again, Hurston consistently employed and conveyed authority in terms of "You are there, because I was there."[29] This narrative mode aided in her representation of her presence in the field and was not an unusual mode for social scientists to take. For example, Melville J. Herskovits (among Hurston's scholarly mentors and supporters) published, with his wife and fellow scholar Frances S. Herskovits, *Rebel Destiny: Among the Bush Negroes of Dutch Guiana* (1934). Published one year before Hurston's *Mules and Men*, *Rebel Destiny* likewise used literary-style narratives to convey their ethnographic experiences and, more importantly, to convey the attitudes of the people they researched in Dutch Guiana. However, Hernández applies her understanding of Hurston's shifting subjectivities to support her assumption that Hurston's work is not authoritative, writing, "The use of the subjective destabilizes Hurston's ethnographic authority, yet it also provides a vantage point from which to view her shifting allegiances" (1995, 151). Hernández also describes how Hurston's shifting can be explained by her relationships with mentors and how their various perspectives implicitly "circumscribe" her scholarship (148). Her focus on Hurston's personal history misses the macro-historical trends in literary realism that shaped both Hurston's and the Herskovitses' ethnographic productions.

In "Defining Feminist Ethnography," Kamala Visweswaran also responds to James Clifford's charge that feminist anthropologists offered limited contributions to discussions concerning experimental ethnography. She rightly argues that in discussions of what constitutes experimental ethnography there was a tendency to quote male canonized writers only. Additionally, she builds on Strathern's description of feminist considerations of the relationship between self and other. Visweswaran says, "It is not a little ironic that cross-cultural and class 'others' have finally been acknowledged within the women's movement, while feminists in anthropology, the bastion of cultural relativity, insist on maintaining an us/them split that does not call into question their own positions as members of dominant Western societies" (1988a, 2). Visweswaran underscores the benefits of understanding experimental ethnography for the feminist project in anthropology and more broadly:

> In experimental ethnography, "pursuit of the other" becomes problematic, not taken for granted. The text is marked by disaffections, ruptures and incomprehensions. Skepticism, and perhaps a respect for the integrity of difference, replaces the ethnographic goal of total understanding and representation. Feminist anthropology, I would argue, stands to benefit from re-evaluating its assumptions about "the other" in terms of experimental ethnography. (3)[30]

Visweswaran then considers possibilities for feminist considerations of experimental ethnography, including a consideration of Hurston's literary productions as ethnography. In "re-reading and assigning new value to texts ignored or discarded," she describes potential contributions of professional ethnographers Jean Briggs, Hortense Powdermaker, and Laura Bohannon for how their ethnographies employed first-person narratives as strategies of "both communication and self discovery" (1, 4). She also argues that these ethnographies reveal the problematic dynamics that the role of gender played in their fieldwork "long before it was fashionable" (6).

In addition, Visweswaran notes the absence of native/indigenous anthropology in the discussions of George Marcus and Dick Cushman's "Ethnographies as Texts" (1982) and questions how experimental the male proponents of experimentalism are willing to get since, "to accept native authority is to give up the game" (Visweswaran 1988a, 7). Here Visweswaran "push[es] at the limits" of the us/them split (Gordon 1988, 8).[31] However, her call for indigenous perspectives argues for the consideration of literature as a source for these native perspectives: "Novels by Zora Neale Hurston or Paula Gunn Allen, or short stories by Cherrie Moraga would never be considered anthropology in the old canon. But perhaps they can in the next one" (Visweswaran 1988, 8). She suggests a reading of, and quotes from, Hurston's *Their Eyes Were Watching God* (Visweswaran 1988, 8). In effect, when she defines and "assigns new values" for feminist ethnography, the bias toward "experimentalism" moves Visweswaran beyond a consideration of Hurston's ethnographic works. Instead, she considers Hurston's recently canonized and much celebrated novel as ethnographic. Because of poststructuralist critiques of ethnography, fiction is privileged as more definitively challenging the "objective" claims and us/them split in ethnography. Visweswaran ignores the ethnographic significance of Hurston's ethnographies because, ironically, within her framework they too closely represent (as ethnographic representations of her fieldwork experience) traditional ethnography.

This "turn" in Visweswaran's arguments illustrates how these debates about the role of feminism in theorizing ethnography are largely about who gets to define the "center" and how vying for the center potentially remarginalizes the marginalized under different conditions. Visweswaran's consideration of Hurston's *Their Eyes* as an example of indigenous literature illustrates the popularity of Hurston's novel. However, the tendency to evaluate Hurston's literature over her anthropology has a particular effect on the consideration of her ethnographic work within feminist anthropology. Hurston's fiction is read conceptually, while her ethnographies are considered for their textual experimentation.

Visweswaran's argument foreshadows a later critical turn that marginalized Hurston's anthropology. Feminist anthropologists, in response to Clifford and Marcus's *Writing Culture: The Poetics and Politics of Ethnography*, defined an experimental focus in their development of a feminist anthropological canon with similar repercussions for Hurston's reception.[32] For example, in "Writing Culture, Writing Feminism: The Poetics and Politics of Experimental Ethnography," Deborah Gordon addresses the perspective of "participant/observer/interpreter" concerning the debates regarding experimental ethnography and feminist anthropology (1988, para. 4):

> For feminists, particularly feminist anthropologists and ethnographers, an important problem with experimental ethnographic authority is its grounding in a masculine subjectivity which encourages feminists to identify with new modes of ethnography, claiming to be decolonial, while simultaneously relegating feminism to a strained position of servitude. This kind of subordination is not located in marginalization nor does it indicate a conspiracy to silence feminists. Rather it is a management of feminism produced out of masculine feminism with specific troubles for feminist ethnographers. (para. 3)

It seems that by "masculine subjectivity" Gordon means that demands for theoretical discussions concerning the poetics and politics of textuality have hegemonic interests at their center. If by "masculine" she means that (powerful) white men were calling for feminist anthropologists to consider experimental ethnography, then she ignores the many men and women of color who also called for experimental approaches to authorize native viewpoints on culture. Again, Hurston's work, as a Black anthropologist who foregrounds Black voices in her ethnography, may be viewed as highly problematic (or simply erased) within a framework that does not consider varied political interests for her use of experimental forms in a vindicationist project that works to revise racist representations of Black culture.

However, the crux of Gordon's argument is to suggest that a dependency on "assumptions from Western critical theories which have been developed and utilized in cultural studies" effectively de-center feminist concerns (para. 5). She looks to debates within film theory and criticism, notes criticisms that challenge binary representations of art as falling into two separate and distinguishable categories, and suggests that a "parallel" categorization occurs in feminist exchanges that, in response to poststructuralism, set up hierarchies of binary opposition between experimental and conventional anthropological authority (para. 6).[33] Gordon then describes how Clifford's assertions regarding feminist contributions to experimental ethnography create an impractical dilemma: "Feminism must produce innovation that is distinct from any other; if it doesn't live up to this impossibility then it ceases to be either feminist or innovative" (para. 14). Therefore, she offers a number of possibilities for feminist anthropologists in response to Clifford's charge: (1) Feminists can self-reflexively situate themselves in their ethnographies "in relationship to the Western epistemology Clifford critiques"; (2) "feminist[s] might persuade experimental ethnographers that women also write experimental ethnographies"; (3) feminist anthropologists might "look at how their [ethnographic] questions and research agendas tie in with macro and global relations"; (4) they can consider the ideas of women of color concerning identity politics as "a form of subjectivity and relationality which is neither 'always, already' positioned nor transcendental but actualized with an ongoing movement of political prioritizing. Agency and intentionality are not opposed to structure here"; and (5) finally, she argues that they can "push at the limits of form/content split" and consider studies made by "Third World Women." She states: "Third World Women suggest rich possibilities for linking Western and Third World feminist writers who are embedded in and wish to speak to diverse audiences" (paras. 18–22).

These various possibilities as outlined by Gordon are also possibilities for a critical reception of Hurston's ethnographic authority: (1) Both *Mules and Men* and *Tell My Horse* self-reflexively reveal her relationship to the West; (2) her work is clearly experimental based on contemporary (and historical) definitions; (3) she illustrates and directly addresses macro processes and global relations in her work; (4) her "identity" as an "indigenous" researcher shifts subjectivities in ways that reveal her "political prioritizing" of certain perspectives and critiques; and (5) she resists a form/content divide, as her experimental ethnographic form both foregrounds the racial and gendered politics of Black people throughout the African diaspora, including Jamaica and Haiti and regions in the U.S. South, and illustrates her negotiations of both ethnographic subjectivity and authority. Although Hurston's work and its production should be compared within its specific historical contexts, any comparative consideration of her work in contemporary terms should consider how it is in strong alignment with the possibilities of a feminist experimental ethnography. It is this alignment of Hurston's work with the interests of feminist and native anthropology that informed early calls for her consideration as an anthropologist within the discipline (Mikell [1990] 1999, 66).

In a direct response to Strathern's (1987) essay regarding the relationship between feminism and ethnography (as well as experimental ethnography), Judith Stacey asks "Can There Be a Feminist Ethnography?" Stacey illustrates her loss of ethnographic "innocence" resulting from what she describes as a feminist bias toward experiential research ([1988] 1991, 115). She describes in a series of examples from her fieldwork experience how intimate access to informants'/respondents' personal lives, rather than detached observation (typically attributed to male, positivistic research), potentially exposed her respondents to "more dangerous form(s) of exploitation" (113). Like Strathern, Stacey's concern with the politics of difference in fieldwork is motivated by a desire to avoid exploiting research respondents. However, both Strathern and Stacey locate difference solely between two entities (never within one complex subject) and assume a straightforward power imbalance that always favors the researcher. Readings of Hurston's ethnographies within this framework might suggest that her representations of difference and power are one-dimensional and politically problematic instead of complexly situational. Hurston's ethnographies reveal how as self and other, researcher and cultural respondent, an ethnographer's power and difference (race, class, and gender) shifts depending on their social contexts. Both Gordon's and Hernández's articles make this point about Hurston's work, but they do so in terms of the influence of Hurston's complicated relationships with individual mentors and patrons, while eliding a broader discussion of the historical contexts of Hurston's work during the Harlem Renaissance and its contributions to early American anthropology. Their readings also do not consider a practice of writing about culture in realistic ways in both the anthropological and literary traditions (Clifford 1983, 124–26, 133, 142; Elliot 2002, xviii).[34] Gordon, for example, suggests that Hurston's mode was out of sync with contemporary expectations of ethnography, and she comments that some of Hurston's detailed lists "harken back to earlier styles of reporting." In fact, during the same period that Hurston produced her ethnographies, other anthropologists and social scientists employed a pastiche style of ethnographic reporting that included lists of beliefs or practices (Gordon 1990, 157; Lamphere 2004, 129–31). Gordon also seems to criticize Hurston's work for its "documentary effect": "There is a documentary effect produced not of a 'culture,' but of a collection of diverse materials" (1990, 150). If so, then Hurston can also be appraised for the way her work writes against culture and reveals culture as dynamic, fluid, and contestable (Abu-Lughod 1993, 13).[35]

Frances E. Mascia-Lees, Patricia Sharpe, and Colleen Ballerino Cohen, in "The Postmodernist Turn in Anthropology: Cautions from a Feminist Perspective" (1989), offer a direct response to George E. Marcus and Michael M. J. Fischer's *Anthropology as Cultural Critique: An Experimental Moment in the Human Sciences* (1986) and Clifford and Marcus's *Writing Culture: The Poetics and Politics of Ethnography* (1986) that challenges the poststructuralist foundations of reflexive ethnographies:

> At this profoundly self-reflexive moment in anthropology—a moment of questioning traditional modes of representation in the discipline—practitioners seeking to write a genuinely new ethnography would do better to use feminist theory as a model than to draw on postmodern trends in epistemology and literary criticism with which they have thus far claimed allegiance. (Mascia-Lees et al. 1989, 7)[36]

They argue that feminists have a long tradition of theorizing about what postmodernist anthropologists claim to have discovered: "that culture is composed of seriously contested codes of meaning, that language and politics are inseparable, and that constructing the 'other' entails relations of domination" (11). In addition, they assert, "The exclusion of feminist voices in Clifford and Marcus's influential volume and Clifford's defensive, convoluted, and contradictory explanation for it are strategies that preserve male supremacy in the academy" (16–17).[37] In response to Marilyn Strathern's (1987) argument concerning the tensions between the feminist and poststructuralist camps, they argue:

> Our suspicion of the new ethnographers' desire for collaboration with the "other" stems not from any such refusal to enter into dialogue with that "other," but from our history and understanding of being appropriated and literally spoken for by the dominant, and from our consequent sympathetic identification with the subjects of anthropological study in this regard. (Mascia-Lees et al. 1989, 21)

They also challenge the aims of new ethnography and experimental ethnography to include "intertextuality, dialogue, and self-referentiality" and say, "These new ways of structuring are more subtle and enigmatic than traditional modes of anthropological writing: they may serve to make the new ethnographies more obscure and, thus, difficult for anyone but highly trained specialists to dispute" (10). Therefore, within this critical context, and in practice, Hurston's singular embodiment of shifting and combined subjectivities (between self/ other, native/anthropologist) within her ethnographies may be met with "suspicion." In addition, her use of "intertextuality, dialogue, and self-referentiality" may be received as particularly obscuring rather than potentially revealing.

I summarize the aforementioned arguments to illustrate the poststructuralist and feminist debates concerning the advent of poststructuralism into anthropology in general and feminist anthropology specifically. These debates foreground the reception of Hurston's ethnographic work in two ways: (1) they provide a critical context for why readings of Hurston's work during this era focused on form over content or on textuality rather than content analysis; and (2) they explain, in part, a critical bias for readings of Hurston's shifting subjectivities. Complicating this bias are scholarly readings of Hurston's ethnographic work that overdetermine the effect of her race and class social position in evaluating the authority of her ethnographic productions, marginalizing her work as methodologically inadequate.

Histories and Hurston:
Canon Making, "Transferences," and Erasures

The debates in feminist anthropology regarding poststructuralism had significant impacts on canon formation within the field. Calls for *Their Eyes Were Watching God* to be read as anthropology foreshadowed the potential effects of the "postmodern turn" not only for Hurston but also for the feminist project of canonical inclusion that she represents, even across disciplinary boundaries. The Walker effect positioned Hurston within Black feminist literary criticism as central to a Black feminist literary tradition. In mainstream literary criticism, her status morphs from a central source to a convenient and sometimes token reference for considerations of *the* Black women's experience. In the discussion that follows, I will discuss how the Walker effect is apparent in inverse; not only is Hurston read as a literary figure while eliding her anthropological contributions, but Walker is read as an anthropologist. As such, I further reveal the terms of Hurston's unusual reception within anthropology (shaped by its poststructuralist reception), which also reveals a logic of token inclusion that inevitably, and more broadly, excludes. I think here of McDowell's discussion in "Transferences: Black Feminist Thinking: The 'Practice' of 'Theory,'" which, like Barbara Christian's "The Race for Theory," considers the ways receptions of poststructuralism come to represent hegemonic theory and enact a delimiting influence on the work (and authority) of Black feminist criticism (McDowell 1995b, 168; Christian 1987). Within anthropology, "transferences" that emerge with the uses of poststructuralism (theory as text) result in an erasure and marginalization of anthropologists like Hurston and the content of their productions (McDowell 1995b, 174; Harrison 1995, 242).

For example, Ruth Behar and Deborah Gordon's anthology *Women Writing Culture* (1995) provides a response to Clifford and Marcus's (1986) *Writing Culture,* asserting that feminist anthropologists have in fact made significant contributions to experimental ethnography. In the introduction, "Out of Exile" (1995), Behar describes the contexts that gave rise to the publication of *Women Writing Culture.* She says that the text is "born of a double crisis" in feminism and identifies two key texts that challenged feminist anthropology: *Writing Culture* and *This Bridge Called My Back* (Moraga and Anzaldúa 2015). The former claimed that feminists had not contributed to discussions or debates concerning reflexive or experimental ethnographies, and the latter called for more than token consideration of women of color in feminist anthropology as well as challenging a divide between creative and scholarly writing (Clifford and Marcus 1986, 3–6, 7). Behar claims that *Women Writing Culture* seeks not to tokenize and notes that "not only were women anthropologists excluded from the project of *Writing Culture* but so too were 'native' and 'minority' anthropologists" (1995, 8).

In a discussion of the politics of canon formation, Behar notes the "erasure" of Margaret Mead from Clifford and Marcus's *Writing Culture,* a general "erasure" of women's contributions in anthropology, the "canon wars" in literary studies, and a lack of similar debates within the field of anthropology. Drawing on arguments concerning canon formation posited by literary theorists Toni Morrison and Hazel Carby, Behar argues for a gender-diversified canon that should seek not only to "add the work of excluded writers to standardized reading lists but also to examine *how the process of marginalization has shaped the works produced within the dominant culture*" (1995, 10; emphasis mine).[38] Behar quotes Morrison's question: "What intellectual feats had to be performed by the author or critic to erase me from a society seething with my presence, and what effect has that performance had on the work?" (Morrison 1989, 12). However, Behar misinterprets the meaning and import of Morrison's quote when she inaccurately revises the question as "how the process of marginalization has shaped the works" of African American productions. Ironically, Morrison's question is fundamentally different from Behar's in that Morrison implicates the agency of the individual critic or author in erasing the African American presence. Behar's revision writes a different question that leads her to define a different set of critical conditions and propose a different set of solutions regarding the politics of canon inclusion and exclusion.

I have previously argued how, in Hurston's case, feminist anthropologists developed arguments about Hurston's marginalization that have become primary rationales for the authoritative failures of her work. They in effect ask "how the process of marginalization has shaped the works" of Hurston, instead of asking, as Toni Morrison did concerning the erasure of African Americans from U.S.–American literature, "what intellectual feats had to be performed by the author or critic to erase me from a society seething with my presence, and what effect has that performance had on the work" (1989, 12). Some of the conclusions of the aforementioned arguments, although not framed as descriptions of Hurston's current potential import, make de facto statements about the authority of her ethnographic work while ignoring its cultural content. The rhetorical effect silences the potential for considerations of Hurston's illustrations of and critical discussions about culture. While Hurston's racial marginalization and financial hardships are worth noting, her material circumstances were neither peculiar nor do they adequately encapsulate the import of her work. However, as Morrison suggests, the process of challenging the canon (the primary arbiter of professional authority) requires questions posed to the erasing critic or author to reveal the "intellectual feats" of canonical exclusion.

For Behar, Margaret Mead is the central symbol of the "erasure" of women from the anthropological canon. Behar notes Clifford's "slip of the pen" as he relegates, in the introduction to *Writing Culture*, Mead as "the one who plays with the children and questions the villagers, not the one who writes the texts" (Behar 1995, 9). Although Mead is perhaps America's most widely read anthropologist, Behar claims that her "reputation as a serious scholar has been damaged by her image in the discipline as a 'popularizer'" (9). To further support her discussion concerning the erasure of women from the anthropological canon, Behar notes the work of Catherine Lutz, who describes "how both female and male authors tend to cite more often the presumably 'theoretical' writing of men, while women's writing, which often focuses on gender issues, is cited less frequently and usually in circumscribed contexts" (9).[39]

Behar also notes the canon debates in literature and a popular alarm (as evidenced in a *Time* magazine article) that the canon was changing such that Alice Walker might replace Shakespeare. Anthropologists remained silent during these debates (9–10). In arguing for the expansion of the anthropological canon, Behar revealingly asks, "Why is the *culture concept* in anthropology only traced through Sir Edward Tylor, Franz Boas, Bronislaw Malinowski, Claude Lévi-Strauss, and

Clifford Geertz? Could the *writing of culture* not be traced, as the essays in this volume suggest, through Elsie Clews Parsons, Ruth Benedict, Margaret Mead, Ella Deloria, Zora Neale Hurston, Ruth Landes, and Barbara Myerhoff to Alice Walker?" (12; emphases mine). She also says, "The essays in this volume offer one entrance into the debate, retelling the story of American anthropology in ways that allow us to imagine what Alice Walker might say, not only to Shakespeare but also to Evans-Pritchard and Mead" (12). Through these excerpts it is possible to trace Behar's own slip of the pen, from "culture concept" to "writing of culture," where, concerned with responding to the debates around ethnographic experimentalism, she argues that marginalized women anthropologists should be recuperated into the anthropological canon on the basis of their textuality rather than for their contributions to defining cultural concepts.

In introducing Graciela Hernández's essay on Hurston, Behar praises Hurston's work in primarily textual terms:

> Hernández reveals how the multiple voices of Hurston as ethnographer, writer, and community member are subtly mediated by the use of a storytelling style that gives power to the spoken words of her informants over the written words of her own text. Hurston's return to her home community in Eatonville, Florida, with the "spyglass of Anthropology" obtained in Morningside Heights forced her to negotiate the relationship between ethnographic authority and personal authenticity. Out of that negotiation came a text about African American folk culture that was postmodern before its time in enacting an exemplary hybridity that combined engaged scholarship with a nuanced portrait of Hurston's own intellectual process. (Behar 1995, 18–19)

Behar acknowledges Hurston's text as "exemplary," "engaged," and "nuanced." However, Hernández's essay, as I have previously discussed, focuses mostly on Hurston as the primary subject of *Mules and Men* and does not provide a sustained discussion of its specific contributions to anthropological/folklore knowledge within the contexts of its production.

The other essay concerning Hurston, although tangentially, in Behar and Gordon's collection is Faye Harrison's "Writing Against the Grain: Politics of Difference in the Work of Alice Walker" (1995). In her introduction, Behar explains Harrison's focus on Walker:

> Alice Walker has long written fiction that is in dialogue with anthropology. It is Walker who, in writing about her own search for Hurston in the 1970s, restored her to anthropology, which had cast her into oblivion, revitalizing interest in her work not just as a fiction writer but also as an anthropologist and a folklorist. Aware that Hurston's precarious position in anthropology has as much to do with her being black as with her writing in creative ways

that go against the grain of conventional ethnographic reporting, Walker has chosen to stay out of academic anthropology and to enact a corpus of fictional works that embody and expand upon anthropological concerns. (Behar 1995, 20)[40]

Harrison's essay describes how Walker's novel *Temple of My Familiar* (1989) can be read as a subaltern history (in the vein of Eric Wolf's *Europe and the People without History* [1982]) that illustrates "the agency of the colonized (especially the women) and of counterhegemonic Western women" through a "cultural critique" of Western notions of marriage, family, racial and ethnic identity, intellectual authority, and the discipline of anthropology (Harrison 1995, 237–41). Harrison describes Walker as an "anthropological interlocutor" and argues that, beginning with Walker's discovery of Hurston and her use of Hurston's *Mules and Men* to inform her writing of the short story "The Revenge of Hannah Kemhuff," "Walker's fiction is ethnographic and ethnohistorical, even if not as deliberately or as self-consciously as Hurston's was" (234–35).

Harrison's critical consideration of Walker's novel provides a systematic discussion of the macro processes of global, political, and economic forces interacting with the micro processes of the personal interactions of Walker's fictional characters. In Harrison's treatment, Walker's characters, who populate and speak in her fictional worlds, matter. Their experiences and their knowledge inform Harrison's reading of cultural concepts within the novel. In contrast, Hernández's treatment of Hurston's *Mules and Men* privileges Hurston's presence in the ethnography over respondent knowledge. Despite Hernández's thesis that one of Hurston's strengths is her use of dialogue, Hurston's respondents are virtually silenced, as is the data that Hurston collected from them. What matters most in Hernández's discussion of Hurston's text is the complicated politics of Hurston's subjectivity.

Subsequently, within this collection of essays Walker is the raced and gendered cultural author and cultural other whose canonical intervention into literature represents the possibility of a new feminist history for the anthropological canon. Behar explains, "I needed to refigure the canon of anthropological knowledge as it is defined and passed on from one generation to the next in the academy. I needed another past, another history. So I looked for models in the text of those women ethnographers who came before us" (1995, 13). In effect, the junctures of two historical moments (Walker's popularity largely associated with Hurston's recuperation, and poststructuralist reading of literary texts as ethnographic) delimit considerations of Hurston's analytical and critical discussions in her ethnographic work. Hurston's analytical anthropology is materially erased and replaced by theoretical considerations of Walker's literary work.

Although Harrison's essay does not focus on Hurston's anthropology, she does consider (and signifies on) the canonical repercussions of the focus on textual readings that her essay enacts. Harrison notes that Walker is only one of many "subaltern" intellectuals who can be read in the way that she reads *Temple of My Familiar,* and she questions the impact that postmodernism has on the reception of "Third World anthropologists": "The postmodern 'fetishizing of [textual and rhetorical] form' and its sharp separation from intellectual content may be responsible in part for the near failure to engage the many substantive analyses and critiques that Third World anthropologists have produced" (1995, 242).[41] Harrison's statement is incisive, although she does not directly name how her own essay and Hernández's are examples of the very phenomenon against which she cautions. However, her critique, by indirection, continues with an argument for the recuperation of Black anthropologists and writers in textual terms: "If form is to be prioritized, how can the virtual invisibility of Hurston, John Gwaltney,[42] and interlocutors like Walker be justified?" (242). With this statement, Harrison underscores the continued exclusion of Hurston's anthropology (and others) notwithstanding the precedence given to experimental approaches in feminist anthropology. Overall, Harrison's critique highlights that Walker's (and Hurston's) presence within the anthology illuminates the absence of many Black anthropologists in terms that fail to note their conceptual contributions. The publication of Irma McClaurin's *Black Feminist Anthropology: Theory, Politics, Praxis, and Poetics* (2001a), which I will discuss in the epilogue, would later redress the absence of Black women anthropologists in anthropological canon making. Its production was a response to the marginalization and erasure of a Black feminist presence in canons of anthropology and feminist anthropology. Significantly, *Black Feminist Anthropology* resists Hurstonism by including a community of anthropologists whose shared vindicationist goals align them in a tradition (a community) of Black feminist praxis (McClaurin 2001b, 15).

Unfortunately, *Women Writing Culture,* which foregrounds the perspectives of diverse women anthropologists, enacts a dynamic of inclusion and exclusion that it seeks to challenge and revise. The relationship between the treatment of Hurston's and Walker's work in Behar and Gordon's collection of essays, which was marketed as a canonical intervention into anthropology, reveals the transference of literary and ethnographic authority with striking repercussions for Black women anthropologists.[43] It primarily asserts a presence of diverse women in the anthropological canon on the basis of textual experimentation. However, its slippages, evidenced in the patterns of its focus and treatment of Hurston and Walker, ironically transfer Hurston's nominal place in a canon (beyond discussions of textual form) to Walker. Hurston remains a highly innovative but complicated ethnographer who, in poststructuralist terms, subverts and "debunks" and "destabilizes" her own authority (Hernández 1995, 160–61), while Walker is held up as presenting cultural content and concepts as anthropology's "interlocutor" (Harrison 1995, 234–35).

Because of the efforts of feminist anthropologists to recuperate her legacy, Mead has a safe place within the larger anthropological canon for having contributed to the development of ideas about cultural concepts. Any consideration of Mead's work in textual terms does not negate her contributions. For example, both Mead and Ruth Benedict have been featured within anthologies for their contributions to the discipline. During the period of Hurston's heightened reception in poststructuralist terms, the first edition of R. Jon McGee and Richard L. Warms's *Anthropological Theory: An Introductory History* (1996) lists Margaret Mead and Ruth Benedict as the sole women contributors under the heading "Cultural Theory in the Early Twentieth Century." More recently, with the seventh edition (2020) of the anthology, Hurston joins Mead and Benedict.[44] The entry from chapter 4 of *Mules and Men* (Hurston [1935] 1978, 64–81) is occasioned by editorial notes that describe Hurston's autoethnographic form and "pride" for the Black communities she studied (McGee and Warms 2020, 137). There are extended notes that focus on Hurston's use of vernacular and her distinctive narrative styles in *Mules and Men* (McGee and Warms 2020, 182), the historical contexts of the location (Polk County, Loughman, Florida), and the influence of Boas's methodology on Hurston's presentation of the folktales. These are important aspects of her work, but there is no sustained reference to her distinctive conceptual contribution as an anthropological folklorist. In addition, other editorial notes refer to her telling "lies" to gain access to information from the community, offer extended details regarding Hurston's patronage support and her "dramatic and tumultuous life," and narrate how her reception by Harlem Renaissance contemporaries and patronage influenced her work (136–38, 178–89). Indeed, as in Gordon's (1990) comparative assessment of Hurston's and Mead's work and *Women Writing Culture*, Hurston's conceptual contributions to anthropological folklore, having never been fully considered, are largely ignored in a discussion that centers her narrative approach and biographical details in a reading of her work. Furthermore, in an anthology that defines theory, these conventional receptions leave the reader to question whether Hurston advanced or produced a theory of culture—in particular, of African American culture.[45] Of course, Boas warned against developing grand theories. However, Hurston worked to develop and advance concepts regarding Black culture (Hurston [1934] 1995; Mikell 1982, 221). She also worked to make conclusions, collect "new facts," and provide analysis and "opportunity for serious study" (Hurston 1947, 437–38).

The narrow focus on text during this era of Hurston's recuperation within feminist anthropology means that Hurston's work is "othered" rather than considered as the product of and negotiation of intellectual choices (Morrison 1989, 9). The rereading of Hurston's work occurred during a period when some feminist anthropologists launched defensive responses against poststructuralist claims that it provided the more ethical model of fieldwork. These concerns shaped a critical bias within feminist anthropology, encouraging readings of Hurston's shifting subjectivities and limiting a consideration of her work in broader historical terms. Those terms include, but are not limited to, a consideration of her anthropological research of folklore as grounded in the contemporaneous methods and theories of social change of the discipline (Boas 1920; Boas [1928] 1986; Boas [1932] 1983; Boas [1935] 1978; Herskovits 1937c; Redfield, Linton, and Herskovits 1936). Instead, critical evaluations of Hurston's ethnographies as either definitively "undisciplined" or extra-experimental shaped her reception in the field. In addition, feminist anthropologists were concerned with the ethics of the practice of experimental ethnography, and with defending their ability to evaluate women in "other" cultures without employing experimental modes. They argued that these modes obscured rather than revealed power inequities. Therefore, feminist anthropologists received Hurston's shifting rhetorical stances with skepticism and as examples of the limits of experimental anthropology. Hurston's marginalized status as an anthropologist was further secured by these critical concerns.

The shift in Hurston's reception (by both literary scholars and feminist anthropological scholars) brings into sharper focus the maintenance of authority and exclusion in the academy. As evident in the receptions of both Hurston and Walker alike, disciplinary debates around poststructuralism reveal the hegemony's ability to maintain systems of inequality. Where Hurston is inscribed as powerful and central, the communities that she symbolically represents are marginalized (duCille 1994, 596). Within feminist anthropology, where Hurston is marginalized, the limited terms in which she is admitted into the canon also reflect the hegemony's ability to marginalize or effectively erase the communities she represents (Black feminist anthropologists). As Black feminist critics on both sides of the disciplinary divide note, the politics surrounding the uses of poststructuralism threatened to render obsolete the work of marginalized groups at a point when they were gaining access to the academy and shaping with authority fields of study that centered their scholarly perspectives (Harrison 1995, 242; Christian [1987] 2000, 281; McDowell (1995b), 168–69).

Hurston's literary presence, marginalization, and erasure within the feminist anthropological canon are a material and symbolic representation of these dynamic processes.

Nonetheless, Hurston's ethnographies were anthropological projects that spoke to prevalent theories of Black inhumanity and inferiority by writing against existing cultural concepts and representations of Black social life. In this way, she advanced research about Black humanity that stressed complex cultural practices, community diversity, cultural change, and innovation as proof of a civilized existence. Of course, Hurston was not alone or the first in her advancement of this cultural concept, nor was the field of anthropology the first disciplinary or scholarly field concerned with advancing this concept. Frederick Douglass, for example, offered a response to ethnological studies concerning Black inhumanity in 1854 in "The Claims of the Negro, Ethnologically Considered: An Address before the Literary Societies of Western Reserve College, at Commencement, July 12, 1854," which countered ethnological science of the period and argued for "Negro" humanity. Moreover, making a canonical claim for Hurston's special theoretical contributions is problematic. Since, according to Morrison, "canon building is empire building," the process itself would involve assigning a primacy to Hurston's views over other scholars in a hegemonic movement that asserts a politics of inclusion, marginalization, and exclusion (1989, 8).

For purposes of evaluating Hurston's ethnographies, I resist a hierarchical engagement with knowledge production and instead engage a relativistic method that seeks to understand Hurston's contributions within the historical contexts of their production. This approach recognizes and foregrounds Hurston's membership within a community of scholars committed to challenging representations and knowledge production on African American sociocultural life. Chapter 5 investigates the complex politics of Hurston's literary and ethnographic authority within contexts that recognize critical arguments and interests shaping both the content and form of her ethnographic productions and the productions of other noted social-scientific ethnographers who recognized and acknowledged Hurston's conceptual contributions to anthropological folklore.

5

Mules and Men

"Negro Folklore . . . Is Still in the Making"

Contemporary Black feminist anthropologists have called for a consideration of Hurston's anthropology within contemporary critical frameworks such as global or transnational perspectives (Mikell [1990] 1999, 66; Bolles 2001, 31). This approach, they suggest, might inform the disciplinary consideration, if not contemporary recuperation, of Hurston's ethnographies within the anthropological canon. I offer an alternative response to that call, which instead considers Hurston's ethnography *Mules and Men* within the historical contexts of its production. These contexts include a demand for studies among early African Americanists that would appeal to non-academic audiences by featuring narrative dialogue in ways that paralleled the widely popular literary realism found in fiction of that time, along with a critical interest in treating these narratives as data to illuminate traditional beliefs, knowledge, attitudes, and practices of Black people.[1] Hurston's representation of African American culture in *Mules and Men* challenged common myths of Black inferiority. She demonstrated that, while shaped by the legacies of slavery, plantation life, and African retentions, Black cultural traditions are not determined by these contexts. They remain dynamic and evolve: "Negro folklore is still in the making" (Hurston [1934] 1995, 836). Hurston's assertion that African American culture is generative and complex challenged prevalent attitudes that "Negro" culture was essentially derivative and uncomplicated in its expression.

Readings of Hurston that do not explore the more immediate professional context in which she worked tend to obscure the critical conversations with which she engages within and through her ethnographies. In addition, as her letters reveal, Hurston was aware that she was producing ethnographic works for a popular audience that would include specialists and generalists who would "reference" her findings in future studies (Kaplan 2002, 308, 389).[2] Therefore, I must ask, should we compare Hurston's professional/ethnographic authority against a standard that she never sought to emulate? When Hurston wrote *Mules and Men*, for example, are we to assume that she was without critical agency, wholly subject to the demands of her publisher, patrons, and mentors? Should we presume that she was merely resigned to write a "text" that, consequently, defied ethnographic conventions and eclipsed its cultural content, as so much of the literature concerning her ethnographic production and anthropological experiences suggests? Can we, instead, imagine that Hurston put pen to paper and deliberately crafted (from her exhaustive field notes) a distinctive statement about Black folk life and culture within her ethnographies? Can we imagine that her content (and approach) was informed by, and even revised, prevailing concepts of culture during the period? What were those concepts? What was her statement? This chapter reveals some of the ways that *Mules and Men* can be read as an ethnographic representation of Black folk life and culture when the historical contexts of its production are more closely considered and when Hurston's intellectual agency is centered.

Hurston's ethnographies are often evaluated as highly unusual, receiving either "twice as much praise or twice as much blame," in Hurston's words, because they are read apart from trends in the study of African American culture during the era of their production ([1928] 1995, 827). It is helpful, rather, to think of Hurston's *Mules and Men* as entering a conversation with scholars of Black culture who comprised a distinctive interdisciplinary field of study that sought to evaluate and revise critical scholarship and popular representations of African American life. In general, they developed vindicationist approaches to evaluating culture to better define, describe, and ameliorate racial and gender disparity in a post-slavery American society and to challenge normative beliefs concerning the racial and cultural inferiority of people of African descent (Baber 1999, 193; L. Baker 1998, 107, 162; Franklin and Collier-Thomas 1996, 1–16; Harrison 1992, 240–41). These African Americanists, who are defined by their commitment and approach to the subject area, often experimented with and blurred genre conventions as they applied diverse methods that might reveal new data and, in the process, revise representations of African American life and culture. In a challenge to evolutionary theories of human development that definitively characterized Black people as primitive, African Americanists considered history and tradition as significant contexts for understanding Black culture in America and presented first-person narratives from local respondents as a valuable source for this data.

In addition, literary realist fictions that documented African American life were popular in the 1930s for their "storied" representations of folk life and culture. Hurston and other social scientists could expect that representing their qualitative data in a similar style, as realistic representations of African American thought, feelings, and wisdom, would attract wide readership and thus help to revise widespread stereotypes concerning Southern African Americans. Although a strongly held and shared goal of the African Americanists, revising these stereotypes was no easy feat. White reading audiences, both in literature and in social science, often found it hard to believe that people of African descent acquired wisdom, possessed human feelings, and could express sophisticated thoughts. Hurston reports, in "What White Publishers Won't Print," that Julia Peterkin's characterizations of Gullah life in *Scarlet Sister Mary* ([1928] 1998) were met with skepticism by a reader who protested "and everybody knows that Nigra's don't think" (Hurston [1950] 1995, 952). Nonetheless, Hurston and other social scientists, including Charles S. Johnson and Hortense Powdermaker, incorporated narratives and dialogue gathered from Black respondents within their social scientific studies of African American life and culture. In order to better reveal the contexts of Hurston's experimental mode and ethnographic authority, as well as her distinctive representation of African American culture, I compare Hurston's *Mules and Men* with Johnson's *Shadow of the Plantation* (1934) and Powdermaker's *After Freedom: A Cultural Study in the Deep South* ([1939] 1993). Hurston, Johnson, and Powdermaker were all members of a dynamic social-scientific community committed to the study of race relations in the United States. Johnson (1893–1956) was an American sociologist, Powdermaker (1900–1970) was an American anthropologist trained in the British school of anthropology, and Hurston, of course, was an American folklorist and anthropologist, educated in the Boasian school of anthropology.[3]

Although we can compare Hurston's *Mules and Men* to the ethnographies of other women anthropologists of the era (like Margaret Mead or Ella Deloria) for the ways gender and ethnicity influenced their methods and subject matter, comparing Hurston with her contemporaries who studied race relations in the United States provides a more specific historical context in terms of the time periods covered, the publication receptions, the shared field of specialization, and the associations between these scholars.[4] My comparison of these scholars across racial and gender lines (Black male, Black female, and white female) shows how such siloed examinations might elide scholarly communities, methodologies, and research interests. Johnson, Powdermaker, and

Hurston were contemporaries, and my comparative approach provides a more stable foundation from which to evaluate Hurston's distinctive contribution to the scholarship on African American culture during the mid-1930s. Johnson and Powdermaker researched, wrote, and published their ethnographies from the late 1920s to the late 1930s, during the same period as Hurston. All three ethnographies focused on the lives and culture of African Americans in the rural South and, therefore, they shared a common subject area and likely attracted similar audiences. In their use of fieldwork research, and in their focus on respondent commentary as central to representing cultural meanings, they employed similar "experimental" methodologies. In addition, their interests in addressing "the Negro problem" in America put their works in conversation with each other in the documenting of sociocultural change.

All three ethnographies were published within five years of one another and were likely read by each of the other authors as well as by other scholars in the field. Each scholar had some documented interaction with the others as part of the community of scholars, writers, educators, and artists with research interests in Black life and culture. For example, Powdermaker consulted with Johnson while gathering data on African American culture and literature at Fisk University (Williams and Woodson 1939, xviii). Johnson subsequently gave a favorable review of Powdermaker's ethnography in a 1939 issue of *The New Republic*. Charles Johnson was the founder of *Opportunity: A Journal of Negro Life*, the literary arm of the National Urban League, which documented the Harlem Renaissance, in which Hurston published several award-winning pieces.[5] Johnson is credited with having invited Hurston to New York while she was a student at Howard University. Hurston frequently corresponded with Johnson, and they were familiar with each other's research. Johnson visited Hurston while she was completing fieldwork in New Orleans under the apprenticeship of "Dr. Jenkins," a prominent hoodoo doctor (Hurston [1935] 1978, 234). These connections are real and indicate professional networks if not relationships. Placing their works in conversation with one another (as the authors actually were) offers a critical perspective on Hurston's ethnographies that allows us to hold questions concerning her "professional" authority.

Each employed "innovative" approaches, but they brought different disciplinary perspectives to the issue of race and race relations in the U.S. South and held divergent views on the impact of history on African American culture: Johnson's ethnography advanced that African Americans' progress toward assimilation was hindered by the experiences of slavery in America. His ideas concerning social and economic experiences of African Americans in the South were related to critical discussions concerning whether African Americans retained any traces of African beliefs, knowledge and practices following the experience of slavery. These discussions included the "Herskovits-Frazier debate." Powdermaker's ethnography work was generally informed by Bronislaw Malinowski's views "that culture determined behavior" (Williams and Woodson 1939, xxiii). However, she was also influenced by recent critical discussions by Herskovits concerning acculturation, particularly his coauthored "Memorandum for the Study of Acculturation" (Redfield et al. 1936), which she cited in her study.[6] However, unlike Herskovits, Powdermaker viewed acculturation as a one-directional process, whereby white culture strongly influenced, if not determined, Black culture and Black culture had little, if any, acculturative impact on white culture (Fraser 1991, 406; Williams and Woodson 1939, xxiv). Like Johnson, Powdermaker viewed African American culture as largely shaped by slavery, and she minimized the role of African survivals in African American culture. By contrast, as noted, Hurston moved beyond Herskovits's views to advance the ongoing creation of folklore phenomena within Black communities. In addition, Hurston's perspective and approach stands apart from her contemporaries Johnson and Powdermaker because of her treatment of African American life in a context beyond a plantation economy and because she relied exclusively on ethnographic data. She shares with Johnson an interest in representing the original voices of those she studied. Powdermaker largely summarized respondent commentary, but Hurston shares with Powdermaker a consideration of class dynamics.

The distinctive qualities of *Mules and Men* are best revealed when examined within a community of African Americanists working to revise representations and scholarly records of African American culture. In the discussion that follows, I offer a comparative assessment of their ethnographies (inclusive of prefatory endorsements) and an assessment of subsequent critical reviews, respectively. For Johnson's *Shadow of the Plantation* and Powdermaker's *After Freedom*, I consider both the prefatory endorsements and critical reviews following their publication. Genevieve West's study of the concurrent reception of *Mules and Men* covers much ground in illustrating how early critics of *Mules and Men* received Hurston's work in terms that fail to realize "that Mules and Men contains three years of anthropological research" (West 2005, 81). Hurston's publisher, Lippincott, wanted a work that would appeal to a broad audience. Informed by Lippincott's sensational advertising, reviews of *Mules and Men* in the 1930s were uneven and sometimes racially charged. For example, comparisons to Joel Chandler Harris's *Uncle Remus: His Songs and His Sayings* (referenced by Boas in his preface) were tinged with rhetoric of racial stereotypes, leaving critical reviewers to largely question the authority and significance of Hurston's work (West 2005, 77–87). Taking into account the problematic reception of *Mules and Men* during its recuperation within the field of anthropology in the 1990s, I offer a sustained discussion of Boas's prefatory endorsement of *Mules and Men* and a significant and neglected critical review by Melville Herskovits that defends its critical authority. Their analysis and endorsement shines light on ways of reading the first half of *Mules and Men*. In addition, I offer ways of reading the second half of *Mules and Men* in terms of its ethnographic methodology, given Hurston's significant familiarity with medical discourse. With this broad comparative discussion of Hurston's ethnography, I illustrate and underscore Hurston's contributions to a larger field of African American studies, including her specific challenge to social-scientific (and common) knowledge and attitudes concerning African American life and culture. In addition, I demonstrate the contemporaneous and explicit academic and professional authority conferred to her ethnography by her peers, who largely shared her conceptual views on Black culture, notwithstanding polarized popular and academic reviews of her work.

Sociologist Charles S. Johnson's *Shadow of the Plantation* combines statistical, survey, ecological, historical, and interview responses to describe the economic and societal vestiges of U.S. slavery in African American life. Set in a small African American community in Macon County, Alabama, Johnson's analysis focuses on the impact of the plantation economy on behavior and customs in the community. Johnson argues that many aspects of African American social life are "disorganized" due to the devastating impact of slavery: "Patterns of life, social codes, as well as social attitudes, were set in the economy of slavery" (1934, 16). He also argues that the failing plantation economy limits the possibility of stable social institutions for this community (16).

Johnson uses excerpted commentaries from individual community members throughout the work to support his observations of social life in Macon County. While he describes social institutions in the community and the impact of a declining agricultural economic system on African American life and culture, he is also concerned with realistically representing "folk culture" and "the folk" through the use of quoted respondent material. To achieve his objective of realism, Johnson transcribes the folk vernacular of Southern African Americans, taking care to phonetically reflect the dialect of his respondents. For example, Johnson excerpts the following quotations to reflect common practices and cultural meanings ascribed to divorce within the community:

"My husband done cross de line; don't hear nothing. He may be living or dead. Ain't dat divorce?" (1934, 72)

"I divorced my first wife and I'm separated from the other one, but she ain't divorced. We didn't fuss or nothing, we just decided to quit intelligent." (76)

Johnson offers these examples and others as evidence of the community's "confusion" about legal divorce and their belief that a physical separation essentially constitutes divorce (71). Although Johnson does not elaborate on the use of the term "intelligent" by the last respondent, I interpret the passage to mean they did not have a difficult separation that might require intervention and codification through a formal judiciary process. Involving the court system in their personal lives would have been risky for Black Americans living in the Jim Crow South, and, therefore, "quit[ting] intelligent" meant avoiding interpersonal violence and structural racism.[7] In another passage a respondent refers to legal divorce as "revorce," which, by my reading, indicates that the practice of a legal divorce might be thought of as redundant, given that many practiced a local custom of providing a slip of paper with a handwritten declaration of divorce from a witness in the community as sufficient evidence of divorce (72).

In addition to representing common experiences and attitudes concerning unregulated and informal divorces, of interest to scholars concerned with Black family and marriage patterns, these quotations portray folk vernacular expressions that draw readers in, allowing them to engage the immediacy of the research event by hearing the respondents speak in their own words. Johnson carefully transcribes the rhythm and intonation of each individual's speech pattern, which functions to realistically portray this aspect of African American culture. Some excerpts "sound" like and are written like Standard English, while others are written phonetically to signify dialect speech. Johnson does not translate the dialect of his respondents into Standard English, which suggests his understanding that these responses as spoken hold some fundamental value in communicating Black cultural meaning.

Ironically, some of the "folk culture" examples that Johnson presents contradict his thesis that African American cultural life is largely destitute in the wake of slavery. In some instances, his narrative selections portray African American culture as creative, resilient, and resistant in the "shadows" of plantation life. For example, Johnson provides a transcript of the "The Funeral of Brother Jesse Harding," which he includes in its entirety "because it reflects many facets of community life" (1934, 162). Brother Jesse Harding, a successful businessman and landowner, reportedly differs significantly from the "spirit of the community," which held "little property," as he had a shrewd approach to business that included "exacting payments of debt to him" (162). The community fails to provide an adequate response to the minister's call for outward expressions of grief, and the episode resounds with implicit cultural meaning: "Under different circumstances, perhaps, his life would have been considered worthy of emulating for his thrift and foresight. But not in this community. The people came to the funeral, but there was neither praise nor sorrow over his passing" (162). Johnson's empathetic description of the funeral is highly literary and sometimes humorous. His description of Brother Jesse Harding is reminiscent of Hurston's description of Joe "Jody" Starks in *Their Eyes Were Watching God*, whose approach to doing business and relating to his neighbors in the all-Black town he founded left his neighbor Sim Jones feeling that "Joe Starks is too exact wid folks. All he got he done made it offa de rest of us" (Hurston [1937] 1998, 49). The narrator describes Joe Starks's difference from the community as being "like seeing your sister turn into a 'gator" (49). Although Starks's burial was "the finest thing Orange County had ever seen," Hurston's implicit critique of businessman Joe Starks stands in contrast to Johnson's admiration for businessman Jess Harding. Hurston offers a different reading of the class tensions in Black towns through the voices of community members, whose critiques raise questions about power and property and the costs to the community. As Hurston's narrator declares, "But any man who walks in the way of power and property is bound to meet hate" (48).

Whether this aspect of Hurston's *Their Eyes* was directly influenced by Johnson's sociological study is unclear, but I offer this comparative reading to underscore the shared quality of Johnson's sociological and Hurston's fictional use of realistic dialogue. These and other "folk culture" considerations within *Shadow of the Plantation* were not typical for a sociological treatise during this time. In fact, they were unusual enough to warrant sociologist Robert E. Park's defense of their significance in his introduction to Johnson's ethnography. Park was a sociologist and an early and distinguished member of the Chicago school of sociology. His introduction is a conventional and significant endorsement of Johnson's research focus, method, and approach, which provides an "apology" for the study's experimental form and advances critical frames for the work's reception by readers. Park notes that the study is sociological in its use of survey data and statistics while being anthropological in its claims to study "non-material" folk culture (1934, xiv). He seems to have anticipated that the combination would produce confusion for readers expecting one approach or the other, and his introduction defends the use of each method to the anthropologist and the sociologist, respectively.

To sociologists, Park defends Johnson's use of ethnographic descriptions and quoted remarks in an endorsement of Johnson's innovative contribution: "Undoubtedly the *most* revealing portions of the present study are the candid comments of the peoples studied on their own lives. As recorded here, in the language and accents in which they were uttered, most of these statements have the character of a human document" (1934, xviii; emphasis mine). Park also approvingly notes that the passages could have been written by authors of realistic fiction such as Julia Peterkin, author of *Scarlet Sister Mary* (1928), and DuBose Heyward, author of *Porgy* (1924) (Park 1934, xix). His comparison suggests that these realist fictions had some ethnographic authority for the social scientific community.

To anthropologists, Park explains and defends the role of survey data:

> Although it describes itself as a study of "social and cultural change," the materials on which this study is based are not those [with] which anthropologists are familiar or are likely to approve. As a matter of fact, the study starts with a different tradition—the tradition, namely, of the rural sociologist, who conceives his community rather as a statistical aggregate than as a cultural complex. (xvi)

More specifically, he elaborates on the importance of survey data for the study of African American culture in particular:

> There were other reasons why a study of Negro culture should assume the technical form of a survey besides the desirability of starting with the available information in regard to the region. One was the character of the Negro community itself, and of the very tenuous lines of connections which hold the rural population into any sort of solidarity that could be described as communal. Another was the fact that the Negro community is so completely interpenetrated and dependent upon the dominant white community that *it is difficult to conceive of it as having any independent existence.* (xvii; emphasis mine)

Park attributes the difficulties of studying African American culture in terms that define that culture as completely dependent upon white society. For Park and Johnson, African American cultural change does not happen in relation to, in resistance to, or apart from white culture, but as subject to white culture. Park's description of a dependent African American community frames Johnson's discussion of the conditions of African American folk life and culture in a post-slavery plantation economy. Johnson describes an impoverished rural South whose culture is determined by economic impoverishment and the catastrophe of slavery.

For Johnson, the total loss of cultural traditions began with slavery:[8]

> The Negro of the plantations came into the picture with a completely broken cultural heritage. He came directly from Africa or indirectly from Africa through the West Indies. There had been for him no preparation for, and no

organized exposure to, the dominant and approved patterns of American culture. What he knew of life was what he could learn from other slaves or from the examples set by the white planters themselves. (C. Johnson 1934, 3)

Johnson's interests are to revise popular representations of plantation life that fail to render the harsh material realities of both the old and present-day system.[9] However, his analysis of African American culture is biased by this assessment when he applies this broad lens to a discussion of nonmaterial cultural practices, finding them to be unoriginal:

> Their dialect is in part a survival of the English colonists, their superstitions most often are borrowed from whites, their religious beliefs are in large part the same as [those] held by isolated whites, their folk lore is scarcely distinguishable from that brought over from Europe by the early colonists, their religious emotionalism is similar to that commonly demonstrated in white Methodist camp meetings until very recently. (4)

For Johnson, African American folk culture is largely derivative of European or white culture rather than a cultural exchange across groups. In contrast to Melville Herskovits's views on African survivals, cultural practices, beliefs, and knowledge among the group Johnson studied, which he regards as representing all Black folk groups of the South, are survivals of the former plantation system. Of course, Johnson's survivals do little to support communal solidarity and expressions noted in Park's introduction as missing from this group.[10]

Remarkably, despite Johnson's summary dismissal of African survivals, *Shadow of the Plantation* includes a brief reference to the presence of newly arrived Africans within the Macon County community that indicates a more dynamic exchange of cultural practices than Johnson had anticipated. Johnson describes the Africans as distinctive from the rest of the community and notes that an older community member referenced them as forming their own tightly knit community (C. Johnson 1934, 22, 23). Despite language barriers within the group, this community organized to protest and resist work. Quoting eighty-five-year-old Cass Stewart, Johnson reports:

> "I was wid de Africans. Dey couldn't understand what dey was saying dey-selves. I seed dem salt-water niggers down on my home near Selma. I knowed a man down dere working 25 acres, couldn't work wid half of 'em 'cause when you made one of 'em mad you made all of 'em mad." (23)

Johnson admits, "This situation provides an unexpected link with Africa which might indeed yield traces of other transplanted cultural traits" (23). He also footnotes the use of African West Coast pidgin English by another resident (23).

The presence of newly immigrated enslaved Africans among first- or second-generation enslaved African Americans suggests possibilities for the ongoing transmission of cultural knowledge, beliefs, and practices from Africa to the Americas. This passage also counters both Park's and Johnson's arguments (and supports Herskovits's argument in *The Myth of the Negro Past*) that a sense of African community was lost in the wake of slavery, through its illustration of communal organization and resistance even among enslaved Africans who did not share a common language (Herskovits [1941] 1990, 1). Despite his illustration, Johnson does not pursue the issue of an African presence or African cultural retentions among the Black community members. Doing so would have challenged or significantly complicated his argument that African American culture was essentially copied from white culture.

Johnson's use of Black vernacular and dialect is ornamental, serving not as a link to an African past or as an example of cultural change but as evidence of an otherwise intangible African American community and culture. Nevertheless, it would be a significant element in terms of *Shadow of the Plantation*'s reception because of the demand for literary and cultural realist works. Johnson's narrative ethnographic content struck a chord with critical audiences, who described it as the one bright note in an otherwise bleak study. Sterling A. Brown, in the *Journal of Negro History*, writes, "The portrait he gives is almost unrelieved in its grimness" (1936, 70),[11] and later, underscoring the knowledgeable insights of the respondents, "These bits of folk-speech, bearing witness to an ironic awareness, are some of the few gleams that dart across the shadow" (73). Likewise, Holland Thompson describes *Shadow of the Plantation* (in the *Journal of Southern History*) as a sociological study and notes that Johnson's "frequent verbatim quotations" "produced an interesting and illuminating book out of what might have otherwise been a dull and prosy account of a depressing subject" (1935, 106).[12] Howard H. Long, the assistant superintendent in the Department of Research for the public schools in Washington, D.C., reviews Johnson's work in the *Journal of Negro Education* and describes Johnson's Macon County as "an eddy of fatalism" (1935, 124). Similarly to Sterling Brown, Long notes the importance of Johnson's inclusion of dialogue for revealing another perspective on the folk culture: "The sheer sordidness of it all is brightened here and there by quotations from illiterate minds which send out a gleam of hope and of satisfaction that human nature can withstand so much adversity and still survive" (125). B. B. Kendrick, writing for the *Annals of the American Academy of Political and Social Science*, regards the study as generally representative of Black life in the South: "This Alabama community is more or less typical of the entire [B]lack [B]elt" (Kendrick 1935, 290). Finally, Ruth Landes's "Review"

(1935) in the *Journal of American Folklore,* provides a description of Johnson's key findings and offers no commentary on its use of dialect. Altogether, reviews of *Shadow of the Plantation* reveal support for Johnson's conceptual approach and for his use of folk-speech.

In contrast to Johnson, Zora Neale Hurston shared Melville Herskovits's views about African survivals in America. Her folklore research reliably cataloged data concerning African American folktales and religious practices so that it might be a source for cross-cultural considerations of African cultural diffusion. Her use of folk-speech received mixed reviews during its initial publication (West 2005, 81–90). During its subsequent recuperation in the 1990s, *Mules and Men* is celebrated as creative and especially experimental, but its conceptual contributions to anthropology are largely ignored. However, Hurston employed "authentic" or reliable representations of Black Southern speech in her depictions of African American culture, and through a "problem focused methodology," she moved beyond representations of culture as a seamless whole to create dynamic representations of group conflict and consensus (Lamphere 2004, 129).[13] Illustrating African American culture in this way was an important conceptual contribution to the field of anthropology, given the way more static portrayals of Black culture and character stereotyped each of these elements.

Like other scholars who studied with or were influenced by Boas, Hurston was less concerned with defining grand theories regarding race and culture and more concerned with describing specific cultural practices. Boas advised his students to delay the theory-making aspect of research. He felt that defining and defending universal theories did more to entrench scientific inaccuracies and inequality than they did to accurately inform scientific knowledge (as with the case of evolutionary claims of the biological inferiority of "Negroid" peoples). Cultural relativism and historical particularism informed Hurston's work and, of course, served as a practical impetus and method for her analysis of Southern African American culture. However, Hurston also made conceptual statements about Black culture that challenged pervasive views (like those held by Johnson and E. Franklin Frazier) in terms of African American acculturation and assimilation within American society (L. Hill 1996, 8).[14] Her essay "Characteristics of Negro Expression" ([1934] 1995), published one year before *Mules and Men,* informed by the data she gathered on Black folk culture, reveals Hurston's views on the originality of Black culture even as its members "mimic" and "imitate" the larger American culture (L. Hill 1996, 8).[15] Rather than viewing Black cultural practices as failed assimilations of white American culture, Hurston advances that Black culture is aesthetically original in its manipulation and revision of cultural influences including popular American culture (Hurston [1934] 1995, 837–39): "He [the Negro] has *modified* the language, mode of food preparation, practice of medicine, and most certainly the religion of his new country, just as he adapted to suit himself the Sheik hair-cut made famous by Rudolph Valentino" (838; emphasis mine). While Hurston, influenced by Herskovits, viewed African American folklore as retaining African survivals, she advanced African American culture on its own terms as dynamic, diverse, and inventive in relation to itself and to broader cultural influences.

In addition, Franz Boas not only authorizes *Mules and Men* with a prefatory endorsement, but he also provides clues as to how readers should access the cultural data embedded within the larger narratives. Boas praises the ethnography for providing "the intimate setting in the social life of the Negro [that] has been given very inadequately" in prior representations of African American folklore (Boas [1935] 1978, x). Prior representations, whether produced by armchair anthropologists or represented in plantation literature, were ubiquitous and greatly shaped American ideas and attitudes concerning African American identity in all forms of popular and scientific media. Theories about African American inhumanity predominated scientific discourses on race, with cultural and literary productions reinforcing these discourses of African American inferiority (L. Baker 1998, 14–17). Regardless of the various advancements that African Americans made, these attitudes about Black inhumanity and inferiority persisted. In social sciences such attitudes were reinforced through scholarship questioning whether African Americans possessed distinctive cultural practices.

In the case of African American folklore, representations of folktales were bounded in literature by stereotypical settings, often with Southern plantations as the institutional backdrops that strongly linked their subject matter and practices to representations of subservient performance. For example, Joel Chandler Harris's *Uncle Remus: His Songs and His Sayings* (1880), which Boas notes as having a "strong attraction upon the imagination of the American public," were widely assumed to represent not only "authentic" folktales but also an essentialized African American character through the representation of Uncle Remus (Boas [1935] 1978, x). Published folktales were bounded by caricatured language that greatly exaggerated folk-speech and further emphasized folktales and folk tellers as primitive or lacking complexity. As Genevieve West describes, Boas's reference led early critics to compare Hurston's ethnography with Harris's tales even though Boas does not "explicitly compare the two" (West 2005, 79).

Beyond his cursory references to *Uncle Remus* and Hurston's ability to establish rapport with her respondents, Boas endorses *Mules and Men* for its ethnographic form and content: "To the student of cultural history the material presented is valuable not only by giving the Negro's reaction to every day events, to his emotional life, his humor and passions, but it throws into relief also the peculiar amalgamation of African and European tradition which is so important for understanding historically the character of American Negro life, with its strong African background in the West Indies, the importance of which diminishes with increasing distance from the south" (Boas [1935] 1978, x). In addition to highlighting Hurston's contributions to studies of acculturation, he highlights that the folklore is revealed more distinctly, as in the sculptural method that provides greater focus and dimension, through Hurston's attention to social context.

Contemporary scholars have read *Mules and Men* in "relief" (against setting) as they consider historical and socioeconomic contexts of the sawmill camps and lumberyards where the folktales are told, illuminating the tales' contextual meanings (Meisenhelder 1996, 277; Nicholls 1999, 467; Patterson 2005, 128–58). This approach expands rather than contracts our understanding of the meaning of the numerous folktales presented within *Mules and Men*. For example, I argue that the many tales told about "John" and "Massa" (presented in chapter 3 of *Mules and Men*) and other tales told about the natural environment, when isolated from their contexts as in a close reading, only elicit separate meanings for each individual folktale. Apart from their social contexts, each tale's meaning resonates on only one narrative level and is fixed in its meaning and significance. Thus, read individually, the tales illuminate very little concerning the "social life of the Negro" that Boas praised as distinctive in Hurston's work (Boas [1935] 1978, x). However, when read within their shared social contexts, the folktales' meanings are multidimensional. Such readings illustrate their function as ritualized narratives that represent and mediate conflict, resistance, community, and individual variation and that give clues as to the unique cultural histories of the individuals and communities portrayed.

Mules and Men is set in the socioeconomic context of lumber and turpentine camps, which distinguishes Hurston's study from Johnson's within a declining plantation economy. In the wake of the Civil War, with the end of slavery and facing a waning cotton industry, planters began to mine Florida forests for lumber and turpentine (Patterson 2005, 55). By the time Hurston arrived to the Loughman Camp, the lumber and turpentine industries were failing due to deforestation (131). Historian Tiffany Ruby Patterson describes how the Black workers in the sawmill camps worked in slavery-like conditions. Racial violence and other forms of labor control were customary "horrors" of life in turpentine and lumber camps and included "debt peonage, convict leasing, lynching, and whitecapping (a term that referred to white vigilante gangs who invaded black communities in masks)" (56).[16]

Within this socioeconomic context, the folktales told in part 1 of *Mules and Men* challenge or subvert white power and economic oppression (Meisenhelder 1996, 277; Nicholls 1999, 467). One of Hurston's accounts narrates a description of the workers walking to a lumberyard only to be turned away from work. The numerous "John" and "Massa" tales the workers tell during their walk are veiled critiques of the "straw boss" who controls labor in the camp (Meisenhelder 1996, 271; Nicholls 1999, 472).[17] As John outwits Massa, the tales function as a psychic relief for the group of men from their oppressive work conditions (Nicholls 1999, 273). In addition to the competition between "John" and "Massa" in many of the tales, the individual men and women offer other competing stories on various folk subjects. Many of these tales and contexts have been summarily discussed in contemporary criticism, and more attention can be given to the socioeconomic and ecological contexts of the tales. Susan Meisenhelder, for example, refers to these tales as illustrating verbal contests between the individuals (1996, 275). However, folktales about hot weather, big insects, and rich and poor land are not merely subjects for "verbal contests" but also reveal the impact of ecological histories on folktale subject matter. For example, several tales are told about mosquitoes (Hurston [1935] 1978, 108–109):

> "Yeah," put in Joe Wiley, "we seen a man tie his cow and calf out to pasture and a mosquito come along and et up de cow and was ringin' de bell for de calf."
>
> "Dat wasn't no full grown mosquito at dat," said Eugene Oliver, "Ah was travellin' in Texas and laid down and went to sleep. De skeeters bit me so hard till Ah seen a ole iron wash-pot, so Ah crawled under it and turned it down over me good so de skeeters couldn't git to me. But you know dem skeeters bored right thru dat iron pot. So I up wid a hatchet and bradded their bills into de pot. So they flew on off 'cross Galveston bay wid de wash pot on their bills." (108)

On the surface the dialogues appear simply to be competitions in exaggeration and humor. Yet their purpose for the tellers goes beyond idle amusement.[18] The prevalence and variety of folktales about mosquitoes (and other insects) and the metaphorical richness that the tellers employ indicate the extreme conditions in which the men and women labored and traveled. In the subtropical climate where they worked, a mosquito is more than a nuisance. Malaria was a significant public health issue in the United States during the early twentieth century, so much so that the Communicable Disease Center (which would later become the Centers for Disease Control) was founded largely to control insect-borne diseases that posed a significant risk to military personnel in the U.S. South and the Caribbean (Parascandola 1996, 549). Among U.S. states, Florida had one of the highest mortality rates due to malaria deaths (Blanchard 1934/1935, 76). For the workers in Hurston's ethnography, who worked outdoors and often near wetlands, the persistent nuisance of mosquitoes was a lethal threat. The hyperbole and rich metaphors found in these tales symbolically underscore the mosquito's prevalence and pestilence. They also illustrate the adaptive strategies of the folk tellers to transform a dangerous nuisance into humorous emotional relief through creative expression.

Regarding tales about the fertility of land, Nicholls argues, "Since the workers live in company-owned shacks in a corporate compound, their brags about fertile farmland are out of place. . . . Their values project an alternative modernity . . . of fictive property" (1999, 475). Then again, in talking about the rich or poor property of "my ole man" (Hurston [1935] 1978, 110), readers learn that within a generation or two, these migrant laborers have shifted economies from landownership (or sharecropping) to industrialized labor. Given that during this period the lumber industry was in decline, their folktales reflect a material nostalgia for an agricultural economy they once participated in, which offered a less migratory, if not less difficult, lifestyle. For example, the tellers trade tales of their fathers' rich farmlands. Joe Wiley describes how his father would not use "commercial-nal" (a term used to describe commercial fertilizer) to make his land more fertile (110). In response, Larkins White raises the competition by switching to a discussion of the poorest land and describes how a piece of land too poor for farming was donated to build a church. However, after the church was built, the land was so poor that it required "ten sacks of commercial-nal before dey could raise a tune on dat land" (111). Here, the folk exchange underscores not only the incredible wit of the teller but also the difficult labor of farming and, perhaps, the avoidance of ineffective commercial fertilizer by skilled farmers who took great pride in working their land.

The women and men go fishing after being denied work for the day. Meisenhelder refers to this scene as a space where more playful folktales are told (1996, 275), while Nicholls asserts that it is recreational time still "regulated by the company" since "they persist in telling stories" about the bosses as they fish (1999, 475). Significantly, fishing is also an informal economy that provides an alternative source of food and wealth (by selling fish to other camp members) and, as such, is a form of economic resistance in favor of a more communal economy. Fishing provides an alternative and ample sustenance, unregulated by the camp bosses, that the men and women rely on when they decide (however covertly) they don't want to work at the mills. However, some of the folks are more successful at catching fish than others. As stated by Hurston's respondent Presley, "All them that caught fish got fish. All them that didn't got another chance" (Hurston [1935] 1978, 143). The community in *Mules and Men* share in a fish fry from the string of fish that Cliffert, one of the younger men, catches (143). Hurston also includes the rules of eating fish as described by Mr. Allen, one of the older men of the "swamp gang," who paternally offers advice to the younger men in the group (143–45). The detailed description of hand washing, prayer, putting only one piece of fish on one's plate at a time, and carefully removing the fish meat from the bone from tail to head (for both aesthetic effect and to keep from having a mouth full of bones) all testify to the passing down of cultural values or lore with regard to proper etiquette and communal respect from one generation to the next. However, the younger generation may reject these rules, as illustrated by both Hurston and Cliffert, since she relays that they ate the fish "rough-and-tumble with no holds barred" (147).

The arrangement of the folktales may lead skeptics to question Hurston's ability to recall each folktale, or to suggest that she fabricated the orderliness of the tales or even the tales themselves. However, folktellers possess skills of memory, revision, and improvisation as the individual members share their competing versions of more common tales. Hurston is careful to delineate their order and to underscore the authority of the tales. Joe Willard, for example, cries out, "Let *me* talk some chat. Dis is de real truth 'bout Ole Massa 'cause my grandma told it to my mama and she told it to me" (Hurston [1935] 1978, 78). Both men and women vie for the opportunity to share stories, and Hurston was careful to capture differences across generations in the swamp gang. Since a predominant attitude was that African American people had no community (Park 1934, xvii), Hurston's illustration of a respect for knowledge passed down from older to younger generations was intended to challenge this attitude.

The tales and exchanges, therefore, illustrate not only competing discourses between men and women, across generations, and (in terms of content) between the tellers and their bosses, but also discourses of community. These discourses of community reflect some homogeneity, in that they are told among the group and shared as collective knowledge and experience. They are also heterogeneous in that they connect individuals through competition as individual community members vie for collective agreement over the best or most believable folktale. The rules of the folklore exchanges and standards for bad, best, and better tale seem to depend on the extent to which someone can effectively combine hyperbole, metaphor, and believability within a tale.

All three are confirmed, in context, when the last tale in a series resonates with others in the group: "Everybody liked to hear about the mosquito. They laughed all over themselves" (Hurston [1935] 1978, 109). Group consensus (through shared laughter) confirms a good folktale and may end that folktale theme as the next teller transitions to another theme. In this example, the teller who picks up after the group laughter transitions topics from mosquitoes to fertile and infertile farmland. In addition, off-theme interruptions and errors are met with objection and correction, since collaborative revision is a part of the collective, social, and ritual experience of telling folktales. Significantly, Hurston was also clear to assert the distinctive quality of the folk stories apart from any European influence in ways that move beyond the views of Frazier and Herskovits. Briefly commenting on the telling of some "European tales undiluted," she asserts, "Others had slight local variations, but Negro imagination is so facile that there was little need for outside help" (Hurston [1935] 1978, 21). Here, of course, Hurston employs the term "facile" to mean skillful and to assert the originality of many of the folktales she collected.

Hurston's conceptual argument and approach provides an opportunity to consider how her ethnography worked to revise representations of Black people. If she had chosen a more traditional form for the folklore included in the first part of *Mules and Men*, it likely would have been published as a compendium of folktales and folk rituals. However, that presentation would not have fully represented the social contexts and multiple meanings required to analyze her data.[19] Folklore compendiums of the time presented folktales as static, bounded by pages of taxonomic lists. For example, Stith Thompson published several volumes of *Motif-Index of Folk-Literature* throughout the 1930s, which cataloged folktales, ballads, and other folklore in a motif classification system that provided easy access for scholars but set folklore apart from its varied social contexts. The motif lists made information about folklore accessible but presented tales as disassociated items, separated from the individuals telling the tales and from the contexts or settings of their storytelling. Such representations of folktales and folk tellers froze each of them as potentially unchanging and uncomplicated. In effect, the representations of folktales in many literary representations and taxonomies of folklore "trafficked in generalizations" (Abu-Lughod 1993, 7) that may have supported the presumption of African American inferiority through static difference. Generalizations are intrinsic to the project of defining cultures as discrete units and are problematic because they "smooth over contradictions, conflicts of interest, doubts, arguments, not to mention changing motivations and historical circumstances" (9). Static representations of culture present an illusion of group consensus and group cohesion, making it easier to create and objectify the "other" (12). *Mules and Men* worked against cultural generalizations by showing individual behavior within a cultural context, through illustrating individual "competitive artistry . . . rather than the existence of a unified cultural scheme" (Elliott 2002, 176).

Less critical attention has been given to the second part of *Mules and Men*, which consists of Hurston's study of hoodoo practices in New Orleans. Scholars often note this section as having been added to the work at the request of the publisher to make it longer, since much of its data had already been published in "Hoodoo in America" in the *Journal of American Folklore* (Dorst 1987, 305n1; Meisenhelder 1996, 285; Walters 1999, 353). An exception is a 1980 review of the reissue of *Mules and Men* (along with *Their Eyes Were Watching God*) by John Roberts in the *Journal of American Folklore* that draws our attention to Hurston's methodology. He describes Hurston's approach as "most effective in this section in keeping the reader from reaching easy conclusions concerning the practice and efficacy of hoodoo. The initiation rituals which Hurston underwent to become a hoodooer are described with much detail and allow for easy comparison for similar rites in other cultures" (Roberts 1980, 464). In addition, Hurston would likely have been familiar with Newbell Niles Puckett's *Folk Beliefs of the Southern Negro*, which characterized hoodoo practices in stereotypical terms, including reference to Black folks' speech as "Mutilated English" (Puckett 1926, 13, 154). Whereas Puckett pretended to be a hoodoo doctor in order to obtain his data (Hemenway [1977] 1980, 87), Hurston's study of Southern hoodoo would be the first to provide descriptions of rituals and material culture based on her full immersion as a participant-observer (Hazzard-Donald 2013, 10). Hurston's representations of hoodoo align with her overall approach in *Mules and Men*: she avoids overgeneralizations and instead focuses on particulars in order to humanize the communities and individuals she portrays, contradict stereotypes, and provide a reference for future research.

Not unlike Karen McCarthy Brown in *Mama Lola: A Voudou Priestess in Brooklyn* ([1991] 2010), which received positive critical reviews for its experimental ethnographic approach, Hurston was initiated and practiced rituals under individual hoodoo doctors in order to gain access to data concerning hoodoo practices. The first-person narration, therefore, relates Hurston's description of what she experiences under the tutelage of each hoodoo doctor. Generally speaking, the narrative of each chapter focuses on Hurston's experience with one hoodoo doctor. Hurston introduces each doctor, providing historical or biographical background data on their significance and specialty, she recounts the work that she performed for each doctor in exchange for the training she received, and she describes specific rituals that each doctor practiced and that she herself experienced. The rituals are often framed by the individual contexts in which they were performed. Hurston describes in detail the conversations between hoodoo doctor and patient, which follow a typical pattern: An individual has a specific health problem, relationship problem, or social dispute, which Hurston reports in detail. The doctor then prescribes an appropriate ritual, the details of which Hurston also describes. Finally, the outcome, usually positive, is described. Taken together, these descriptions illustrate the effectiveness of the ritual practice, the skill of the hoodoo doctor, and the social legitimacy of hoodoo religion.

Remarkably, Hurston illustrates typical "medical" protocol of hoodoo as indicated by its practitioners and patients, generally adhering to a Western medical explanatory model in her narrations.[20] Each discussion of specific ritual "healing" is not unlike a medical case study presentation that involves collecting patient histories in terms of symptoms, causes, treatment, and prognosis, and Hurston systematically illustrates how hoodoo doctors function as holistic (mind, body, spirit) health-care providers who service individuals with a variety of culturally specific ailments. Hurston would have been very familiar with this model from her own personal experiences: She briefly worked as a doctor's assistant, was married to medical student Harold Sheen, had a brother who was a physician and another who was a pharmacist, and experienced a series of illnesses that may have informed her familiarity with a case study method for presenting medical knowledge (Haas 2000, 210).[21]

John Dorst and Graciela Hernández emphasize the conflicts and risks that Hurston likely negotiated as a participant in healing rituals, such as fasting naked for days at a time (Dorst 1987, Hernández 1995). However, their critiques focus more on Hurston's experiences as an ethnographer and less on the data she collected. Despite these highly sensationalized experiences, Hurston's voice is often dispassionate and detailed in her descriptions of each ritual. For example, she methodically describes Dr. Duke's ritual for "uncrossing" or removing evil influences/spirits from an individual:

> Take seven lumps of incense. Take three matches to light the Incense. Wave the incense before the candles on the altar. Make client bow over the incense three times. Then circle him with a glass of water three times, and repeat this three times. Fan him with the incense smoke three times—each time he bows his head. ([1935] 1978, 232)

The narrative continues with the same specificity for the entirety of the ritual. By providing such details of various ritual elements taught to her, Hurston sought to represent hoodoo as a complex and sophisticated belief system. Stereotypical representations of hoodoo as backward and primitive were the norm. In contrast, her descriptions, although sensationally marketed by her publisher (West 2005, 78), were themselves free from hyperbole.

Hurston buttressed these descriptions with documentation of the experiences of individuals who might provide additional proof of, or authority for, her experiences. For example, she notes the experiences of sociologist Charles S. Johnson, who, as previously mentioned, visited her while she was in New Orleans:

> Dr. Charles S. Johnson, the well-known Negro sociologist[,] came to New Orleans on business while I was there and since I had to see Dr. Jenkins, he went with me. Without being asked, Dr. Jenkins told him that he would receive a sudden notice to go on a long trip. The next day, Dr. Johnson received a wire sending him to West Africa. ([1935] 1978, 234)

Two "Drs." meet, in reality and within a single paragraph of Hurston's work, for readers, especially social scientists, to consider. One is a doctor of sociology authorized by academic study and the recent publication of *Shadow of the Plantation* the year before. The other doctor is a "two headed doctor" authorized by second sight and his ability to intervene on behalf of clients in legal conflicts (230). Hurston describes their interaction to convince readers of the legitimacy of Dr. Jenkins's second sight. Some readers might query Dr. Johnson to confirm if the event happened as reported, while others, noting Dr. Johnson's reputation, might take Hurston's description at face value. In either case, she employs Dr. Johnson's authority as a respected social scientist to support Dr. Jenkins's authority and the larger authority of her own research. In addition, Hurston's concern for the representation of hoodoo as a valid belief system practiced by a diverse group of communities is likewise reinforced when she also reveals that most of Dr. Jenkins's clients are white and upper-class people (234). Given the common perception that hoodoo was practiced by lower-class and uneducated Black people, which reinforced its stereotyping as backward and primitive, Hurston's statement asserts its legitimacy through its patronage by white wealthy people, as well as by an educated Black professional. This assertion also underscores the sharing of cultural practices between Black and white communities.

Three appendices build on Hurston's exploration of hoodoo—"Formulae of Hoodoo Doctors," "Paraphernalia of Conjure," and "Prescriptions of Root Doctors" (Hurston [1935] 1978)—and together suggest her significant research about the practice of folk medicine.[22] Within her discussions in the glossary and appendices, Hurston defines the meanings of common terms and related folk beliefs and practices. Regarding paraphernalia of conjure, Hurston writes, "It would be impossible for anyone to find out all the things that are being used in conjure in America. Anything may be conjure and nothing may be conjure, according to the doctor, the time and the use of the article. What is set down here are the things most commonly used" (284). She describes the paraphernalia with methodical detail and is careful not to draw grand conclusions, thereby assuring the appendix's usefulness as a resource for future comparative analyses. In the following passage, Hurston describes the utility of folk medicine for whites and Blacks and makes a useful distinction between hoodoo doctors and root doctors:

> Folk medicine is practiced by a great number of persons. On the "jobs," that is, in the sawmill camps, the turpentine stills, mining camps and among the lowly generally, doctors are not generally called to prescribe for illness, certainly, nor for the social diseases. Nearly all of the conjure doctors practice "roots," but some of the root doctors are not hoodoo doctors. One of these latter at Bogaloosa, Louisiana, and one at Bartow, Florida, enjoy a huge patronage. They make medicine only, and white and colored swarm about them claiming cures. (288)

Hurston also provides a list of folk treatments gathered in Florida, Alabama, and Louisiana for a range of "folk-illnesses," including gonorrhea, syphilis, flooding (excessive menstruation), and poisoning. In the section on poisoning, Hurston notes that many do not believe in the effectiveness of a medical doctor's treatment for poisonings related to "fixes." A person is "fixed" by another through the use of charms or coming into contact with foreign substances. The fixer intends to either exert some control over the victim's behavior or to physically harm them:

> Often the patient is organically sound. He is afraid that he has been "fixed," and there is nothing that a medical doctor can do to remove that fear. Besides, some poisons of low order, like decomposed reptiles and the like, are not listed in the American pharmacopoeia. The doctor would never suspect their presence and would not be able to treat the patient if he did. (291)

Here Hurston theorized a "nocebo" effect whereby "beliefs and expectations sicken and kill" (Hahn and Kleinman 1983, 17). In addition, she illustrates a sophisticated understanding of chemical properties of folk substances along with their probable physiological and possible psychological effects. In general, she describes what contemporary medical anthropologists Robert A. Hahn and

Arthur Kleinman define as "'culturogenic' or 'ethnomedicogenic' disease and healing" (3). They theorize "Belief kills; belief heals" and assert:

> It is our thesis that a society's ethnomedicine *constructs* medical reality in that it informs both patient and practitioner about how symptoms and conditions are distinguished, what course they run in syndromes and why, how these conditions may be ameliorated, and how symptoms and their dynamics fit in a larger order of agency, power, and value (16).

Hurston describes folk health practices with a similar framework and includes discussions about cultural motivations and constraints to individuals seeking medical care. Her insight into folk beliefs and practices went beyond sensational representations of hoodoo through her case study approach to individual occurrences of folk illness and holistic healing.

Notwithstanding the exhaustive fieldwork and documentation presented in *Mules and Men*, as mentioned previously, reviews of the work were shaped by comparisons to Joel Chandler Harris's *Uncles Remus* (West 2005, 79–81). One such emblematic review and a significant (but often ignored) rebuttal offers an opportunity to underscore the professional authority of Hurston's ethnography. Joseph J. Williams's review in *Folklore* (1936) offers a cursory dismissal of the significance of Hurston's folktale findings.[23] Comparing *Mules and Men* to *Uncle Remus*, Williams writes, "The reader will be due for a surprise. There is little here of the old tribal folklore and even less of distinctly African tradition" (329). Williams rightly argues that many of Hurston's folktales have no association with "African origins," but he also indicates a bias toward a cultural evolutionary and racist perspective in his evaluation. He says, "The book really yields a valuable account of our Southern United States Negro of the present day. And as such it may be accepted as a phase of folklore, but only as a foundation of what is to come in a later development of the race and not as any indication of what went before" (330). Williams seems to promote Frazier's and Johnson's argument that African American culture presents no significant occurrences of African survivals. He also challenges the authority and character of the folk tellers themselves by directly referencing them as liars: "Miss Hurston's associates make no pretense as folklorists. They openly prefer to be regarded as professional liars" (330).

Melville Herskovits, who would later author *Myth of the Negro Past* (1941), offers a definitive response to Williams's review. In the June 1937 issue of *Folklore*, Herskovits provides approximately three pages of a detailed critical response to Williams's claims. First he challenges Williams's claim that "there is practically nothing to remind us of African origins" (J. Williams 1936, 329). He asserts that specific tales from Hurston's collection are also found in various locations in the coastal South, the Caribbean, and in Senegal, Africa (Herskovits [1941] 1990, 220). Given Herskovits's vindicationist interest in defining the significance of Africanisms, his defense of Hurston's work in these terms is connected to his larger research interest in documenting African survivals and defining a process of acculturation. Herskovits also defends the merit of Hurston's work beyond the influence of *Uncle Remus*, referring to the publication as a "historical accident," which suggests it is more cultural artifact than an unbiased work of social science.[24] He also directly challenges Williams's conflation of the cultural reference "lies" with pretense or deceit, given his reference to the folk tellers as "professional liars" (J. Williams 1936, 330). Herskovits responds:

> Just because the tales told by Miss Hurston's informants are called by them "big old lies," this emphatically does not mean, as Father Williams maintains, that these tellers of stories "prefer to be regarded as professional liars," or that "a gathering of story-tellers becomes a veritable Ananias club." To term these creative artists who draw on their imagination "liars" is an egregious reading of European meaning into the use of a term sanctioned by long traditional usage in Africa itself, as well as in the New World. Need one recall to Father Williams the opening disclaimer of Rattray's Ashanti informants that reads, "We do not really mean, we do not really mean (that which we are going to say is true)"?[25] Or is it not significant that in Dutch Guiana a riddle is called a *lei-tori*, a "lie-story"? In neither case, however, is there any implication that the teller of a tale is "lying" in the European sense of the term. (Herskovits [1941] 1990, 221)[26]

Williams's review, and Herskovits's response, provides a model example of the complex and problematic contemporaneous reception of Hurston's *Mules and Men*. In particular, Herskovits's defense should inform contemporary receptions of Hurston's ethnographies, alluded to previously, that use the perverse version of "lies" in order to either implicitly or explicitly question Hurston's ethnographic authority. Nonetheless, in this case, Hurston's work was explicitly received as an example of stereotypical African American culture. Williams challenged the originality, validity, and reliability of Black culture and of Hurston's research. He did not recognize African survivals within *Mules and Men*, he equated cultural meanings within the ethnography to long-held attitudes concerning African American character, and he questioned the reliability of native respondent cultural practices. His rationale, dependent on a common stereotype of Black people as naturally deceitful, substantiates Herskovits's defense and concern that "the myth of the Negro past is one of the principal supports of race prejudice in this country" (Herskovits [1941] 1990, 1).

Williams suggested that Hurston's contribution was not unlike more sensational and stereotypical literary representations of Black life in the U.S. South. In contrast, Boas and Herskovits, as scholars in the field of anthropology and folklore studies, presented *Mules and Men* as making distinct contributions to cultural knowledge. Boas lauded Hurston's ethnography for providing a sense of the social contexts in which folktales are told and for providing examples of acculturative processes in the merging of European and African cultural elements. Herskovits defended Hurston's contribution as important data that connected folklore practices of "New World" Black people to folklore practices throughout the African diaspora. His defense, and Boas's endorsement, underscores that Hurston's *Mules and Men* should be received as a distinctive contribution to the study of African American culture, one that ultimately extended her mentors' conceptualizations of cultural change.[27]

Beyond Johnson's *Shadow of the Plantation* and Hurston's *Mules and Men*, and considering respective claims to their innovative approaches to ethnography, Hortense Powdermaker's *After Freedom: A Cultural Study in the Deep South* can be viewed as an ethnographic outlier. She advanced her ethnography as experimental, and she emphasized her use of respondents' life stories and interviews as an important source of data for her study of Black life in the rural South. However, she neither represented the regional dialect of her respondents nor did she extensively include (verbatim) their narratives, which affected the terms of the work's reception.[28] In addition, Powdermaker's views on acculturation were met with some skepticism in ways that highlight Hurston's conceptual contributions and ethnographic authority.

Set in "Cottonville," the fictionalized name she gives to Indianola, Mississippi, Powdermaker's study illustrates racial attitudes and sociocultural practices of Black and white, male and female members of the largely agricultural community. She observes that while there are class distinctions within each racial group, these differences do not correspond with each other in terms of shared practices, attitudes, and beliefs. Whites are divided into the aristocratic class, the middle class, and poor whites ([1939] 1993, 14). African Americans are divided into upper class, middle class, and lower class (60). She considers the social attitudes of each racial group toward the other, and she also considers variations in racial attitudes across class divisions within each racial group.

Figuring largely in Powdermaker's account of these differences is the process of acculturation, particularly of the town's Black community members. For Powdermaker, acculturation is a one-directional process whereby African American culture over time becomes more like white culture. Her ethnography describes a diverse white community, but she suggests a white normative culture to which African Americans emulate, aspire to, or stand in marked contrast to.[29] Regarding the various classes within the Black population, she writes, "It is the upper middle class that has the greatest degree taken over both form and meaning" of "white American patterns" (61). The middle class and lower class follow in decreasing order such that "the lower class follows the fewest, and most of those in form merely" (61). In effect, she conflates class status with cultural affinity. Her study imposes an evolutionary bias in defining acculturation and the various class distinctions (in attitudes and behaviors) that she argues this process produces in African Americans of Cottonville.

Despite weaknesses in her views concerning acculturation, Powdermaker's attention to class differentiation works to provide a complex sense of culture process (Williams and Woodson [1939] 1993, xxvi) in large part due to the greater class diversity of the community she studied. By contrast, Johnson's *Shadow of the Plantation* is largely silent on class and focuses exclusively on "the folk," which are represented as a homogenous community. *Mules and Men*, however, illustrates class dynamics within the Black community in a number of exchanges. For example, Hurston negotiates her entry in the field by telling some of her respondents that her car and expensive dress are benefits from a bootlegging life, revealing her understanding of class politics as a barrier to gathering data from respondents. As mentioned previously, she notes class distinctions among patrons of hoodoo doctors as a way of dispelling stereotypes that only the uneducated and the poor believe in and practice hoodoo. In addition, the folktales that feature contests between Ole Massa and John are metaphors for a class struggle between whites who run the lumberyards and the Black men who provide its cheap and dangerous labor (Hurston [1935] 1978, 73–82; Nicholls 1999, 472–75; Meisenhelder 1996, 271–73). Again, critical audiences are instructed by Boas to read beyond stereotyped representations of African American folklore and to read in "relief," or in historical context, the implicit meanings of the tales (Boas [1935] 1978, x).

A cursory review of Hortense Powdermaker's *After Freedom* by contemporary readers might suggest that it is a standard anthropological ethnography, as it observes many of its conventions in both its method and mode of presentation. Powdermaker completed twelve months of fieldwork from 1932 to 1934, during which she observed and interviewed community members and participated in daily activities of the Cottonville community. In contrast to Hurston's *Mules and Men*, which provides an extended narrative of her fieldwork experience and organizes its chapters with titles that direct researchers to specific folktales and rituals, Powdermaker's ethnography is organized into broad sociocultural categories and chapter titles that describe individual social institutions apart from their sociocultural contexts: "The Social Scene," "Economic Considerations,"

"Cohesion and Conflicts in the Negro Family," "Religion and Superstition," "Education," and "The Negro's Response to the Situation."[30] In keeping with a functionalist approach, these divisions are made to illustrate culture as a whole operating and maintained through these various institutional parts. Like Johnson, Powdermaker references data from other studies, including statistical government data about Mississippi and Cottonville. She also gathers data for her study about racial attitudes of whites concerning Black people using a "Questionnaire on White Attitudes toward the Negro," noting, "The author is indebted to Dr. Charles S Johnson for permission to use this questionnaire, which he had employed in a study of public opinion" (Powdermaker [1939] 1993, 381). The inclusion of statistical data makes Powdermaker's study a kind of disciplinary complement to Johnson's *Shadow of the Plantation*. These various sources triangulate her data to support her research findings concerning the material and interpretive culture of Black life in Cottonville. They are also employed to more fully consider the interrelationship between Black and white racial attitudes: "Today, as in the past, the Negro lives in no isolated black community. To understand his life there must be an understanding of the Whites who form so large a part of it" (Powdermaker [1939] 1993, xliv). In contrast, Hurston's "Part 1" of *Mules and Men* is a local-level study, concerned primarily with documenting folklore practices, attitudes, and behaviors of Black respondents within a political economy of the sawmill and lumberyards. Countering Powdermaker's assertion, the camps were geographically isolated communities, predominantly Black, and drew workers from a variety of Black communities throughout the South. White people figure in *Mules and Men* (often symbolically as "Massa" in some of the folktales), but they are materially peripheral in her representation of the workings of African American folk life.

Despite Powdermaker's use of traditional ethnographic conventions and sociological methods, she describes her study as an experiment within the first sentence of the ethnography: "This study was conceived as an *experiment*: to apply to a segment of contemporary American society the training and methods of a cultural anthropologist and whatever perspective had been gained through fieldwork in civilizations other than our own" ([1939] 1993, xliii; emphasis mine). Because of similarities between *After Freedom* and other sociological considerations of African American life, Powdermaker is careful to describe how her work is distinctive in its application of methods typically used for the study of cultures outside of the United States: "The purpose was not to make a survey in terms of statistical units or of abstract institutions, but rather to study the living forces of a culture: their present functioning and their impact on the individuals who comprise the community" (xlvi–xlvii). In contradiction to her use of statistical data, and even the organization of her ethnography, Powdermaker argues that her ethnography represents "the living forces of culture" through a consideration of attitudes expressed in interviews through which "the bulk of the data was obtained" (xlviii).[31]

Despite her commitment to representing "the living forces of culture," she does not represent dialect or narrative dialogue. Powdermaker used formal questionnaires and also elicited life stories from respondents (xlviii), and this data is presented as third-person narrations of individual life stories. She includes some quoted statements, but on the whole her writing has a distant, journalistic effect. For example, she excerpts the following passage to illustrate the prohibitive effect of water taxes on the already impoverished income of Black residents: "A woman speaks of going back to sharecropping. She has had only bad luck with it and hardly hopes to break even, but says that 'at least you don't have to pay rent and water taxes'" (132). The effect is of reading Powdermaker's edited field notes of her ethnographic field experience set off from her larger descriptive analysis. Regarding the inclusion of narrative data, Powdermaker offers the following statement in a footnote:

> In offering case material, this study uses quotation marks only where the exact words were remembered. Often, while the precise wording was not recalled, colloquialisms used by the informant, and the general cast of expression, have been recaptured. Where possible these have been preserved, so that much of this material is to be regarded as a sort of indirect quotation. This has not been set off from the rest by type or punctuation, but will undoubtedly be apparent to the reader. The initials employed for convenience of reference in some of the longer illustrations are without exception fictitious. (xlviii)

Unlike Charles S. Johnson's *Shadow of the Plantation* and Zora Neale Hurston's *Mules and Men*, Powdermaker does not attempt to consistently render the "precise wording" of her informants. Instead, she uses the term "colloquial," perhaps to distinguish her studies from those that specifically attempt to render regional dialect. Powdermaker's focus on both Black and white respondents may have been one reason for her omission of phonetic representations of language in her ethnography. The attention to each as a separate cultural form would have required that she have expertise in American dialect variations, which she did not. Gertrude Fraser (1991) suggests that Powdermaker indicated in her professional memoir, *Stranger and Friend* (1966), that her choice of Mississippi as her next site to do fieldwork, following her research in Lesu, was determined in part by her assumptions that a study of African American culture would be more linguistically accessible. One of her other options was a study of Hassidic Jews, which she rejected because she knew neither Hebrew nor Yiddish (Fraser 1991, 405). Ironically, Powdermaker assumes that she knows the language or vernaculars of African American culture. That she does not textually render the words of her respondents results in a loss of cultural meaning. Although representations of regional and racial patterns of dialect had been the subject of literary fictions and critical discussions, Powdermaker underestimated the importance of language in the study of American culture. Her representations of Southern folk life erase these distinctions and instead provide "general casts of expression" ([1939] 1993, xlviii).[32] Even though Johnson and Powdermaker both acknowledged the importance of language as a source of African survivals, Johnson was more familiar with dialect as a representation of folk culture, and his use of dialect was generally praised in critical reviews (S. Brown 1936, 73; Thompson 1935, 106; Long 1935, 125).

The larger expectations of ethnographic form and content can be read through some of the critical reviews of Powdermaker's work, as some suggested that critical audiences expected an ethnography of African American culture to provide more descriptive and contextual detail (Bond 1939, 201; Du Bois 1939, 137; Duffus 1939, BR3; C. Johnson 1939, 196; Waller 1940, 505).[33] In some instances, because her ethnography lacked a dialogic form, Powdermaker's work was received as conventional and less accessible as compared to other social-scientific productions on African American life and culture. Some reviews revealed an expectation for a more self-reflexive ethnography with more details concerning the researcher's experiences in the field.[34] In addition, reviews by Herskovits (1939) and Carter G. Woodson (1939a) criticized Powdermaker for her failure to consider African survivals in her description of Black culture. Herskovits asks, "Does Negro history really go no farther back than 'before freedom'—to slavery times?" He proposes that corporal punishment of children, religious possession, and the central role of the mother in the African American family could all have a connection to West African practices. Herskovits notes that he chose these examples because "such matters are by no means only of academic interest," and he suggests that in order to dispel stereotypical views of African Americans, research should account for connections to an African past to explain cultural attitudes and behaviors. Otherwise, he argues, "the failure to probe carry overs of an earlier tradition . . . throw[s] explanations of present-day Negro behavior askew" (Herskovits 1939, 299). Woodson likewise questions the absence of a discussion of African survivals, and he also challenges the constructed authority of Powdermaker's third-person objective narrative:

The author believes that she has discovered these Negroes of the South. Their culture is derived historically from that of the dominant whites. Not much is said here about the survival of the African traits in America, although the Negro is presented here as temperamentally different from his white neighbor. (1939a, 220)

Despite different views on acculturation, it was generally acknowledged that representations of social contexts should be featured in any studies of African American culture. Prefatory statements by Robert E. Park in Johnson's *Shadow of the Plantation* and by Franz Boas in *Mules and Men*, as well as Herskovits's defense of *Mules and Men*, suggest that contextual representations of Black life were an important element in early African Americanists. Reviews of *After Freedom* corroborate that audiences expected an ethnographic work on African American culture to evaluate its findings through representations of social contexts and to, in some instances, provide more descriptive detail than Powdermaker's ethnography provided.

Beyond detailing specific textual interactions among Johnson, Hurston, and Powdermaker, my analysis underscores the significance of informal, formal, familial, and institutional networks that shaped Hurston's disciplinary practices, claims to authority, and critical receptions. As discussed in chapter 4, readings of Hurston's critical reception in the late twentieth and early twenty-first centuries consistently argue for the restrictive impact of Franz Boas, Charlotte Osgood Mason, and Alain Locke on the mode, method, and quality of her work. The repetitive consideration of this by now infamous trinity of the iconic Hurston paints them as a primary constraining influence on Hurston (Gordon 1990, 154–55; Hernández 1995, 151–53; West 2005, 43–48; Patterson 2005, 159–82).[35] The influences of her mentors and patrons have been referenced to explain Hurston's "experimental" productions. However, this chapter has shown that while Hurston's *Mules and Men* is innovative and distinctive, its experimental form is not surprising, given the historical contexts of its publication. Charles Johnson's *Shadow of the Plantation* and Hortense Powdermaker's *After Freedom* also offered experimental methods to the study of African American culture, life, and race relations of the U.S. South in the 1930s, and all three ethnographies offered contextual considerations of Black life toward redefining the complexity of African American culture. They all received critical reviews, both positive and negative, that indicated a demand for cultural literary works.

These reviews illustrate complex receptions to ethnographic experimentation in representing African American culture. Johnson's reviews were largely positive, perhaps setting the stage for Hurston's experimentation in *Mules and Men*. Hurston's ethnography moved beyond Johnson's *Shadow of the Plantation* in its sustained use of narrative dialogue. The reception of *Mules and Men* was mediated not only by the races of respective reviewers (West 2005, 81–90) but also by their varied responses to Lippincott's stereotypical marketing. While Lippincott's marketing of *Mules and Men* may have influenced reviewers, others looked beyond sensational jacket copy and newspaper ads and described the importance of Hurston's work, both in literary realistic terms and in terms that conveyed her contributions to knowledge on African American folklore (Chubb 1936, 181; McNeill 1936, 224). Significant also to understanding Hurston's professional authority is Herskovits's defense of Hurston's scholarship in the wake of critical reviews from popular critics and lay folklorists. Powdermaker's *After Freedom* offers a different perspective on "experimental" ethnography within the context of studies of African American culture and life. Her claim to provide a new and useful method for understanding Black life and culture was met with mixed reviews. Some reviews indicate that her work was considered authoritative, but it was also challenged on the grounds that it did not offer a distinctive and particularly revealing method.

The questions that frame this chapter, examining *Mules and Men*'s reception and professional authority in its historical contexts, ultimately begin with my consideration of Hurston's literary and ethnographic reception from the 1970s through the 1990s. That period marked a rise in the popular interest in Hurston's life and work along with the concurrent and significant critical consideration of her literary and ethnographic work in the fields of literature and anthropology. In considering Hurston's reception across these fields, there are a number of parallel cultural phenomena to consider. In both periods, attention to Hurston's experimental ethnographic form is framed by publishers' demands for accessible scholarly works. The 1935 publication of *Mules and Men* followed trends in literary realism and a growing interest in qualitative data in the social sciences; its reissue and reconsideration occurred over subsequent periods (including the 1990s) when discussions about experimental ethnography again took center stage. Parallel socioeconomic contexts shaped its reception in both eras, including publishers' responses to market trends. Hurston's prolific publishing career during the Great Depression may have been buoyed by the fact that publishers, challenged by a declining readership and tight market, preferred works that sold broadly as opposed to those that would appeal only to scholars of folklore and anthropology (Richard 2011, 9).[36] A similar preference for cultural productions that could bridge a sales divide between academic and general audiences was also a factor in the late 1980s and early 1990s, across several periods of economic recession, when the economic vitality of publishing houses (especially university presses) was in question.

It is perhaps not an accident that publishers would again favor experimental ethnographies, as midline or trade texts, for their marketability across lay and academic audiences. As well as being promoted for their appeal to general audiences, such works were marketed to the academy as highly accessible texts suitable for introductory courses, with the added bonus that they also function as symbols of multicultural inclusion (duCille 1994, 594).[37] Finally, experimental ethnography was legitimated as a groundbreaking and politicized method in ethnographic form and cultural representations, which contributed new knowledge in the field of anthropology. In understanding Hurston's iconic place in American cultural imaginations across time, these parallels in socioeconomic contexts and economic rationales are significant and deserve future consideration.[38] Ultimately, to understand her very real contribution to the field of American anthropology, we should consider both Hurston's ethnographic methods and conceptual arguments in their rightful historical contexts.

6

"Burning Spots"
Reading *Tell My Horse*

Not a strictly scientific work, but burning spots from the ensemble.
—Zora Neale Hurston, letter to Guggenheim Foundation

Hurston published *Tell My Horse: Voodoo and Life in Haiti and Jamaica* in 1938, four years after the end of the U.S. occupation of Haiti. *Tell My Horse* is an ethnography of cultural practices related to folk beliefs in Jamaican and Vodou cosmology in Haiti. The data on Jamaican folk beliefs and Haitian Vodou is framed and reframed by Hurston's commentary on the historical and political contexts of both island nation-states, but the larger ethnography represents Hurston's social-scientific commitment to the diasporic study of African-derived folk culture and belief systems. *Tell My Horse* extends Hurston's collection of religious and folk practices from the U.S. South, as represented in *Mules and Men*, to the Caribbean. As in *Mules and Men*, Hurston's conceptual approach to the study of cultural practices in Haiti and Jamaica illustrates how shifting social and historical contexts give rise to new cultural forms, particularly in her analysis of Haitian Vodou.

Some early assessments during the period of Hurston's canonical consideration focus on the form of Hurston's ethnography and imagine her as wholly unable to negotiate institutional and individual barriers to produce a "successful" or "authoritative" work (Gordon 1990; Dutton 1993). Despite her extensive training and experience as an anthropologist, and notwithstanding popular and critical receptions of her work, *Tell My Horse* (like *Mules and Men*) provokes questions for many critics regarding Hurston's social-scientific authority: Why did she not produce a "strictly scientific" work? Are her expressive narratives an indication that she was really (and only) a writer at heart? The ability to employ and evaluate satire and irony require great skill, and Hurston obviously took delight in using her wit to convey analytical and critical discourse in *Tell My Horse*. However, her use of these narrative elements (especially in her description of Jamaican and Haitian politics) is taken by some critics to indicate that her ethnographic approach lacked the requisite objectivity. And what should readers make of the political commentary that frames Hurston's discussions of folklore and Vodou? A number of critical assessments of *Tell My Horse* favor discussions that rigorously analyze Hurston's political positions, in part to revise imbalanced and sometimes unfavorable assessments of her commentary on Haitian and Jamaican politics. However, the critical attention given to Hurston's political views in *Tell My Horse* also sidelines discussions of her transcriptions and analyses of observed daily and ritual practices. In addition, since Hurston never published a standard, as opposed to experimental, ethnography, although she published significant research findings in peer-reviewed journals, another question begs to be answered: Has Hurston proven her knowledge of social-scientific methods and rules of the conventional ethnography? Finally, and most significantly, does *Tell My Horse* offer general readers and social scientists original research, and what is the significance of this research?

In order to make critical room for future discussions of Hurston's conceptual contributions to the field of anthropology, this chapter discusses selected contemporary receptions of the political content of *Tell My Horse*. In addition, given the critical record concerning Hurston's experimental forms, it addresses received attitudes that she was unable to present her anthropological findings in an authoritative ethnographic narrative mode, focusing on her distinctive contribution to representations of Haitian Vodou in *Tell My Horse*. Although many emphasize the iconic author's "unorthodox" form, *Tell My Horse* presented to both readers and scholars of her era a bold statement regarding Haitian cultural production and Vodou. Significantly, it also offered a direct counterargument to anthropologist Melville Herskovits's focus on acculturations of West African customs with French (and Catholic) customs in his commentary of Vodou as described in *Life in a Haitian Valley* ([1937a] 2007).

In analyzing Hurston's political views expressed in *Tell My Horse*, many scholars have argued that Hurston offers readers a controversial commentary on the American occupation of Haiti from 1915 to 1934, but they differ in the amount of intellectual agency they imagine she has as a scholar in shaping the narrative effect of this ethnography (Trefzer 2000, 299; Duck 2004, 136; Rowe 2000, 254–56; Mitchell 2013, para. 2). Some argue that Hurston's views support the American occupation and are therefore largely, although ambiguously, imperialist. Others argue that Hurston's narrative tone and use of satire, irony, and historical and political allusions should be more faithfully engaged in order to fully describe her attitudes about the American occupation. Doing so, they argue, reveals Hurston's sustained critique of political corruption and confirm her interests as an advocate for those most oppressed.

John Carlos Rowe's 2000 treatment of *Tell My Horse* suggests that Hurston held conflicting opinions. On one hand, she might have believed that U.S. aid to Haiti was the best course of action for Haiti's peasant population, given what it provided in the development of various infrastructures that improved education and transportation. On the other hand, he argues, she also offers indirect criticisms of the United States.[1] Rowe's sustained reading of *Tell My Horse* convincingly argues that Hurston's ethnography of Haiti should be read with attention to her interest in irony. He argues that the "'coding' of her narratives should be understood as her primary mode of narration, whose purpose is to transform attitudes and feelings, together with preconceived ideas" (256). Rowe reads Hurston's rhetoric as strategic. He argues that she is a social idealist who, while critical of the United States, expresses a fundamental belief in democracy (255). Rowe comments that the juxtaposition of seemingly contradictory perspectives on Haitian Vodou, for example, indicates Hurston's political position: "The folkloric purposes of Voodoo in Accompong [a historical Maroon village in Jamaica] are clearly meant to serve as positive contrasts with the use of Voodoo by Haitian dictators to consolidate their power" (274).

Annette Trefzer notes the same contradiction but describes Hurston's rhetorical position as more problematic than Rowe does. She notes, "As a black American ethnographer working on the cultures of the Caribbean, Hurston seems caught between defending the U.S. Imperial 'possession' of Haiti and simultaneously critiquing it by highlighting spiritual possession of Haitian voodoo rituals as a strategy of resistance to colonial politics" (2000, 299). She later describes Hurston as "trapped by rhetorical U.S. justifications for the occupations" (301, 302). Trefzer reads Hurston's seemingly pro-U.S. sentiment as a defense against the "anti-U.S. sentiment" she encountered while in Haiti and as a response to the extreme poverty that she witnessed, and she concludes that Hurston's rhetoric problematically repeats American justifications for the occupation of Haiti (302). Trefzer also argues that Hurston significantly contributes to representations of Vodou in her attention to spirit possession as an act of resistance for the Haitian peasantry and as a transnational phenomenon that connects people of African descent in the U.S. South to the Caribbean (310–11). However, it is not clear whether Trefzer sees Hurston as consciously producing the effect of contradictions between her seeming praise of the U.S. occupation alongside her illustration of her anthropological observations of how peasants and elites regard that occupation. For Trefzer, the seeming contradiction of Hurston's ethnography "ultimately mirrors the culture and politics of the ethnographer more than that of her subjects" (299).

Mary A. Renda concludes that within *Tell My Horse* Hurston "reinforced exotic discourses, while critiquing them in the same breath" (2001, 300). Leigh Anne Duck emphasizes that, in discussing the U.S. occupation, Hurston "carefully restricts her praise to its material accomplishments" while leaving her commentary on its social and political impact interwoven throughout the ethnography (2004, 136). Daphne Lamothe is interested in what she calls the "narrative dissonance" evident in *Tell My Horse* (2008, 141–59). Echoing Gordon's arguments regarding Hurston's ethnographic authority, Lamothe comments, "Because she was doubly marginalized as an African American and a woman, her efforts to perform the ethnographer's role became a delicate and fraught operation" (143). And not unlike Annette Trefzer's point, Lamothe reads Hurston's ethnography as an example that explains "the social and political attitudes that influence the production of anthropological knowledge in the United States" (144).

Jeff Karem's analysis of the holograph of *Tell My Horse* largely confirms John Carlos Rowe's assessment of its anti-colonialist interests. Karem's review of Hurston's revisions reveals edits that indicate Hurston's interest in managing the reception of her criticism of Haitian politics and minimizing any sensational receptions of the Vodou practices (2011, 70–73). He convincingly argues that "Hurston explicitly crafted and revised the manuscript to foreground the contrast between traditional bourgeois politics and populist resistance, with the goal of using the example of Haiti to privilege the latter" (71). Karem further argues:

> This perspective has the conservative effect of leaving the U.S. occupation uncritiqued, but it is also radical in casting a skeptical eye on traditional "Talented Tenth" politics. Hurston's complex position is consistent with her contention in other works that it is through vernacular culture, rather than conventional politics, that African-descended peoples of the New World can best keep their traditions and advance their interests. (71)

Ernest Julius Mitchell (2013) decisively argues that Hurston's political views are on the whole anti-colonialist. Through a reading of Hurston's many political essays, Mitchell shows that she had an ongoing interest in international affairs, which includes pointed critiques of American domestic policies and imperialism. Mitchell's discussion of *Tell My Horse* confirms that Hurston's subversive commentary categorically criticized the U.S. occupation of Haiti (1915–1934). In particular, he argues that the chapter "Rebirth of Nation," an allusion to D. W. Griffith's *Birth of a Nation* (1915), includes a comparison of the marines to the Klan and the assertion that Hurston's "contrarian" position in a debate with an upper-class Haitian citizen revealed the complex and contradictory reception of the U.S. occupation by Haitian peasants and the ruling class. The discussion ends with her agreement with her debater's final statement: "'What can a weak country like Haiti do when a powerful nation like your own forces its military upon us, kills our citizens, and steals our money?'" (Mitchell 2013, 7, quoting Hurston ([1938c] 1995, 350).

For all of its complexities and contradictions, a number of scholars agree that *Tell My Horse* offers an irreverent cultural critique not only of Haitian and Jamaican politics but also of the racial politics of the United States. Mitchell reminds us that Hurston's essay "Seeing the World as It Is" (1941), confirms that Hurston's anti-imperialist commitment includes her willingness to criticize American foreign policy, noting her declaration, "I will fight for my country, but I will not lie for her" ([1938a] 1990, 792). However veiled or dissonant Hurston's rhetoric might be in *Tell My Horse*, her critical perspectives reveal her strategic interest in challenging unchecked power in Jamaica, Haiti, the United States, and France. True to the Boasian school of anthropology, she was engaged in a cultural critique while also working to chart new ground in the study of religious beliefs in Jamaica and Haiti.

Readings that primarily describe Hurston's position as imperialist or ethnocentric, even as they work to grapple with her distinctive rhetorical style, reveal a kind of confirmation bias that delimits opportunities to analyze her ethnography more fully. Whether one agrees or disagrees that she presented imperialist and even ethnocentric views on the U.S. occupation of Haiti and Haitian and Jamaican culture, the extensive critical attention given to this issue occludes a more pointed discussion of her ethnographic findings in *Tell My Horse*. The focus on Hurston's political views is a pragmatic one, as her rhetorical narrative modes present distinctive challenges for readers (especially of today) who are interested in deciphering her critical position on the occupation of Haiti and who perhaps are influenced by the conventional and complex receptions of her ethnographic work. There is a current interest in mapping out transnational and global discourses in her work, and this reception echoes and rejects themes shaped by the postmodern turn in anthropology, which largely receives Hurston as a writer about culture rather than a scholar in anthropology.[2] Contemporaneous reviews of *Tell My Horse* were less concerned with questions of Hurston's political positions and more concerned with her methodology and the validity and significance of her findings, especially given Lippincott's racist marketing (West 2005, 132–39).[3] Notwithstanding its mixed reception, the disciplinary interest of African Americanists in challenging the "armchair anthropology" and literary works that patently reproduced stereotypes of Black culture shaped Hurston's commitments. Historian Carter G. Woodson's review, for example, noted, "She went among the people in their daily walks, won their confidence and moved them to speak to her out of the depths of their hearts. She can give, then, the inside story of voodoo on these islands, for she saw these scenes enacted and participated in them herself" (1939b, 117). He also stressed, "She is regarded as a novelist, but at the same time she is more anthropologist than novelist" (116). Noting her methodology, he also stressed, "She did not collect stories from books" (117).

However, some critiques of Hurston's ethnographies within the field of anthropology leave open the question of her attention to anthropological methods. Instead, they focus on her ethnographic authority and her own representations of her subjectivity (insider/outsider) as a researcher doing fieldwork. In addition, many of these assessments either evaluate her work against contemporary standards of ethnographic production or describe her work as distinctively experimental and ahead of its time. But how did Hurston perceive the standards necessary for ethnographic authority, and, in particular, how did she perceive the standards for reliable and valid anthropological methods in the study of African-derived belief systems in the United States and the Caribbean?

Hurston discusses her research approach in both *Mules and Men* and *Dust Tracks on a Road*. In *Mules and Men* she notes the importance of having the "spyglass of Anthropology" and refers to her training at Barnard College under the direction of Dr. Franz Boas. Within a few deft sentences she authorizes her critical perspective, and although she underscores her Barnard experience, it is not lost on readers that her personal knowledge of her field greatly enhances her ability to gather the material covered. Likewise, Franz Boas's preface to *Mules and Men* assures readers of the importance of Hurston's "identity as a Southern negro" and her significant contribution to the study of "the true inner life of the Negro" ([1935] 1978, xiii-xiv). Hurston's "Research" chapter in *Dust Tracks on a Road* underscores the specific import of her training in Boasian methods: "His instructions are to go out and find what's there. He outlines his theory, but if the facts do not agree with it, he would not warp a jot or dot of the findings to save his theory" ([1942] 1995, 143). Boas was committed to challenging pseudo-scientific approaches to the question of racial difference, which defined and supported racial hierarchy. This required a method that relied heavily on observation and documentation of cultural change as well as historical contextualization using reliable sources (Boas 1920, 313–14), Hurston likewise took on this commitment and approach.

More specifically, evidence of Hurston's methodological rigor can be found in her review of *Voodoo in New Orleans* (1946), authored by Robert Tallant (1909–1957). Tallant's work purported to offer an authentic account of "Voodoo." However, Hurston took him to task for the shallowness of his research and the inaccuracy of his claims. In her review of Tallant's work, published in the *Journal of American Folklore* in 1947, Hurston writes:

> *Voodoo in New Orleans* is offered by Robert Tallant, the author, as the most authoritative work on the subject. The student of folklore therefore expects to find first, properly authenticated material unpublished before, and the answers to the following questions: 1. What is Voodoo? 2. What is its esoteric background? 3. Who were and are the exponents and carriers of this culture in New Orleans? 4. From what sources did the author gather his material? 5. What is the historical background? 6. What inferences have been drawn to add to the sum total of human knowledge? (436)

Hurston goes on to detail an extended critique of Tallant's study. I excerpt and annotate it here at length, since it enumerates Hurston's methodology and her commitment to a rigorous approach to research:

> 1. Hoodoo is nowhere defined in the text, except by implication. . . .
> 2. The author makes no attempt to establish the esoteric background by a comparative study of the African religions, nor the developments in Santo Domingo. He merely quotes several writers of fiction who wrote about occurrences brought to public notice. . . .
> 3. The best efforts of the author were in digging out of the newspaper files the names of the best known Hoodoo "doctors" of the past. No light is thrown upon those numerous others, however, who did not for one reason or another attract the notice of the press or the police. . . . There is no study of the current Hoodooists of New Orleans. There are merely some rumors about them. What their methods and procedures are, the author does not tell us.[4] . . . However, if the author had witnessed every ceremony of Hoodoo in Louisiana as he claims, the story would have been different. In order to witness the ceremony, he would have had to be a hoodooist himself. . . .
> 5. The author offers not one valid source of information for a serious work on folklore. . . . His Haitian borrowings of the Zombi (*Magic Island* and *Tell My Horse*), and the little coffin of the Sect Rouge (*Tell My Horse*), and the

translation of the invocation to Legba (*Tell My Horse*, p. 103) do not escape the notice of the trained eye, though nowhere does the author acknowledge his indebtedness.

6. The historical background is not to be trusted since the author is not even informed about matters that are in the common school histories of the United States. (1947, 436–38)

Hurston's fifth point highlights that Tallant did not credit her work, and her sixth point further challenges the validity and reliability of Tallant's research, as she describes a number of significant historical and factual errors. Finally, she addresses his failure to offer any new interpretation of the information presented:

> 7. The author arrives at no conclusion.
> *Voodoo in New Orleans* is totally exterior so far as Hoodoo is concerned. There is no revelation of any new facts, nor any analysis of what is already known. It is rather a collection of the popular beliefs about Hoodoo from the outside. The snake-worship sex-orgies, Greek Pythonesses, and goat-sacrifices, proceeding from false premises, and governed by hasty generalizations. It offers no opportunity for serious study, and should be considered for just what it is, *a creative-journalistic appeal to popular fancy.* The late Lyle Saxon says in the foreword, "... So much nonsense has been written about Voodoo in New Orleans...." *Voodoo in New Orleans* in no way tends to abate the nuisance. (Hurston 1947, 437–38; emphasis mine)

This review, in effect, stands as Hurston's statement on ethnographic methodology. She establishes her standards for methodological rigor and, specifically, the importance of participant observation, including ritual initiation, in order to fully and reliably document the religion. She also underscores her commitment to social scientific discovery. Ironically, some assessments of Hurston's ethnographies suggest that her work should be characterized as more creative and journalistic than social scientific and that she does not fully demonstrate her understanding of anthropological methods in *Tell My Horse*. These assessments assume that Hurston's rhetorical stance, including the use of satire and irony, reflects the research methods and theory applied in her collection and analysis of cultural data, which are, as noted, under-evaluated.

Of particular note is Hurston's statement that a researcher should be initiated to gain credible information on hoodoo practices. Hurston was herself initiated in the practices of hoodoo and Vodou, which she brought to bear in her discussions about whether zombies are in fact real or are simply part of the cultural lore and where she, as in her discussions of hoodoo in *Mules and Men,* advanced pharmacological explanations (Hurston [1938b] 1990, 196; Hurston [1935] 1978, 291). In addition, Hurston offers detailed descriptions of Vodou ceremonies wherein she indicates her firsthand participation in the building and dedication of a *hounfour* (a Vodou temple) and her preparation into the "second step towards the priesthood" of "Canzo," or Kanzo. By describing a second-degree initiation, she confirms her own first-degree initiation and suggests her imminent initiation as a "Canzo." Thus, at the writing of the ethnography Hurston was one degree away from becoming a Vodou priest, or Mambo.

Hurston also offers a discussion of the distinctions between the Rada and Petro spirits (1947, 164–67) that serves to contradict common stereotypes of the essential evilness of all of the Vodou loas. She stresses the utility of the Petros in relation to their great power to protect, and not simply in terms of their potential for great revenge if they are not served properly, a significant distinction, given stereotypes of Vodou. She indicates that people serve these loas (who have the potential to do both good and harm) when they are in need of fast and powerful results for very difficult situations. In a remark that signifies on European beliefs about evil, she quotes Houngan (priest) Louis Romain, who states, "They lend you big support or give you something to protect you in order that nothing will happen to you and that no one will cause you to be sick, and the demons or the devil will be unable to do you anything in the night" (Hurston 1947, 167). The passage reminds an audience unfamiliar with Haitian Vodou that beliefs concerning good and evil are not unique to Haitian Vodou, and that the Iwas/loas are neither demons nor devils in the Christian sense. She details how, in return for their work and protection, the loas require considerable sacrifice in the form of larger, and more expensive, animals (167): "The Petros work for you only if you make a promise of service to them," and those who fail to deliver on their promise then are punished with illness and death (167).

Throughout these discussions, Hurston underscores the education and character of the Vodou leaders under which she trains: Mambo Madame Isabel Etienne, Houngan Dieu Donnez St. Leger, and Houngan Louis Romain and his wife, Mambo Madame Romain. Hurston's interest here is to challenge stereotypical representations of Vodou culture, rituals, and practitioners as wildly disordered and wicked. She also describes the process by which animals to be sacrificed are ritually cleaned and perfumed (Hurston 1947, 171). Scholars of Hurston's ethnography focus on her discussions of her fearful corporal response to animal sacrifice (153) as evidence of her nonobjective approach to her study, because they are moments when she describes her own reaction to the event. The inordinate focus on her responses to animal sacrifice, offered ritually upon the death of a houngan, and her description and photograph of a zombie are quite remarkable, given the extensive details and data she provides regarding Haitian Vodou, including descriptions drawn from her personal experience at ritual events. Rather than providing evidence of Hurston's ethnocentrism, her elaborations can be read as fulfilling the conventions of ethnographic realism, as she intends to both mirror and mediate reader receptions of animal sacrifice for a general audience. In effect, Hurston is better able to educate a 1930s audience about the specificity and orderliness of the ritual experience because she realistically narrates episodic moments of her own interpretations and reactions as a non-native observer and participant, respectively. These include the emotions of awe, fear, and anticipation during a ritual ceremony, which are, incidentally, also experienced by local participants and are not indicative of ethnocentric judgment (Hurston ([1938a] 1990, 144).

In a letter dated January 6, 1937, to Dr. Henry Allen Moe, secretary of the John Simon Guggenheim Memorial Foundation, Hurston requested additional funding to continue her research and provided a detailed outline of the form that *Tell My Horse* might take. Her appeal described *Tell My Horse* as "not a strictly scientific work, but burning spots from the ensemble" (Kaplan 2002, 389). By "burning spots" Hurston suggests that she has highlighted what she assesses are the most important aspects of her research findings rather than provide a "strictly scientific" ethnographic production. Her metaphor of burning spots is not a declaration of her interest in the sensational but rather an indication of how she selected significant scientific information from the "ensemble" of what she faithfully collected and recorded. What, then, are "the burning spots," that she intended to be read as her definitive conceptual contribution to the study of Haitian Vodou?

One significant answer lies in the title of the ethnography, which directly signals Hurston's interest in critique and also alludes to Hurston's interest in foregrounding the active and original creation of Haitian folklore. "Tell my horse" is the translation of the Haitian Creole phrase *parlay cheval ou*, which a Haitian peasant utters when possessed by Guede, a Vodou loa of the dead. The phrase signals the possession and justifies the often biting critiques that individuals thus possessed may speak about almost anyone but especially those who have a higher-class status. As Hurston explains, Haitian peasants can claim they are not responsible for any scathing remarks they make against more powerful members of their community, including the Creole elite (Hurston [1938] 1990, 221). Hurston describes the loa Guede in the following manner:

> Gods always behave like the people who make them. One can see the hand
> of the Haitian peasant in that boisterous god, Guede, because he does and

says the things that the peasants would like to do and say. You can see him in the market women, in the domestic servant who now and then appears before her employer "mounted" by this god who takes occasion to say many stinging things to the boss. You can see him in the field hand, and certainly in the group of women about a public well or spring, chattering, gossiping and dragging out the shortcomings of their employers and the people like him. Nothing in Haiti is quite so obvious as that this loa is the common deification of the common people of Haiti. The mulattoes give this spirit no food and pay it no attention at all. He belongs to the black and the uneducated ones at that. He is a hilarious divinity and full of the stuff of burlesque. This manifestation comes as near a social criticism of the classes by the masses as anything in all Haiti. Guede has another distinction. It is the one loa which is entirely Haitian. There is neither European nor African background for it. It sprang up or was called up by some local need and now is firmly established among the blacks. (219–20)

Following this description, Hurston also provides an etic description of the material culture of the loa, including its ritual and symbolic settings and performance:

The people who created Guede needed a god of derision. They needed a spirit which could burlesque the society that crushed him, so Guede eats roasted peanuts and parched corn like his devotees. He delights in an old coat and pants and a torn old hat. So dressed and fed, he bites with sarcasm and slashes with ridicule the class that *despises* him. (220; emphasis mine)

In these passages, Hurston speaks of the functional significance of Guede for a community that has little voice. Haitian peasants mounted by Guede can more freely ridicule the economically and politically powerful elites. The public aspect of this ridicule unites the peasant population against their shared oppressors. In other examples, Hurston illustrates ways in which Guede offers opportunities for intra-community critiques within the peasant class and suggests that other loas, like Grande Libido, have this same potential for class resistance (236). In addition, her choice of the word "despises" should not be glossed, as it further illustrates the nature of the hierarchy that shapes and maintains the lower socioeconomic status of the Haitian peasant and reveals Hurston's empathy with the peasant class's social predicament (222, 236).

Many scholars have noted the significance of the title *Tell My Horse* to understanding Hurston's controversial narrative approach. They argue, for example, that her narrative ambiguity concerning discussions of Haitian politics is signified by the ethnography's title. Mary Renda says, "The book may have constituted for Hurston a kind of back talk against the authority of that audience.

Hurston took her title from the formulaic utterance of a Haitian god, or *loa*, Papa Guede, whose primary characteristic is the audacity of his back talk. Through his 'mounts' or 'horses'—that is, those he possesses—Guede talks back brazenly to the powerful, beginning always with the words, 'Tell my horse'" (2001, 289). Annette Trefzer likewise notes the significance of the title's cultural allusion: "Like the Haitian peasant population, who had to resort to disguising their ideological insubordination, the black American writer traditionally had to find her own ways of negotiating between dominant narratives and social critiques" (2000, 305). Daphne Lamothe asserts, "Just as she begins the narrative by signifying her own trustworthiness as a narrator of the kind of 'truth' her audiences expected, so does she suggest that her own informants possess fluid subjectivities that refuse the reader assurance of authentic and accurate reportage that would allow him or her to understand this other culture in absolutist terms (2008, 155).

In these ways, the title aptly announces Hurston's interest in documenting folk culture in terms of the culture of the Haitian peasant, and the loas mode of discourse aligns with Hurston's own affinity for signification and literary veiling. The title also announces Hurston's explication of a distinctive cultural element, which adds greatly to our understanding of her conceptual contribution to anthropology.[5] Hurston's study specifically states, "Guede has another distinction. It is the one loa which is entirely Haitian. There is neither European nor African background for it. It sprang up or was called up by some local need and now is firmly established among the blacks" ([1938] 1990, 219–20). Given this critical assessment of Guede's unique Haitianness, Hurston then offers a detailed discussion of Guede's geographical origins:

> The spirit Guede (pronounced geeday) originated at Miragoane and its originator's especial meeting place was the bridge across the lake at Miragoane, where the Department of the South and West meet. These people who originated this cult were Bossals who were once huddled on the waterfront in Port-au-Prince in the neighborhood of the place where all of the slaves were disembarked from the ships. There came to be a great huddle of these people living on a very low social and economic level in the stretch flanking the bay. For some cause, these folk had gained the despisement of the city, and the contempt in which they were held caused a great body of them to migrate to the vicinity of Miragoane, and there the cult arose. It is too close to the cult of Baron Cimeterre not to be related. It is obvious that it is another twist given to the functions of that loa. The spirit of Guede is Baron Cimeterre with social consciousness, plus a touch of burlesque and slapstick. (222)

Hurston's title not only signifies her narrative approach, as some scholars have noted, but also clearly signals her distinctive ethnographic contribution to acculturation studies. In brief, Hurston asserts that Haiti's history, politics, and socioeconomic conditions created the context for its own loa, originating from the "folk" of Haiti and not simply from a merging of European tradition and African survivals.

Guede is the only loa for which Hurston describes a specific historical origin. She describes all of the loas more broadly: "Who are the loa, then? I will not pretend to call the name of every mystere in Haiti. *No one* knows the name of every loa because every major section of Haiti has its own variation. It has gods and goddesses of places and forces that are unknown fifty miles away. The heads of families of gods are known all over the country, but there are endless variations of the demigods even in the same localities" ([1938] 1990, 114). Hurston's interest, then, in describing loas sui generis is to illustrate that not all of them can be described as syncretic or acculturated aspects of West African deities with French influence.

This assertion challenges the standard discourse in acculturative studies as defined by Melville Herskovits, who was the leading anthropologist in the study of the African diaspora. Herskovits does not mention Guede's origins but only describes Guede's (or Gede's) role as a "gossip" who disrupts rituals ([1937a] 2007, 167, 196) and a "handy-man" to Baron Samedi, the loa of the cemetery, who has "the final say" in matters of death (113, 250). Herskovits's study seeks to define the survivals of West African religions as they came in contact with European or French cultural tradition and customs (47–64). He summarizes, "Two historical facts must be kept constantly in mind in making this analysis, for without them, what follows would be meaningless. The first is that vodun derives from a background of African theology and ceremonialism. The second is that the Negroes have continuously been subjected to the influence of Catholicism during the centuries that have passed since their introduction into the island" (141). Herskovits's descriptions of "the Haitian" and his characterization of Vodou reflect his dedication to essentially defining Vodou as a mixture of a belief in a Christian and Catholic God alongside African loas (142).

Hurston, however, offers a radically different definition of Vodou. She defines Vodou as "a religion of creation and life. It is the worship of the sun, the water and other natural forces, but the symbolism is no better understood than that of other religions and consequently is taken too literally" ([1938] 1990, 113). She asserts that Vodou is more than "a pagan religion with an African pantheon" and refutes the idea that the Haitian loas are "the Catholic saints done over in black." She explains further: "Neither are their attributes the same" (113–14).

Hurston acknowledges the existence of Catholic references in some of the Vodou rituals, but she places far less emphasis than Herskovits on Catholicism's role in shaping Vodou's cosmology (142). She states, "Nominally Haiti is a Catholic country, but in reality it is deeply pagan" (91). Later still she describes Haitian Vodou as more than an extension of African spirituality, while also refuting the importance of visual representations of Catholic saints:

> Some of the other men of education in Haiti who have given time to the study of Voodoo esoterics do not see such deep meanings in Voodoo practices. They see only a pagan religion with an African pantheon. And right here, let it be said that the Haitian gods, mysteres, or loa are not the Catholic calendar of saints done over in black as has been stated by casual observers. (114)

Her attention to this concern, for example, is illustrated with her description of the attributes of Erzulie Freida, one of many Vodou loas whose attributes she describes at length. She writes, "She has been identified as the Blessed Virgin, but this is far from true. Here again the use of the pictures of the Catholic saints have confused observers who do not listen long enough" ([1938] 1990, 121). Another example, near the end of the ethnography, in the chapter titled "Parlay Cheval Ou (Tell My Horse)," illustrates Hurston's documentation of the tenuous relationship between the Catholic Church and indigenous religious or spiritual practices in Haiti. Hurston describes a story of how in 1884 local Haitians began to worship at a palm tree, where they reportedly saw a vision of a "beautiful, luminous virgin" with "gorgeous wings" (230–31). Many locals congregated at the site and reported that they were healed of their ailments (231). Hurston says, "The Catholic Church was neglected. So the priest became so incensed that he ordered the palm tree to be chopped down, but he could find no one to chop it" (231). The priest attempted to cut the tree down himself with a machete, "but the first blow of the blade against the tree caused the machete to bounce back and strike the priest on the head . . . [and] he soon died of his wound" (231). She describes this location as "this great shrine of Haiti" located at the cascade of Saut d' Eau (230–31). Her discussion of this story offers a valuable emic perspective on the complex relationship between the institution of the Catholic Church and the ongoing development of Haitian religious culture.

In contrast to Hurston's ethnography, Herskovits's *Life in a Haitian Valley* ([1937a] 2007) is a standard study that closely follows ethnographic convention in both its content and organization. It begins with a description of its setting in Mirebalais, maps out broader historical contexts (African and colonial European), and defines his theoretical approach. He then describes aspects of the daily life of the Haitian farmer (male) as well as chapters on family organization before moving into his more focused discussion of Haitian religion. However, Herskovits avoids any sustained discussion of the occupation of Haiti, leaving Sidney Mintz to note in his introduction to the 2007 edition, "The book does not deal with the occupation; it is barely noted in the introduction. But Herskovits was surely aware of the effects of the occupation on his Haitian colleagues" (v-vi). For Herskovits, the political context of Haiti is not at all central to understanding Vodou, since everything can be understood by "working the amalgam" of African and French Catholic beliefs and practices (47–64).[6]

Regarding Hurston's definition of the "endless variations" of the loa, anthropologist Andrew Apter claims, "Zora Neale Hurston was one of the first to grasp the elusive polymorphism of the Haitian loa in her more personal (and in many ways proto-experimental) ethnography of Vodoun" (1991, 249). Apter's "Rethinking Syncretism" reconsiders Herskovits's assumptions about the acculturative process of syncretic exchange of cultural practices and meanings. He argues that Herskovits's theories of acculturation depend too closely on a positivist model that essentially understands the exchange of cultures in the African diaspora as occurring between pure Africanisms and Europeanisms and that he failed to see Africanisms as themselves a product of cultural exchange and syncretic acculturation (237–40). Apter continues:

> The cosmological principles that render such polyvocalities possible and intelligible are grounded in Yoruba notions of "deep knowledge" (imo jinlè), referring to the privileged access of powerful priests and priestesses to hidden truths and secrets. I will return to the power of such knowledge in due course. For now, it is enough to point out that within this ritually safeguarded space of interpretive possibilities, official dynasties and genealogies are revised, deities are repositioned to express rival political claims, and the deities themselves are fragmented and fused into multiple and singular identities. Small wonder that Herskovits had trouble with his lists, since even in Nigeria, no òrisà cult, community, or Yoruba kingdom (let alone two individuals) would produce the same list or pantheon of òrisà. (249)

Here Apter contests Herskovits's attempt to create a taxonomy of *òrisà* within a Yoruba cosmology.[7] His general discussion of Herskovits's critical weaknesses has great implications for Hurston's methodological approach and her subsequent findings regarding the Haitian cosmology. For Hurston, Haiti's culture is mediated by its immediate local and national historical contexts, as anthropologist Gwendolyn Mikell has noted (1982, 222–26). Hurston's Haiti is highly gendered and influenced by the politics of color consciousness, and her analysis of the highly political production of cultural meaning and associated rituals within Haiti presents its resistance to syncretic influences of the Catholic Church.[8]

Hurston's initiations into Vodou authorized her research as distinctive from Melville Herskovits, and they allowed her insight into more fluid and situational aspects of Vodun cosmology. She attended picnics, built religious sites, and generally participated in the social life of the various communities that she visited. Herskovits's *Life in a Haitian Valley* includes an appendix on his methods, wherein he explicitly defines and defends his ethnographic approach in his role as observer and not as participant-observer, the latter being today's ethnographic standard. He presents a veiled criticism of Margaret Mead's use of the participant-observer method in Samoa and notes that the "social visibility" of his whiteness would be a barrier to such an approach: Crossing the "caste lines" of the culture, he argues, would leave the ethnographer open to "ridicule" from cultural groups who, like West African Negroes and their New World Negro descendants, strongly valued "individual identity" ([1937a] 2007, 327). In other words, Herskovits defends his methodology based on the belief that becoming fully integrated in the Haitian social life would be met with derision by the people under study (326–27).

Hurston's subjectivity as a "New World Negro descendant" was received as providing her with greater access to Haitian peasants and Creole elites alike. In the latter instance, then, Hurston studied up, in the sense that she studied people with more structural power in the community, providing her analysis with its complex and complicated assessment of cultural life. But also significant is Hurston's ethnographic (research) authority as an initiate in hoodoo and Vodou religious practice and her knowledge of Creole. By contrast, Herskovits was not an initiate and had to rely on "native" testimony for his ethnography. In addition to outlining his methodological approach, his appendix on methods reads as a defense of his dependence on interviews of "native residents" and his argument against the use of participant-observation by white researchers among nonwhite peoples (Herskovits [1937a] 2007), 324–30). Considering Carter G. Woodson's review of *Life in a Haitian Valley*, then, especially given the terms of his support of Hurston's method in *Tell My Horse*, sheds some light on their different approaches. Although largely positive, Woodson's review expressed a concern with Herskovits's limited research setting as well as his view of acculturation: "The objection raised to a study of this sort is that, losing sight of its scientific import, laymen are liable to consider this the general pattern of life among the people of Haiti. The author [Woodson] would not convey the impression that all transplanted Negroes and their descendants are still Africans, but that this isolated community because of being little influenced by European culture offers an explanation of many other things where differences are less pronounced" (Woodson 1937, 367).[9]

In Hurston's commitment to address the larger political contexts of Haitian Vodou, her study offers an explanation of "many other things." As scholars work to situate Hurston's contributions in anthropology, they should consider and compare these two ethnographies for their perspectives on Haitian Vodou.[10] *Tell My Horse* was published one year after Herskovits's *Life in a Haitian Valley*; both were influenced by the work of Franz Boas, and both focused on the culture of Haitians as African descendants. Hurston's ethnography presents to both lay readers and scholars of her era an outspoken statement regarding Haitian cultural production and Vodou. She offers a counter-narrative to anthropologist Melville Herskovits's focus on acculturations of West African survivals with French (and Catholic) customs as described in *Life in a Haitian Valley*. Critics have considered the meanings of Hurston's signifying play on the loa Guede's infamous utterance, "Tell my horse," and they describe multiple audiences that Hurston navigates and speaks to within this ethnography. I find a new meaning of conceptual significance in this work of anthropological folklore: by signifying her affinity with the "folk" of Haiti, Hurston's *Tell My Horse* talks back to Herskovits's study and to his established views of acculturation, which did not fully consider Haitian cultural practices as "still in the making."

Epilogue
On Icons, Interdisciplines, and Communities

Although in the sixties the works of neglected Afro-American male writers of the Harlem Renaissance were beginning to resurface, for example, Jean Toomer's *Cane*, I was told the women writers of that period were terrible — not worth my trouble. However, because of the conjuncture of the black arts movement and the women's movement, I asked questions I probably would not have otherwise thought of.
— Barbara Christian, "But What Do We Think We're Doing Anyway?"

With this history in mind, the critical question is how can we today claim these women as foremothers of a Black feminist anthropological tradition when a gendered approach, save for Hurston, was not on their agenda?
— A. Lynn Bolles, "Seeking the Ancestors: Onward and Upward into the Twenty-First Century"

One of the commitments of Black women's and feminist studies is to redress the marginalization of Black women's intellectualism and creativity. In this regard, its methodology addresses historical silences and omissions and reveals how practices of erasure and exceptionalism systemically negate Black women's subjectivity and agency. This interdisciplinary project was created and pursued with these concerns in mind, and they largely informed my sustained attention to

Hurston's literary and anthropological receptions. As Hurston states, "Research is formalized curiosity. It is poking and prying with a purpose" ([1942] 1995, 687). In order to address Zora Neale Hurston's intellectual contributions to American anthropology, this work has foregrounded Hurston's research methods, data, and thought, underscoring her contributions to cultural concepts about Black folk life and ways. But first, it was also necessary to consider how receptions of her life and work from the 1970s through the 1990s shaped her relative critical success and marginalization in American literature and American anthropology, respectively. That framing reveals how varied ideological frames and rhetorical tendencies shape Hurston's distinctive status in the U.S. academy across two disciplines, although much (and more) could be said about how studies of Hurston travels across other disciplines and fields. Along the way through this project, my purpose was to underscore the intellectual work of Black women scholars who recuperate her intellectual standing and work into the public and academic record. However, early Black feminist scholars in both fields addressed Hurston's work as just *one* critical intervention as they challenged the exclusionary practices of their respective disciplines and canons. When and where Hurston enters these disciplines—as icon, token, canonized writer, or under-evaluated social scientist—is, of course, in no way a final word on the comprehensive and far-reaching work done to address a myriad of issues through the field of Black feminist studies.

For Black feminist scholar-activists, the work of Black feminist literary studies emerged as one axis of a larger effort to transform the academy and society at large. In particular, their efforts to increase literary output since the 1970s are a lasting testament of their commitment to social justice and their recognition of the significance of literature, various modes of literacy, and the arts in speaking about and against social inequality. The publication of Toni Cade Bambara's *The Black Woman: An Anthology* (1970), long recognized as a "first" contemporary text in Black women's studies, occurred as a radical act born of the movements of the 1960s.[1] Its goals included raising social consciousness in the fight for justice on feminist issues in the United States and abroad and producing work that would support the movement's mission and strategic interests. Bambara's groundbreaking anthology, which included poetry and fiction among political essays, was very clear about the connections between literacy and liberty. She writes, "We are involved in a struggle for liberation. . . . To do that, we might turn to various fields of studies to extract material, data necessary to define that term in respect to ourselves. We note, however, all too quickly the lack of relevant material" (1). The Combahee River Collective, a Black feminist social justice organization founded in 1974, published "A Black

Feminist Statement" in 1979 (written in 1977). The statement listed—among many other activist projects, including "sterilization abuse, abortion rights, battered women, rape, and health care"—its intent to "gather together a collection of Black feminist writing." The organization noted that "black feminists are living in isolation all over the country," and they expressed their strategy to use their writings "as a means of organizing Black feminists as we continue to do political work in coalition with other groups" (B. Smith 1977a, 20–21).

Mary Helen Washington's "Black Women Image Makers" (1974) called for the critical consideration of the works of Black women writers, including an analysis of how their works revised stereotypes of Black women. Alice Walker's *In Search of Our Mothers' Gardens* (1974) implored women to look to everyday activities of women for evidence of women's significant contributions to the arts, including literature. That same year, Pat Crutchfield Exum's edited collection, *Keeping the Faith: Writing by Contemporary Black American Women* (1974), gathered together the writing of Black women to address stereotypical images in the larger society. In the numerous criticisms and anthologies and cross-talks that followed, the field's expanse and import continued and continues amid what Farah Jasmine Griffin's calls its "growth and growing pains" (352) and its radical assertion of a "strategy of reading" that's politically grounded (353).[2]

It was the reception of Barbara Smith's "Toward a Black Feminist Criticism" that prompted a critical conversation within the academy about specifically feminist ways of reading and analyzing Black women's writing. Smith wrote:

> At the present time I feel that the politics of feminism have a direct relationship to the state of Black women's literature. A viable, autonomous Black feminist movement in this country would open up the space needed for the exploration of Black women's lives and the creation of consciously Black woman-identified art. (B. Smith [1977b] 2000, 133)

Expressing her intentions to "make in this essay some connections between the politics of Black women's lives, what we write about and our situation as artists," Smith not only justified her approach through an examination of the reception of works authored by Black women by white critics and Black male critics, but she also offered evidence of the invisibility of Black lesbian writing as an example of Black women's oppression (138–44):

> When Black women's books are dealt with at all, it is usually in the context of Black literature which largely ignores the implications of sexual politics. When white women look at Black women's works they are of course ill-equipped to deal with the subtleties of racial politics. A Black feminist

approach to literature that embodies the realization that the politics of sex as well as the politics of race and class are crucially interlocking factors in the works of Black women writers is an absolute necessity. Until a Black feminist criticism exists we will not even know what these writers mean. (134)

Here Smith echoes and employs the theoretical framework or logic of multiple and interlocking oppression outlined in the Combahee River Collective's "A Black Feminist Statement" as an analytical perspective to redress the omission and biased readings of race, class, gender, and sexuality in works written by Black women writers. She later extends that framework as a rationale for thinking of Black women writers as forming a tradition:

> Beginning with a primary commitment to exploring how both sexual and racial politics and Black and female identity are inextricable elements in Black women's writing, she [a black feminist critic] would also work from the assumption that Black women writers constitute an identifiable literary tradition. (B. Smith [1977b] 2000, 137)

Smith's feminist literary statement extends political interests for readers with its analysis of the critical reception of these works as she outlines an approach that strives to define *a* (and not *the*) tradition.[3] She outlines a list of principles that Black feminist critics could use, each qualified with "might" or "could," anticipating multiple ways of approaching readings of Black women's writings. However, subsequent critics would take Smith to task for her prescriptive readings of Black women's motifs, her reading of Toni Morrison's *Sula* as a lesbian novel, and her call for Black feminist literary critics to work in terms of tradition. Smith's claim that Black women writers could be read as "an identifiable literary tradition" led Black feminist scholars to engage in critical conversations regarding whether and how to read Black women authors in the ways she proposed (Christian 1980; McDowell 1980; Carby 1987b, 7–11; Awkward 1991; duCille 1993; Wall 2005b). Of course, these discussions have been largely academic ones, and rarely did they seriously consider the production of Black literature criticisms for the activist purposes that Barbara Smith outlined in her original statement.

Originally published in the journal *Conditions*, Smith's essay "Toward a Black Feminist Criticism" was an intervention into literary criticism that largely excluded Black women writers. Despite her carefully qualified suggestions for criticism, Smith is definite about the approach that Black feminist literary critics "would" take:

> The Black feminist critic would be constantly aware of the political implications of her work and would assert the connections between it and the

political situation of all Black women. Logically developed, Black feminist criticism would owe its existence to a Black feminist movement while at the same time contributing ideas that women in the movement could use. ([1977b] 2000, 138)

Smith's aims for tradition building are for the purposes of establishing a community of readers and writers and activists who are connected in their diverse interests in the feminist movement(s) to address interlocking oppressions. One goal of this tradition building would be to establish and provide a sense of the diversity of Black women's experience through a consideration of the works of many authors and their many characters; an extended application of her approach may well have avoided the elevation of Hurston as uniquely central to the tradition of Black women writers.

During the advent of poststructuralism literary studies, Barbara Christian modeled such an approach in her reading of the work of Alice Walker, "We Are the Ones That We Have Been Waiting For: Political Content in Alice Walker's Novels" (1986), one year before "The Race for Theory" (1987). Christian's essay, with its focus on Walker's political intent, was informed by her need to affirm a Black feminist literary approach within American literary studies during an age of "radical avant garde" criticism (1986, 421). She comments, "It strikes me ironic that as groups who have traditionally been silenced begin to 'penetrate' the literary market, we learn that neither the world nor meaning exists. That a text is but a reference to other texts" (421). She argues that Alice Walker's representation of "coming to consciousness," as well as her treatment of Black women characters as they resist power in the domestic and public spheres, are ways that Walker appeals to readers' desire for social justice and teaches them how to effect both personal and social change in the face of multiple oppressions. In light of the Walker effect, we can see that Walker's popular reception as Hurston's literary daughter has, in its own way, shaped what general and academic audiences know and remember about Walker's feminist legacy and body of work.[4] However, Christian's reading moves beyond *The Color Purple*, Walker's most celebrated work, in its efforts to read Walker's legacy through the lens of her commitment to social justice.

Where does this brief reassessment of Smith's call for Black feminist literary criticism and Christian's response lead us? If one is to judge the success of the early labors of Black feminist literary critics by today's fruits, then their efforts are indeed successful. For example, Barbara Smith extended the literary goals of both "A Black Feminist Statement" and "Toward a Black Feminist Criticism," co-founding Kitchen Table: Women of Color Press, which described itself as "the only publisher in North America committed to publishing and distributing the writing of Third World women of all racial/cultural heritages, sexuality, and classes" (B. Smith 1989, 12). That press produced a body of significant anthologies that lay a foundation for Black women's studies and illustrated the demand for Black women's literature and criticism. Since that time, a number of literary traditions have been influenced and defined as a result of the pioneering efforts of the production of these and other Black feminist scholar-activists and writers, and they take us well into the twenty-first century. Journalists, poets, clergy, elementary and high school educators, lawyers, and politicians; political scientists, physicians, social workers, and psychologists; visual and performing artists, and, of course, grassroots scholar-activists, routinely draw from the wellspring of Black feminist thought found in the fiction and nonfiction writings of Black women produced across hundreds of years. And with the advent of new technologies, from Black feminist blogs to Black Twitter, the publishing interests of Black feminists have, in some ways, exponentially moved beyond concerns of invisibility (and certainly beyond institutional structures of the academy), although ongoing problems regarding modes of marginality, misinterpretation, objectification, and access remain.[5]

Altogether, this application of literature, this Black feminist literary praxis, emerged, shaped and continues to shape any number of discourses, engagements, and interventions. At this present moment, Black feminist scholar-activists no longer lack relevant material, as Bambara protested, although they must continue to defend their hard-won access to all manner of spaces, including academic ones, in order to do the work. And Black feminist scholar-activists and artists need no longer work in isolation from each other. They form multiple and diverse communities. The legacy these pioneers created continue to support contemporary liberatory efforts to produce contemporary, historical, and speculative literary and cultural work that seek social-justice and to make a lasting and positive difference. In many instances that liberatory effort, as Barbara Christian reminds us in the first epigraph to this epilogue, is as fundamental as creating opportunities for future readers of all backgrounds and interests to examine and study the work of Black women thinkers as authoritative without undue censure.

The second epigraph framing this chapter comes from *Black Feminist Anthropology: Theory, Politics, Praxis, and Poetics* (2001), and it is a reminder of the care that should be taken in defining traditions and canons, particularly for Black feminist anthropologists. Remarkably, efforts to define a Black feminist tradition in anthropology were not codified until the publication of this anthology in the early twenty-first century, although they were born of the same movements that developed Black feminist literary criticisms.[6] That delay might reflect the special gatekeeping constraints within the discipline, which the anthology works to reveal. Edited by anthropologist Irma McClaurin, *Black Feminist Anthropology* provides a collection of critical essays that together define and historicize the terms "Black" and "feminist" within the discipline of anthropology. Its form, featuring autoethnographic essays by individual Black women anthropologists, merges biography and critical analysis to situate the theoretical concerns of Black feminist anthropologists within a discussion of each anthropologist's experience of racism and sexism. Its vindicationist perspective, then, works on two levels: (1) to revise anthropology (through its attention to the politics of canon formation), and (2) to survey the diverse kinds of work that Black feminist anthropologists engage in concerning race and gender in global contexts. Contributors note how their experiences as Black women anthropologists from the West shape not only their interests in research in the African diaspora and other locations but also how their race, nationality, and gender complicate and facilitate their experiences in the field. As such, many of the contributors note the distinct contributions they provide to larger anthropological discussions concerning the politics of fieldwork and knowledge production. In both of these ways, through making readers more aware of their research interests, and in discussing the politics of their presence within a discipline known for having contributed significantly to scientific racism, this text responds to the institutional and critical invisibility of Black women anthropologists in the fields of anthropology and feminist anthropology.

Irma McClaurin consciously situates Black feminist anthropology at the crossroads of two intellectual histories—African American studies and anthropology:

> As part of a Black intellectual tradition, we claim a consciousness that identifies race as a social construction bolstered by a structural reality that is harsh and striking in its economic, political, and social ramifications. To understand how the "race" concept has come to pervade the thinking and policies of U.S. society and resulted in some of the most dehumanizing institutions, practices, and behaviors that defy rationality, morality, and spirituality, we trace our genealogy through the writings of Sojourner Truth, Frederick Douglass, W.E.B. Du Bois, Ida B. Wells, Anna Cooper, Zora Neale Hurston, Katherine Dunham, and St. Claire Drake, to name only a few. (2001a, 9)

In McClaurin's genealogy of Black intellectuals, Zora Neale Hurston is listed as one of many contributors (from a variety of "disciplinary" perspectives) to a Black feminist anthropological tradition. In historicizing the contributions of Black women in anthropology, McClaurin provides a timeline that, while not exhaustive, is "the beginning of an effort to document the contribution of Black women/Black feminist anthropologists" (8n).

Although Hurston is not explicitly placed at the center of this tradition, as she was in some African American and Black feminist literary criticisms, there are strong indications that her work is regarded as particularly influential within the field of Black feminist anthropology. Epigraphs from and about Hurston's work frame "Forging a Theory, Politics, Praxis, and Poetics of Black Feminist Anthropology," McClaurin's introduction to the volume: one from P. Gabrielle Foreman's critical essay "Looking Back from Zora, or Talking Out of Both Sides of My Mouth for Those Who Have Two Ears" (1990), and one from Zora Neale Hurston's "What White Publishers Won't Print" (1950). Foreman's quotation concerns the need for defining a "tradition" as a means of challenging the "silencing" of work by and about Black women (Foreman 1990, 649–66; McClaurin 2001b, 1). In "What White Publishers Won't Print," Hurston critiques publishers for being interested only in works that reify stereotypical attitudes concerning the Negro ([1950] 1995, 954).[7] McClaurin references both quotations to illustrate the academic racism that marginalizes Black women and constrains their participation and reception within anthropology and the politics of defining a tradition within those contexts (McClaurin 2001b, 1–2).

Beyond framing epigraphs, McClaurin's essay makes the occasional rhetorical moves that promote Hurston as central to the Black feminist anthropological tradition. In her historical overview of African American anthropological writings, McClaurin describes Hurston's work as "the apex of this legacy" (2001b, 11–12).[8] The signifier "apex" brings to mind Walker's reclamation of Hurston for literary audiences in terms that denote its singular importance among a body of other artists within the tradition. McClaurin also represents Hurston as a major symbol of the tradition that is defined by her introductory chapter and by the whole anthology: "Through Hurston it is possible to see that the roots of the foundation upon which Black feminist anthropology is built are cross-cultural, historical, interdisciplinary, literary, and deeply ethnographic" (5).

In addition, Hurston's work is mentioned within several of the collected essays. A survey of the index reveals that she is noted more frequently than any other individual anthropologist. More specifically, she is described as marking the beginning of "reflexive and dialogic forms" within anthropology (McClaurin 2001a, 66); as a "genre bending" foremother (Bolles 2001, 39) whose ethnographies reveal innovative methodologies and ethnographic productions (McClaurin 2001a, 72n13) that contemporary Black feminists reference and employ; and as an early example of the experience of doing native anthropology

(Rodriguez 2001, 245). Paulla Ebron describes how her "discovery" of Hurston's biography led her to the field of anthropology and to "Black women as critical voices" (2001, 212). These references briefly nod to the impact of poststructuralist readings of anthropology on the reception of her work, as well as the larger influence of her Black feminist recuperation and legacy. A. Lynn Bolles notes that Hurston's work, like that of later generations of contemporary Black feminist anthropologists, continues to be marginalized from mainstream anthropological discourses and histories, and that her work remains to be critically investigated: "Hurston has yet to be critically analyzed 'as an anthropologist' in the same manner by someone in the discipline. Most works on Hurston seem preoccupied with her personality and literary production, giving little attention to a deep analysis of her ethnographic work and her alternative research methods" (2001, 31).

McClaurin's and Bolles's situating of Hurston within the Black feminist anthropological tradition may seem reminiscent of the Black feminist literary move to define and historicize a matrilineal tradition some thirty years before. However, McClaurin's edited collection features photographs of each contributor and "autoethnographic" discussions of their varied class and racial backgrounds. Therefore, there is a strong impulse to define the tradition as heterogeneous and independent of Hurston's significance. Because the anthology functions primarily as a reader that introduces audiences to the very presence of Black women in the field of anthropology and their critical research interests, little narrative is spent lionizing Hurston's contributions over and above the contributing anthropologists. The multiple anthologies of early Black feminist literary criticisms, in their numbers, make it easier to read for iconic receptions of Hurston as central to the Black feminist literary tradition. This lone anthology does not. In short, it is a space where Black women anthropologists largely inscribe themselves as a community into a dynamic tradition.

Avoiding "Hurstonism," the volume illustrates tradition more broadly, largely refusing to give Hurston a first or central status in its canon (duCille 1993, 80–82), and it highlights the importance of historical context in linking central figures and their works in any delineation of tradition and canon. For example, Bolles's essay "Seeking the Ancestors: Onward and Upward into the Twenty-First Century" (2001) provides brief biographies on the work of Caroline Bond Day, Irene Diggs, Katherine Dunham, Vera Green, and Zora Neale Hurston, clearly ushering in a community of women as foremothers (24–48). Despite admitted concerns that linking these women together in a shared tradition might be labeled revisionist history, Bolles argues that these Black women anthropologists might be linked as feminist foremothers because of their shared interests in vindicationist projects that treated research as a form of activism, their use of historical and comparative methods, and their treatment of racial oppression as intersectional (41). Linking them together as part of traditions acknowledges their pioneering efforts to work within a discipline that has long marginalized the work of Black women while also establishing a history that might serve as a model for current and future Black feminists in the discipline (41–43).

As in Black feminist literary studies, Black feminist anthropologists link their own work to one another via their interests in exploring multiple oppressions (race, class, gender, sexuality) as interlocking, often drawing on the same foundational works, like Toni Cade Bambara's *The Black Woman* (1970) and Patricia Hill Collins's *Black Feminist Thought* (1990), as critical sources. They also remain grounded in multiple sources, which anthropologist Johnnetta B. Cole notes grounds their work in the "tools of literature, sociology, history, and the interdisciplinary arenas of Black studies and women's studies" (Cole x). In addition, McClaurin situates the literature, theories, and practices of Black feminist anthropology as concerned with concepts of "race" as well as concepts of "culture." This means that in addition to reviewing critical literature from anthropology, Black feminist anthropologists also refer to the critical literature and theories of scholars who contributed to the interdisciplinary study of race and culture from outside anthropology, such as history and sociology. Faye Harrison and Ira Harrison have noted that the process of historicizing the contributions of Black scholars to anthropology means acknowledging the contributions of African Americans who contributed to ethnography from across disciplinary borders: "Why should such individuals be denied recognition within anthropology when the acknowledged forerunners (e.g., Durkheim and Morgan) and even some of the founders (e.g., Boas) of the discipline were not trained in anthropology?" (1999, 11). Harrison and Harrison note the systemic institutional racism that either barred access to anthropology or shaped scholars' decisions to choose other disciplinary homes. For example, Frederick Douglass, Martin Delaney, and W.E.B. Du Bois are credited with having produced ethnographies concerning race and culture outside the discipline of anthropology (11). That African American anthropologists, including Black feminist anthropologists, detail this aspect of their intellectual projects reflects a shared concern and experience with challenges to the intellectual authority of Black scholars of race and culture within the field. This approach informs my reading of Hurston's ethnographies against the ethnographic monographs of Charles Johnson, Hortense Powdermaker, and Melville Herskovits as well as my interdisciplinary reading of Hurston's critical reception across literature and anthropology.

Hurston's differing receptions across disciplinary boundaries seem to prescribe a move against feminist icon making, canon making, and tradition building because these activities privilege a special and individualized status of a few token writers and their "classic" works over a broad set of works for critical engagement. Still, traditions, and even icons, and their imagined communities remain important as rhetorical and pragmatic strategies for transforming consciousness beyond the academy. Moreover, disciplines continue to crown their icon(s), codified in anthologies that present "founders" of thought and coded in the informal stories shared in many classrooms, most often, about the lives of great pioneering men. Perhaps it is a "cultural universal" that in creating communities, even academic ones, icons are built. In either case, Hurston chose not to be "tragically colored," but she was aware of the persistence of structural inequality and she was strategic about her engagement with it.[9] I imagine that she would not be astonished by her marginalization in anthropology (or even her lionization in literature), give the complicated receptions of her work during her lifetime. Or maybe, as she said, she would be.[10] Either way, the irony of it all would not have been lost on her.

As Hurston stated in her analysis of the loa Guede, "Gods always behave like the people who make them" ([1938] 1990, 219). For this reason, historical contextualization and a commitment to interdisciplinarity remain central to our project. As we produce transformative ways of reading individual and collective literary and cultural works in the development of intellectual histories, the stories we tell are multiple and are grounded by our diverse communities.

Notes

Introduction

1. "How It Feels to Be Colored Me" was originally published in "The World Tomorrow" in 1928. Deborah Plant reads this essay as an example of Hurston's philosophy of individualism as shaped by her hometown, an "all-Black Eatonville," informed by Booker T. Washington's moral attitude toward anti-Black racism, and further influenced by her studies with Franz Boas in anthropology (Plant 1995, 35–42). Regarding Hurston's studies in anthropology, Plant notes, "To the extent that she could validate and demonstrate the value of African American cultural traditions, she felt her own self self-worth and self-esteem ([2007] 2011, 42).

2. See also Ann duCille, "On Canons: Anxious History and the Rise of Black Feminist Literary Studies" (2006). DuCille provides a brief history of the field and notes that assumptions about "shared experience and common language" were a critical impasse in its development (43).

3. Many scholars have noted how available Hurston's work is now and have discussed the impact of her popularity. These scholars include Hazel Carby and Ann duCille, whose discussions I describe in more detail in chapter 2.

4. West's *Zora Neale Hurston and American Literary Culture* (2005) is largely a treatment of the critical reception of Hurston's major works immediately following their publication and the impact of her publisher's marketing strategies on subsequent reviews of her work. Her later archival work expands and revises receptions of Hurston in terms of her gendered politics and focus on Southern locales, fulfilling Frances Smith Foster's call for a "literary archaeology" that expands our literary corpus. See Foster 2006; West 2014, 2015.

5. See also Maxine Hong Kingston's "Cultural Mis-readings by American Reviewers" (1982), in which she expressed similar concerns about biased readings of her memoir, *The Woman Warrior* (1976). Kingston's memoir, like *Their Eyes Were Watching God* and *Sula*, is now considered a feminist classic.

6. See Cheryl Wall's "Histories and Heresies: Engendering the Harlem Renaissance" (2001) for her discussion of the ways that feminist scholars expanded critical discussions of the Harlem Renaissance to include the oft-neglected and disregarded contributions of Black women writers, including Zora Neale Hurston. Given the "recuperation" of Hurston, which she recounts in part, Wall states, "A book could, and I am certain, will be written analyzing the recuperation of Zora Neale Hurston, the woman and the writer" (66–67).

7. Ann duCille (2005) says that although Hurston's works were out of print, they were circulated among students, family, and friends.

8. Hurston reportedly referred to herself on occasion as "Queen of the Niggerati" (Hemenway [1977] 1980, 44).

9. This essay would later be titled "Looking for Zora" for its publication as the afterword in *I Love Myself When I Am Laughing . . . and Then Again When I Am Looking Mean and Impressive* (1979a) and in *In Search of Our Mothers' Gardens: Womanist Prose* (Walker [1975a] 1983).

10. See Bruce Weber, "Joy and Blues in Florida Piney Woods," *New York Times*, April 25, 2002. In addition, celebrated Black arts poet and musician Mari Evans (1923–2017) authored a musical adaptation of *Their Eyes Were Watching God* titled *Eyes*, which played at Karamu House in Cleveland, Ohio, in the late 1970s.

11. Spike Lee's film *She's Gotta Have It* references Hurston's *Their Eyes Were Watching God* in the original film (1986) version and the revamped 2017 Netflix series.

12. Valerie Boyd (1963–2022) was the Charlayne Hunter-Gault Distinguished Writer in Residence, director of the MFA in the Narrative Nonfiction program, and director of the Giving Voice to the Voiceless grant program. In addition to authoring *Wrapped in Rainbows*, she edited *Gathering Blossoms under Fire: The Journals of Alice Walker, 1965–2000* (2022), published as this work goes to press.

13. Zora Neale Hurston, *You Don't Know Us Negroes and Other Essays* (2022).

14. For example, see author Tayari Jones's foreword in Hurston, West, and Jones, *Hitting a Straight Lick with a Crooked Stick* (2020, ix-x), a collection of Hurston's short stories.

15. See Irma McClaurin, "Zora Neale Hurston: Enigma, Heterodox, and Progenitor of Black Studies" (2012). McClaurin has called for a full study of Hurston's anthropology: "What gets lost in the emphasis on Hurston as a literary figure is the analytical contributions she made as a theorist on Black culture" (59). McClaurin's larger commitment to defining Black feminist anthropology at the beginning of the twenty-first century is discussed in the epilogue.

16. The Smithsonian National Postal Museum credits the stamp as "designed by Howard E. Paine and contains Drew Struzan's portrait of Zora Neale Hurston with a Florida background that represents the setting from her novel *Their Eyes Were Watching God*." https://postalmuseum.si.edu/exhibition/women-on-stamps-part-3-literature-from-abolition-to

-civil-rights/zora-neale-hurston. "Negrotarian" is the term of affection that Hurston gave to whites who were interested in Black life and culture during the Harlem Renaissance.

17. See Hurston's "Characteristics of Negro Expression" ([1934] 1995), where she observes that African Americans, due to their African cultural heritage, like to set and do things at an aesthetic angle: dance, art, and interior design. Some have argued that the essay makes essentialist claims; however, the essay is widely regarded as an example of Hurston's attempt to describe patterns of cultural aesthetics and performance. Also see Lynda Marion Hill's *Social Rituals and the Verbal Art of Zora Neale Hurston* (1996) and Eve Dunbar's *Black Regions of the Imagination* (2013).

18. From United States Postal Service press release, "Postal News," dated January 24, 2003.

19. Although Black women writers like Gwendolyn Brooks and Maya Angelou have been honored with stamps in recent years, thus far Hurston is the one Black woman writer "canonized" by the USPS Literary Arts Series. Her stamp, remarkably, led the way for the recognition of notable Black male fiction writers by the series. Thus far, the series includes James Baldwin in 2004, Richard Wright in 2009, and Ralph Ellison in 2014.

20. Hurston describes her approach to gathering data in *Mules and Men* as discussed in chapter 5.

21. The image on file at the Library of Congress (Lomax Collection) has been updated to reflect that Valerie Boyd's 2003 biography of Hurston notes that the photo is not of Zora Neale Hurston. In Boyd's biography of Hurston, *Wrapped in Rainbows: The Life of Zora Neale Hurston*, Boyd writes, "The picture apparently became mixed up with the library's collection of Hurston photographs, causing archivists to assume it was a shot of Zora. Once it was published as such, scholars continued to perpetuate the error—despite Lomax's notifying the Library of Congress, in 1993, that the photo was not of Hurston" (437).

22. The *American Masters* television series provides its own well-respected canon of key figures in American cultural history. The program is described as "an ongoing series of award-winning primetime specials examining the lives, works, and creative processes of our most outstanding cultural artists." http://www.pbs.org/wnet/americanmasters/about/index.html/.

23. For example, the book covers of Hurston's *The Sanctified Church* (1981) and *Spunk: The Selected Short Stories of Zora Neale Hurston* (1985) feature the image of the misidentified "smiling woman."

24. Its goal is "To celebrate the life and work of Zora Neale Hurston; To celebrate the historic significance of Eatonville; To celebrate the cultural contributions which people of African ancestry have made to the United States and to world culture." Association to Preserve the Eatonville Community, Inc., https://zorafestival.org/about/zora-neale-hurston/.

25. Hurston was born in Notasulga, Alabama, but claims Eatonville as her hometown.

26. The press release for the 2008 festival is titled "ZORA! Festival '08 to Deliver Something for Everyone."

27. "Women's Forum: Women Empowered for Economic Revival beyond the Pandemic and Injustice," January 28, 2021. https://zorafestival.org/schedule-2021/womens-forum/program-description/.

28. The festival centers on a different theme each year and provides an opportunity for discussion about other important figures in the arts and sciences.

29. There is another festival ("Zora Fest") held annually in St. Lucie County, Fort Pierce, Florida, where Hurston died and where she is buried at the Garden of Heavenly Rest.

30. Halle Berry won Best Actress for *Monster's Ball* (2001).

31. Many critics found that the television adaptation flattened the plot to the romantic interests between Janie and Tea Cake and ignored the many social and politically charged moments of the novel.

32. Elaine Showalter states, "Reclaiming our feminist icons is a necessary step in our collective memoir" (2001, 19). Showalter distinguishes between two types of icons: "I intend the term *icon* in its classical sense of 'revered symbol.' But the term has been debased in popular culture to mean a commercialized visual image or nonverbal sound endlessly repeated, packaged, parodied, marketed, and plugged. Nowadays, *icon* is a word usually linked with 'celebrity' or 'superstardom'" (14).

33. In her introduction to the second volume of *Moving beyond Boundaries*, Carole Boyce Davies writes that in the case of Phillis Wheatley and Gwendolyn Brooks, with their repeated inclusion "from anthology to anthology, readers begin to have some familiarity with their names if not with their corpus" (1995, 2: 6–7).

34. Sarah M. Corse and Monica D. Griffin (1997) describe Walker's influence in terms of "cultural entrepreneurship" in their sociological study of the canonization of *Their Eyes*, noting the work of Paul DiMaggio (1982).

Chapter 1. On Firsts, Foremothers, and the "Walker Effect"

I have coined the phrase the "Walker effect" to explain Alice Walker's authoritative presence on both sides of the feminist borders between literary and anthropological studies. The occurrence in anthropology is discussed further in chapter 3. While I explore Walker's early essays in detail in this section, I do not intend to impose a Walker effect in my reading of the subsequent critical literature by Black feminist scholars concerning Hurston's import. Rather, I intend to trace how themes of Black authenticity and Black language that were already present in the Black Arts movement were discursively transferred and amplified because of Walker's popular and commercial impact.

1. Although Walker is much celebrated, she was also often and problematically criticized by Black male critics for her literary representations of Black male violence against Black women and for her portrayal of same-sex relationships in some of her novels. Of course, Walker was not alone. See Wall's "The Writer as Critic in the Emergence of Black Feminism" for a discussion of how Walker and other writers (including Toni Cade Bambara, June Jordan, Audre Lorde, Paule Marshall, and Ntozake Shange) produced works as "artist-critics" (2016, 19).

2. In many other ways, Black women feminist scholars complicated assumptions about shared oppression. In particular, they redefined Black motherhood as complicated by race, class, gender, and sexuality. Sociologist Daniel Moynihan's *The Negro Family: The*

Case for National Action (1965) pathologized the Black family as "matriarchal" and largely located the social inequality of Black people in the United States with Black women's role in the Black family. In response, Black women scholar-activists used their art and their public scholarship to present the complexity of Black women's experiences as neither all-powerful emasculators nor tragic vessels, even as they faced racism, sexism, and other forms of oppression. They also pushed back against separatist strategies in the women's liberation movement that called for women to separate from all men in order to dismantle male patriarchy. Rooted in the Black community and committed to addressing oppressions as interlocking, many sought instead to "struggle together with Black men against racism, while we also struggle with Black men about sexism" (B. Smith [1977a] 2009, 6). Their writings confirm the importance of community solidarity even as they work to critique and challenge misogyny.

3. DuCille's "The Mark of Zora" (2005) offers a brief literary history of Hurston's emergence alongside the emergence of black feminist literary criticism. She discusses how "the legend of Zora" misses this history and notes the significance of Walker's essays and others like them in shaping Hurston's receptions. I provide a detailed and extended discussion of rhetorical representations of Hurston's significance as framed within these works.

4. While I am focusing on the critical literature created by Black women literary critics during this era, it should also be noted that many other cultural productions were created during this period and beyond to represent and extend related themes from Hurston's work for Black audiences. For example, celebrated Black Arts poet and musician Mari Evans (1923–2017) authored a musical adaptation of *Their Eyes Were Watching God* titled *Eyes* (1979), which played at Karamu House in Cleveland, Ohio.

5. Another article within the same issue, titled "Black Folk Spirit and the Shape of Black Literature," begins, "Black folk art is the manifestation of Black spirit, carried on its own momentum from Africa" (Taylor 1972, 31). Referencing the work of many of Hurston's Harlem Renaissance contemporaries, including Sterling Brown, Claude McKay, and Jean Toomer, this article illustrates the period's interest in returning to these authors as "the originators of the concept of Negritude in everything but name, turning to our roots in the 'second Africa' that the Black South had become" (34).

6. The image appears to be a reproduction of a Van Vechten photograph of Hurston in profile.

7. Ellease Southerland also authored "The Influence of Voodoo on the Fiction of Zora Neale Hurston," in *Sturdy Black Bridges: Visions of Black Women in Literature* (1979).

8. The same title is used in the caption beneath Hurston's image on the front cover of this issue.

9. These include but are not limited to Mari Evans's *I Am a Black Woman* (1970); Toni Cade Bambara's *The Black Woman* (1970); Pat Crutchfield Exum's *Keeping the Faith: Writing by Contemporary Black American Women* (1974); Mary Helen Washington's *Black-Eyed Susans: Classic Stories by and about Black Women* (1975); Roseann P. Bell, Bettye J. Parker, and Beverly Guy-Sheftall's *Sturdy Black Bridges: Visions of Black Women in Literature* (1979); Barbara Christian's *Black Women Novelists: The Development of a Tradition*

(1980); bell hook's *Ain't I a Woman: Black Women and Feminism* (1981); Gloria T. Hull, Patricia Bell Scott, and Barbara Smith's *All the Women Are White, All the Blacks Are Men, but Some of Us Are Brave* (1982); Barbara Smith's *Home Girls: A Black Feminist Anthology* (1983); Claudia Tate's *Black Women Writers at Work* (1983); and Gloria Wade-Gayles's *No Crystal Stair: Visions of Race and Sex in Black Women's Fiction* (1984). For extended discussions regarding histories of Black feminist literary criticisms and Black women's studies, see Beverly Guy Sheftall's "The Evolution of Feminist Consciousness among African American Women" (1995a); Farah Jasmine Griffin's "That the Mothers May Soar and the Daughters May Know Their Names: A Retrospective of Black Feminist Literary Criticism" (2007); and Stanlie M. James, Frances Smith Foster, and Beverly Guy Sheftall's introduction to *Still Brave: The Evolution of Black Women's Studies* (2009).

10. One need only note the publication of Alice Walker's *Once* (1968), *In Love and Trouble: Stories of Black Women* (1973b), and *Revolutionary Petunias and Other Poems* (1973d) to get a sense of her prolific output and singular voice. Walker defines "womanist" in *In Search of Our Mothers' Gardens: Womanist Prose* as "a black feminist or feminist of color" (1983b, xi).

11. There are other essays authored by Walker that briefly reference Hurston. See also "A Talk: Convocation 1972," in *In Search of Our Mothers' Garden: Womanist Prose*, where Walker briefly states, "And Zora Neale Hurston, who wrote what is perhaps the most authentic and moving Black love story ever published, died in poverty in the swamps of Florida, where she was again working as a housemaid" ([1972] 1983, 35). I will return to the theme of tragic readings of Hurston later in this chapter. The five described here, however, do so in ways that rhetorically promote Hurston as a central woman writer in Black literary history

12. Additionally, critical essays often paired the two writers together to trace the influence that Hurston's work had on Walker's early fiction. I will discuss this "coupling" later in this chapter.

13. See Carby 1990, 71–93; Corse and Griffin 1997, 176; Gates 1993, xii; duCille 1993, 85; and West 2005, 249.

14. Its headline reads "The Fabulous Zora Neale Hurston; Rediscovering Zora Neale Hurston; ... A Readiness for Someone Who Never Held Back; The Rebellious Novelist, Pioneering Folklorist and Spellbinding Raconteur of the Harlem Renaissance Died in Obscurity in 1960, but Now She Has Become the Center of a New Cult." Jacqueline Trescott, *Washington Post*, May 21, 1978, Sunday, Final Edition.

15. Spillers (2004) notes Walker's essay in an article/review of Barbara Johnson's *A World of Difference* (1987). Spillers also notes the inscription on Hurston's grave marker and typesets it to visually recreate the marker on the page. She notes Toni Cade Bambara's "Some Forward Remarks" in *The Sanctified Church* ([1981] 1998), where Bambara also begins her remarks with the marker as an epigraph (Spillers 2004, 94).

16. Some scholars questioned the predominant attention given to Zora Neale Hurston. Hazel Carby, Ann duCille, Cheryl Walker, and others have questioned and expanded the discussion concerning her place as Black literary foremother and challenged the grounds

upon which arguments are made concerning her particular place at the forefront of the Black woman's literary canon. DuCille in particular has elaborated how some critical reviews of Hurston have affected notions of the Black woman's literary tradition. I will return to this point and her argument later in this chapter.

17. A news article titled "Lost and Found" by staff writer Cynthia Tucker appeared on the first page of the "Dixie Living" section of the *Atlanta Journal-Constitution* on February 3, 1991. Tucker noted the "rise" in Hurston's "literary reputation" and described the "Zora" festival (noting that no last name was needed) held amid what she described as Eatonville's "decline." Tucker suggested that perhaps the town might benefit from the renewed interest in Hurston's work. She concludes the article: "And so it was that Ms. Walker found her unmarked grave in Fort Pierce and bought a tombstone for it. She had it inscribed with these words: "ZORA NEALE HURSTON 'A GENIUS OF THE SOUTH' NOVELIST FOLKLORIST ANTHROPOLOGIST" (1). Like Spillers, Tucker typesets this text to represent Hurston's tombstone on the page.

18. *Ms.* magazine reprinted this essay in its September/October 1997 issue and again in its spring 2002 issue. See Cheryl Wall's "In Search of Our Mothers' Gardens and Our Fathers' (Real) Estates: Alice Walker, Essayist," in *Worrying the Line: Black Women Writers, Lineage, and Literary Tradition* (2005a), for a sustained reading of Walker's work as an essayist.

19. Walker's short story "Everyday Use," published in *In Love and Trouble* (1973), includes a similar theme.

20. Phillis Wheatley published *Poems on Various Subjects* in 1773 and is noted as the first African American to publish a book in the U.S. colonies. Nella Larsen was a writer during the Harlem Renaissance. She was the author of *Quicksand* (1928) and *Passing* (1929), whose subject matter dealt with the issue of skin color, race, gender, and class. The idea of "contrary instincts" will be returned to later in the book, as it plays a part in understanding contemporary representations of Hurston's work.

21. "It is not so much what you sang, as that you kept alive, in so many of our ancestors, *the notion of song*" (Walker [1974] 1983, 237). Imagining Wheatley's African mother, Walker concludes the essay with "Perhaps she was herself a poet—though only her daughter's name is signed to the poems we know. Perhaps Phillis Wheatley's mother was also an artist. Perhaps, in more than Phillis Wheatley's biological life is her mother's signature made clear" (243).

22. "In Search of Zora Neale Hurston" would later be titled "Looking for Zora" for its publication as the afterword in *I Love Myself When I Am Laughing . . . and Then Again When I Am Looking Mean and Impressive* (1979) and in *In Search of Our Mothers' Gardens: Womanist Prose* (1983), perhaps to prevent confusion between the two essays.

23. Hurston describes Eatonville as her birthplace in her autobiography, *Dust Tracks on the Road* (1942); however, public records would later reveal that she was born in Notasulga, Alabama, in 1891. This essay, published in *The Harlem Renaissance Remembered* (1972), edited by Arna Bontemps, is noteworthy for its discussion of the impact of Hurston's anthropological education on her literary work. Robert Hemenway would author *Zora*

Neale Hurston: A Literary Biography in 1977. Alice Walker would write its foreword, "Zora Neale Hurston: A Cautionary Tale and a Partisan View" (1977), to be discussed later in this chapter.

24. The tragicomical scene includes Walker in search of Zora's sunken grave. She calls out to Hurston, "Are you out here?" Walker's friend quips back, "If she is, I sho hope she don't answer you. If she do, I'm gone," in Walker's "Looking for Zora" (305) and "In Search of Zora Neale Hurston" (85).

25. "Canon" here has its own religious overtones and implications as addressed in Barbara Christian's essay "The Race for Theory" ([1987] 2000, 283).

26. For example, Toni Cade Bambara notes the marker in "Some Forward Remarks" in Zora Neale Hurston, *The Sanctified Church* ([1981] 1998); Hortense Spillers notes the marker in "A Tale of Three Zoras" (2004), as does journalist Cynthia Tucker in her article "Lost and Found" (1991).

27. Hurston biographer Valerie Boyd published "Looking for Alice" (March/April 1988) in *Ms.* magazine. The essay signifies on Walker's "Looking for Zora" as Boyd employs similar rhetorical arguments/motifs/movements as found in Alice Walker's essay on Zora Neale Hurston. Boyd visits Alice Walker's hometown in Eatonton, Georgia, to learn more about Alice Walker the writer. Boyd questions why Alice Walker is not celebrated in her hometown. In addition, Boyd draws genealogical lines between herself, Hurston, and Walker. She writes, "Recently it occurred to me that if Zora is my spiritual and artistic grandmother, then Alice—who put a marker on Hurston's weed-choked grave in 1973—is my mother. So I suppose I drove to Eatonton, to borrow Alice's phrase, in search of my mother's garden" (Boyd 1998, 90).

28. The term "Voodoo" is an offensive spelling. I use the term "Voodoo" to reflect the original transcripts of the works by Zora Neale Hurston and others cited in this book. All other references by myself will use "Vodou" to reflect the Policy and Standards Division of the Library of Congress, which as of October 2012 uses "Vodou." The short story is titled "The Revenge of Hannah Kemhuff" (Walker 1973c). Its dedication reads, "In grateful memory of Zora Neale Hurston."

29. Walker's list of "need(s)" might reinforce a stereotypical representation of Vodou, while Zora Neale Hurston's representations attempted to revise and more fully contextualize these rituals in both *Mules and Men* and *Tell My Horse*.

30. Harold Bloom has suggested that Walker describes Hurston as a cultural revolutionary. See Bloom's introduction to *Zora Neale Hurston: Modern Critical Views* (1986a).

31. They include Jean Toomer, Colette, Anaïs Nin, Tillie Olson, and Virginia Woolf. Toni Morrison is the other contemporary Black woman writer frequently mentioned. Morrison is popularly celebrated but in significantly different ways. Carol Boyce Davies offers a brief discussion of Morrison's body of work as engaging "the process of writing oneself into the canon" (1994, 9).

32. Robert Hemenway's biography ([1977] 1980) and Walker's "In Search of Zora Neale Hurston" ([1974] 1983) are often cited as revitalizing the interest in Hurston's work and life.

33. Margaret Walker was a poet and novelist. She authored *For My People* (1942) and *Jubilee* (1966). She was greatly influenced by key writers of the Harlem Renaissance period, most notably Langston Hughes and Richard Wright. Walker would author a critical literary biography of Wright titled *Daemonic Genius* (1988).

34. Critics shunned Hurston during the Harlem Renaissance because her work, in its presentation of rural Black folk life, was judged as not meeting the mandates of Black art in service to the elevation of "the race." "Criteria of Negro Art" by W.E.B. Du Bois ([1926] 1995) and "Blueprint for Negro Writing" by Richard Wright ([1937] 1995) are examples of essays that advocated that writing and art should be aware of themselves always as propaganda and seek to express an explicit "social consciousness" in literary representations of African American life (Du Bois, "Criteria" 103; Wright, "Blueprint" 200–201). Wright's now infamous review of Hurston's *Their Eyes Were Watching God* charged that Hurston's *Their Eyes* portrayed Black life in the minstrel tradition, and he did not consider her work to be "serious fiction" (Wright [1937] 1993, 16–17).

35. This edition featured a foreword by Sherley Ann Williams (1978) and also included the following blurb from Roger Rosenblatt of *The New Republic*: "A good read when the ERA is being discussed and even better in quieter moments." *The New Republic*, founded in 1914, is a progressive political magazine.

36. Literary scholar Mary Helen Washington's introduction, "Zora Neale Hurston: A Woman Half in Shadow," in *I Love Myself When I Am Laughing* (1979) convincingly argues that earlier critics of Hurston often confused her work with her personality. Washington details how aspects of Hurston's personal life were so controversial that they biased critics' readings of Hurston's literary works. However, Washington employs many of the recurring motifs that Walker uses in her essays in representing Hurston's life and work, which suggests that the narrative regarding Hurston's significance was not solely shaped by Walker herself. Washington provides biographical details concerning the unfair critical treatments of Hurston's work related to patron relationships, the "servile" letters that Hurston penned to her financial patron Charlotte Osgood Mason, the controversies of a public and civil trial in which Hurston was alleged to have molested a young boy, controversial statements Hurston made concerning desegregation, and details regarding Hurston's health and illnesses. However, embedded within the reclamation of Hurston, both in Washington's introduction and Walker's dedication to the collection "On Refusing to Be Humbled by Second Place in a Contest You Did Not Design: A Tradition by Now" (1979b) are personal commentaries from Walker and Washington that conflate Hurston's life with her work and that also set her apart from other Black female writers of the same and preceding eras. Walker's dedication does not repeat the "lost and found" motif, but like previous essays, the tragedy of Hurston's death is noted.

37. Both presses published all of these except "On Refusing to Be Humbled" (1979b). This collection also includes "From an Interview," in which Walker briefly discusses Hurston's work and particular influence. Walker mentions that she feels the need for a "real critical treatment and biographical" work on Black women writers that she featured in a course she designed. She states that she is writing "a long personal essay on my own

discovery of these writers (designed primarily for lectures), and hope[s] soon to visit the birthplace and home of Zora Neale Hurston, Eatonville, Florida" (1983a, 256).

38. To be published as a Perennial Classic is to be deemed a part of the American popular literary canon within the publishing industry. Published as the foreword (dated December 1976) to Robert E. Hemenway's *Zora Neale Hurston: A Literary Biography*.

39. Jordan's blurb is located on the back cover of the 1998 First Perennial Classics edition.

40. I have been endearingly referenced as one of Hurston's "granddaughters" because my work focuses on Hurston. Perhaps because of the larger influence of "Hurstonism," I have also been (somewhat playfully) referred to as a "Hurstonite."

41. For example, *Double Stitch: Black Women Write about Mothers and Daughters* (1991), edited by Patricia Bell-Scott, is a collection of creative, critical, and autobiographical writings that focus on Black mother and daughter relationships.

42. As published in *Mothering the Mind* (1984), edited by Ruth Perry and Martine Watson Brownley, which applies the concept of "mothering" toward understanding the role of influential individuals on the works of a number of well-known writers.

43. See Lillie P. Howard's *Zora Neale Hurston* (1980) and "Marriage: Zora Neale Hurston's System of Values" (1977).

44. As mentioned in chapter 1, Ann duCille writes, "I have long been fascinated by the relationship between the arrival of black women and black feminism in the academy in the late 1960s and early 1970s and the reclamation and rise of Hurston as an intellectual subject and a feminist icon. Where would Hurston and black feminist studies be without each other, and how would Hurston wear the feminist mantle?" (2005, 1).

45. More broadly, Gates's theory regarding "literary revision" draws from Hurston's definition of signifying as well as Claudia Mitchell-Kernan's *Language Behavior in a Black Urban Community* (1971) and Geneva Smitherman's *Talkin and Testifyin: The Language of Black America* (1977). See Gates's *The Signifying Monkey: A Theory of African-American Literary Criticism* (1988). The Hurston essay is titled "Art and Such" ([1938] 1988) and is printed for the first time in Gates's anthology *Reading Black, Reading Feminist* (1990) with a postscript by Stetson Kennedy, who had the essay in his possession for over fifty years.

46. See B. Smith, "Sexual Politics and the Fiction of Zora Neale Hurston" (1978b) in *The Radical Teacher* for Smith's reading of the sexual politics of Hurston's exclusion from literary studies.

47. McDowell's commentary, "New Directions for Black Feminist Criticism," on this essay in *The Changing Same* ([1980] 1995) offers a retrospective reading of Barbara Smith's essay, stating that it is "widely and rightly considered the origin and benchmark of the discourse" (17). She explains that her own focus on "female language" was in part due to the critical influence of Annette Kolodny's "Some Notes on Defining a 'Feminist Literary Criticism.'" Kolodny herself worked to intervene into patriarchal discourses of literary criticism within the mainstream (and largely white) academy and argued that critical attention should be given to women writers' "experiments in language" (1975, 85–89).

48. See note 9.

Chapter 2. Signifying "Texts": The Race for Hurston

1. In addition, the journal *Meridians: feminism, race, and transnationalism* was first conceived in 1996, and its first issue was published in 1999 by Duke University Press.

2. See Barbara Smith, "A Black Feminist Statement: *The Combahee River Collective*" ([1977a] 2009); "Toward a Black Feminist Criticism" ([1977b] 2000); and "Sexual Politics and the Fiction of Zora Neale Hurston" (1978).

3. In general, poststructuralism challenges "language, meaning, and subjectivity" as fixed, essentially knowable, and as related and expressed within dynamic social and power relations (Weedon 2000, 19, 20, 21–22).

4. Parallel debates occurred between feminist anthropologist and scholars of postmodernism/structuralism and anthropology. I discuss these debates further in chapter 4.

5. Joyce A. Joyce provides an additional response in "'Who the Cap Fit': Unconsciousness and Unconscionable in the Criticism of Houston Baker, Jr., and Henry Louis Gates, Jr." (1987b). McDowell analyzes these debates at length within "Transferences: Black Feminist Thinking: The 'Practice' of 'Theory'" (1995b, 165–67). See also Michael Awkward's "Appropriative Gestures: Theory and Afro-American Literary Criticism" ([1988] 2000).

6. See Deborah E. McDowell's "Transferences: Black Feminist Thinking: The 'Practice' of 'Theory'" (1995b, 156–75). See also Theodore O. Mason, "Between the Populist and the Scientist: Ideology and Power in Recent Afro-American Literary Criticism; or, 'The Dozens' as Scholarship," *Callaloo* 36 (Summer 1988): 606–15.

7. Johnson cites Roman Jakobson, "Two Aspects of Language and Two Types of Aphasic Disturbances," in Roman Jakobson and Morris Halle, *Fundamentals of Language* (1956).

8. The passages recount Janie's growing disillusion and eventual psychic independence from her second husband, Joe Stark (Hurston [1937] 1998, 71–72), and the ending of the novel, wherein Janie reflects on her journey in the wake of Tea Cake's death (193). In light of the historical contexts of Hurston's studies in anthropology, I provide a reading of this final scene in chapter 3.

9. Christian states, "Instead, I think we need to read the works of our writers in our various ways and remain open to the intricacies of the intersection of language, class, race, and gender in the literature. And it would help if we share our process, that is, our practice, as much as possible since, finally, our work is a collective endeavor" (1987, 53).

10. Johnson cites "Bell Hooks" as Gloria Watkins and *Ain't I a Woman* (1981) to support her discussion of the erasure of Black women ([1987] 1991, 168). Cheryl Wall is noted in an endnote as having discovered that Hurston was older than the age she reported ([1987] 1991, 220–21).

11. See Bloom, introduction to *Zora Neale Hurston (Modern Critical Views)*, ed. Harold Bloom, 1–4.

12. I mean to imply here both "in theory" and "through theory."

13. Gates quotes Victor Erlich, *Russian Formalism: History Doctrine* (1969, 238).

14. Henderson notes the courtroom scene at the end of the novel, in which Janie must speak to multiple (white and Black, male and female) audiences (1989, 121–22).

15. Henderson employs the terms "suppression," "repression," "disruption," "appropriation," and "transformation" (1989, 125).

16. The subtitle is omitted in Henderson's article, as it repeatedly is in critical references to the work, making it easier for critics to ignore that Walker is making a specific argument about Black women's creative expression in the South, notwithstanding the immense diversity of experiences of Black women in the region.

17. The article was originally published in Cheryl A. Wall, *Changing Our Words: Essays on Criticism, Theory, and Writing by Black Women* (1989).

18. Of course, the privileging of *Their Eyes* also marginalizes her non-canonical novels and essays.

19. Again, I echo West's use of the term "convenient" here (2005, 251).

20. DuCille states, "However attractive and culturally affirming, the valorization of the vernacular has yielded what I would argue is an inherently exclusionary literary practice that filters a wide range of complex and often contradictory impulses and energies into a single modality consisting of the blues and the folk" (1993, 69).

21. The predominant attention given to Hurston's work to describe *the* Black feminist literary tradition and poststructuralist readings of her work led readers to privilege Hurston's theoretical authority apart from other Black women writers. In addition, as P. Gabrielle Foreman's "Looking Back from Zora" (1990) and Nellie McKay's "Crayon Enlargements" (1990) suggest and other critics have argued, a predominant focus on Hurston's voice effectively silences the voices of Northern middle-class, Northern proletariat, and Northern nineteenth-century characters in Black women's literary works.

Chapter 3. Deconstructing an Icon: Tradition and Authority

1. It should be noted that during this period Black women literary scholars were working to analyze the literary and cultural productions of nineteenth-century Black women apart from Hurston and on their own terms. For example, see Frances Smith Foster's *Written by Herself: Literary Production by African American Women, 1746–1892* (1993) and Frances Ellen Watkins Harper, *A Brighter Coming Day: A Frances Ellen Watkins Harper Reader* (1990), edited by Frances Smith Foster.

2. Additionally, Spillers says that Alice Walker "reaches behind her most immediate writing predecessor, Margaret Walker, and reclaims the tendentious rhetorical strategies of writers a decade before" (1985, 256). In yet another example of a coupling of Hurston and Walker, *Conjuring*'s introduction is titled "Zora Neale Hurston, Alice Walker, and the 'Ancient Power' of Black Women" by Marjorie Pryse (1985, 1–24).

3. See Genevieve West's "Part Two: 'The Country in the Woman' and 'She Rock'" (2010) and "'Youse in New Yawk': The Gender Politics of Zora Neale Hurston's 'Lost' Caroline Stories" (2014) for her reading of how Hurston's urban migration stories expand her legacy beyond that of a Southern folk writer.

4. See Hurston's "Women in the Caribbean" in *Mules and Men* ([1935] 1978) or Hurston's representation of color and class conflict as depicted in *Their Eyes*, especially in the conversations between Janie and Mrs. Turner on pages 140–43 ([1937] 1998).

5. See Walker, *In Search of our Mothers' Gardens* (1983b, 322–25).

6. As previously discussed, Wallace notes that the publication of Harold Bloom's anthology of collected essays about Hurston signaled her entry into the American literary canon but that it did so at the price of dismissing the feminist and African Americanist readings of her work responsible for introducing Hurston to the canon ([1988] 1990, 175). In addition, in a move away from *Their Eyes* as Hurston's central work, Wallace offers her own "discovery" story of the first time she read Hurston's work *Mules and Men*.

7. Michelle Wallace's mother is award-winning artist Faith Ringgold.

8. In *Passing*, Jack endearingly and problematically refers to Clare as "Nig" in Irene's presence.

9. Cheryl Wall (1948–2020) was the Board of Governors Zora Neale Hurston Distinguished Professor of English at Rutgers University.

10. See Wall's "Zora Neale Hurston's Traveling Blues" (1995d, 139–99). See also "*Mules and Men* and Women: Zora Neale Hurston's Strategies of Narration and Visions of Female Empowerment" (1998, 53–70).

11. During Hurston's early recuperation into the field of Black women's studies, *Sturdy Black Bridges: Vision of Black Women in Literature* (Bell et al. 1979) attended to a "diasporic nexus of critical thought" regarding Black women's writing (xxix). In addition, the collection includes Ellease Southerland's "The Influence of Voodoo on the Fiction of Zora Neale Hurston" (1979), discussed here. The "Analytical Vision" section of *Sturdy Bridges* featured critical approaches to African and Caribbean among writers from the United States, and the collection also features an extensive (if selected) bibliography of African American women writers, Caribbean women writers, and African women writers.

12. The review here is not exhaustive and is intended to illustrate the frequency with which literary scholars discuss Hurston's anthropological training in terms that enhance her literary authority.

13. Hemenway published *Zora Neale Hurston: A Literary Biography* in 1977. As previously noted, parts of this essay were excerpted by Alice Walker in her 1975 essay "In Search of Zora Neale Hurston."

14. Lionnet considers James Clifford's (1986) idea of the "allegory of the salvage" as characterizing Boasian anthropology and influencing Hurston's approach to the writing of her ethnography. Clifford's ideas concerning ethnography would come to impact the critical trajectory of feminist anthropology, readings of Hurston's ethnography, and her authoritative reception. I discuss this further in chapter 4.

15. See LaVinia Delois Jennings's edited collection *Zora Neale Hurston, Haiti, and Their Eyes Were Watching God* (2013) for a collection of critical treatments of Hurston's classic novel within the context of her research in Haiti.

16. The Erzulie *loa* (or *lwa*) are sometimes spelled "Erzili" and "Ezili." I use "Erzulie" unless the referenced author uses a different spelling.

Chapter 4. "Ain't I an Anthropologist?"

1. See Kamala Visweswaran, "Histories of Feminist Ethnography." Hurston's *Mules and Men* is briefly noted as a "travel narrative(s)," and *Tell My Horse* is described as an "ethnography of race" due to its treatment of "race relations" (1997, 602, 604). Both eth-

nographies are periodized within the 1920–1960 nadir, or "disaggregate" period, of the feminist movement. Visweswaran's description of *Mules and Men* as a "travel narrative" and *Tell My Horse* as an "ethnography of race" indicates the lack of agreement within the field concerning the genres of either work. In addition, Visweswaran places Margaret Mead and Hurston together, within the period 1920–1960, as examples of the period's tendency toward ethnographies that shifted between strictly conceptual discussions of cultures as whole societies and "vindicationist approaches that sought to refute cultural or gender stereotypes" (602).

2. See Charles S. Johnson, *Shadow of the Plantation* (Chicago: University of Chicago Press, 1934); Melville Herskovits and Frances Herskovits, *Rebel Destiny: Among the Bush Negroes of Dutch Guiana* (1934); and Hortense Powdermaker, *After Freedom: A Cultural Study in the Deep South* ([1939] 1993).

3. James Clifford, in "On Ethnographic Authority," notes this as "the predominate mode of modern fieldwork authority" (1983, 118). Readers of *Their Eyes* will recall that Janie tells Pheoby, "It's uh known fact, Pheoby, you got tuh *go* there tuh *know* there" (Hurston [1937] 1998, 192).

4. See note 2.

5. Gwendolyn Mikell notes that Hurston's approach to describe culture in terms of personality/types was informed by Ruth Benedict (Mikell 1982, 221).

6. Gordon takes up the Freeman/Mead controversy in more detail in "The Unhappy Relationship of Feminism and Postmodernism in Anthropology" through a close reading of three contemporary reviews of Freeman's work in order to address feminist debates concerning "experimental" ethnography. Describing each review as feminist, she encourages readers to avoid an "easy polemic between 'academics' and 'politics'" and states, "The different priorities of these reviews push us to consider the border between genuine, productive political differences and 'benign sexism'" (1993, 115).

7. In publishing, the term "monograph" is usually reserved for works that are marketed to scholarly/specialist audiences.

8. For example, see Boas, "The Aims of Anthropological Research" ([1932] 1983).

9. Gordon notes that Hurston held no university positions. Hurston was also a playwright, and she staged representations of her folklore data. She taught drama at North Carolina Central University and Bethune-Cookman College, two premier historically Black colleges. Collections of Hurston's plays are now widely available. See Hurston et al., *Zora Neale Hurston: Collected Plays* (2008).

10. As previously mentioned, Gordon describes this aspect of Hurston's work as "ethnocentric" without qualification (1990, 156).

11. The theme of "triple pressures" is repeated in subsequent critical readings of Hurston's work by other feminist anthropologists and Gordon (1990, 158–61).

12. Noted are Edward Burnett Tylor's and Lewis Henry Morgan's ideas concerning the evolutionary development of human civilization in *Researches into the Early History of Mankind and the Development of Civilization* (1865) and *Ancient Society* ([1877] 1963), respectively, as well as diffusionist perspectives as found in Wilhelm Schmidt's *High Gods*

in North America (1933), William James Perry's *Children of the Sun* (1923), and Grafton Elliot Smith's *The Diffusion of Cultures* (1933) (29).

13. Mikell does not provide this example. She cites Hurston's commentary in "The Rooster's Nest" and her commentary on the Haitian personality as having been influenced by Benedict (Mikell 1983, 30). The example provided here is my reading of an excerpt from *Tell My Horse*, which reveals a discussion of Haiti's colonial history by Hurston to be discussed in chapter 6.

14. Mikell's essay was published in *African American Pioneers in Anthropology* (Harrison and Harrison 1999).

15. Mikell notes that this article was published in 1991. It was also published in 1982 in *Phylon* and is noted there as having been originally presented on October 10, 1981, at "The Symposium on the Life and Works of Zora Neale Hurston" at Morgan State University in Baltimore, Maryland.

16. See Graciela Hernández's "Multiple Subjectivities and Strategic Positionality" (1995, 154) and Deborah A. Gordon's "The Politics of Ethnographic Authority: Race and Writing in the Ethnography of Margaret Mead and Zora Neale Hurston" (1990, 162).

17. I will return to a discussion of *Women Writing Culture* later in this chapter for its significance as a production of feminist canon making and revisionist history and its treatment of Hurston's contribution to feminist anthropology.

18. Hernández critiques or revises Gordon's early work by stating that at the time Hurston published *Mules and Men* (1935), she was no longer in a contractual relationship with Mason. She adds, however, "Surely the legacy of those early years of training under her patron left their mark on Hurston's consciousness" (1995, 155).

19. Hernández does not mention Gates's "speakerly text," or Barbara Johnson's "Structures of Address," or other literary discussions of Hurston's storytelling voice here for how her term differs in either definition or application. However, she offers her own work as a literary intervention in response to polar considerations of Hurston's import by Alice Walker and Hazel Carby.

20. This is a common theme in discussions of feminist ethnography. For example, see Diane L. Wolf, "Situating Feminist Dilemmas in Fieldwork" (1996).

21. She mentions the commonly referenced "spyglass of anthropology."

22. I will discuss this aspect of her data in more detail in chapter 5.

23. See note 2.

24. The commonly referenced "spyglass of anthropology" that Hernández mentions is often read as both lending authority and potentially objectifying Hurston's respondents. The latter reading is ironic given Hurston's efforts to reveal communities negotiating cultural meaning.

25. As mentioned previously, these individuals primarily include Franz Boas, her anthropology professor and mentor; Charlotte Osgood Mason, her patron; and Alain Locke, Black scholar and intellectual and editor of *The New Negro* ([1925] 1997).

26. Beyond the field of anthropology, feminist bell hooks argues in "Saving Black Folk Culture: Zora Neale Hurston as Anthropologist and Writer" (1990) that Hurston might

be considered a "cultural critic" and should have been included in Clifford and Marcus's edited collection *Writing Culture*. George Marcus also co-edited *Anthropology as Cultural Critique: An Experimental Moment in the Human Sciences* (1986) with Michael M. J. Fischer.

27. This aspect of the "history" of experimental ethnography is important to my discussion for the ways it brings the relationship between the Harlem Renaissance, Hurston, anthropology, and experimental ethnography full circle. The Harlem Renaissance influenced the Negritude movement, which influenced surrealism and French theorists, whose ideas were imported back as hot, newly "discovered" lit theory (Condé 1990, 1–7). The argument that African Americanists need not use theories (beyond historical contexts of their work) to come to the same conclusions about their analysis of Black culture (made by some Black feminist literary critics in the first chapter) is underscored. There is a global import (and not simply local expression) and import (significance) of African American influence during this time.

28. I have had the experience of being in courses where the question of whether Hurston fictionalized her research is considered at length because of the form and content of her ethnography. The same kind of attention was rarely given to other ethnographies written by non-"native" researchers whose authoritative rhetoric is assumed to be "truthful" rather than constructed in their own distinctive and discursive ways that speak to their subject positionality.

29. See note 2.

30. Visweswaran's argument suggests that understanding Hurston's movements between "self" and "other" within her experimental ethnographies assists the larger feminist project in its work to dismantle hierarchical and powerful notions of "us" and "them" in their critical work.

31. While calling for native authority, Visweswaran does not question whether a native perspective constitutes a critical and analytic approach. She also does not consider the risks involved if a native anthropologist reifies a nationalistic or essentialist identity of the culture in question. Of course, both insider and outsider anthropological perspectives on cultural phenomenon should challenge those aspects of culture that are taken for granted and described as essential cultural differences (Handler 1985, 181).

32. I will discuss these two developments further in my discussion "Histories and Hurston: Canon Making, 'Transferences,' and Erasures" later in this chapter.

33. Referencing the work of Annette Kuhn, Gordon explains that tendentious representations "'take processes of signification for granted,'" while in feminine representation they "foreground the 'meaning production process itself as the site of struggle'" (1988, para. 5).

34. Marcus and Fischer, in *Anthropology as Cultural Critique*, describe how the 1920s and 1930s saw the influence of "social realism" and how its documentary style impacted ethnography and its forms. While they note experimental forms, they are more concerned with the cultural critique that these forms engendered (1986, 125–31). Michael A. Elliot, in *The Culture Concept* (2002), also discusses how "cultural realism" informed both ethnographic and literary works of the era.

35. Here I refer to Lila Abu-Lughod's concept of "writing against culture" in *Writing Women's Worlds: Bedouin Stories* (1993). I will return to a discussion of this concept and its relation to Hurston's method and concept of culture in chapter 5.

36. Marcus and Fischer's *Anthropology as Cultural Critique* (1986) did not directly refute the import of feminism in discussions concerning experimental ethnography but is referenced in this essay by the writers along with Clifford and Marcus's *Writing Culture* (1986) for its focus on experimental ethnography.

37. Mascia-Lees and her colleagues also assert that "feminist theory is an intellectual system that knows its politics" (1989, 8).

38. Both Carby (1989) and Morrison (1989) wrote incisive arguments regarding canon formation during the same period of Hurston's peak critical reclamation and entry into the literary canon as discussed in chapter 2.

39. Behar is referring to Catherine Lutz, "The Erasure of Women's Writing in Sociocultural Anthropology" (1990). Behar notes that Lutz's study should expand to consider anthropologists of color (1995, 26n26). Lutz's "The Gender of Theory" attends more fully to the dynamics of race, class, and gender as she describes how theory asserts authority. She writes, "Thus the move to theory is involved in historical struggles over the authority of women and of minorities of both sexes to speak: the seemingly antihistorical character of theory is a politically conservative move, and so one more likely to be produced by or perceived by the powerful" (1995, 253).

40. While I agree that literature can be read with attention to cultural politics, and that Walker's texts are amenable to a cultural reading, I have not found any references where Walker has expressed a professional interest in anthropology or offered this as explanation for her literary focus and themes. She has discussed, as mentioned previously, her use of cultural and historical sources to inform her fiction and poetry, including findings from Hurston's ethnographies.

41. Harrison quotes James Clifford, "Introduction: Partial Truths" (1986, 21n2).

42. John Langston Gwaltney (1928–1998) was an anthropologist and African American writer. He was the author of *Drylongso: A Self-Portrait of Black America* (1980).

43. See McDowell's "Transferences" regarding how Black women are "fetishized" by theory (1995c, 172).

44. As this book project neared completion, Hurston was included in this anthology, which is often assigned in entry level anthropological theory courses.

45. I am not suggesting that Hurston worked to advance a specific theory, and I recognize the problems with any privileging of theory. See Christian's "The Race for Theory" (1987); Lutz's "The Gender of Theory" (1995); and McDowell's "Transferences" (1995b). Also see Hurston's "Review of *Voodoo in New Orleans*, by Robert Tallant" (1947).

Chapter 5. *Mules and Men*: "Negro Folklore . . . Is Still in the Making"

1. For example, in 1925, Arthur Huff Fauset, an African American anthropologist and folklorist, published his essay "American Negro Folk Literature" in Alain Locke's *The New Negro: Voices of the Harlem Renaissance*. Fauset described the legacy of inaccurate representations of "Negro" dialect and called for a "literary treatment based on a scientific recording [which] will have much fresh material to its hand, and cannot transgress so far from the true ways of the folk spirit and the true lines of our folk art" (Fauset [1925] 1997, 244). Hurston's *Mules and Men* answers Fauset's call.

2. In a letter to Franz Boas requesting that he endorse *Mules and Men* with an introduction, Hurston stated that her publisher "wants a very readable book that the average reader will understand, at the same time one that will have value as *a reference book*" (Kaplan 2002, 308). She further states, "So I hope that the unscientific matter that must be there for the sake of the average reader will not keep you from writing the introduction. It so happens that the conversations and incidents are true" (308; emphasis mine).

3. Hurston received a BA in anthropology in 1928 from Barnard College, where she studied with Franz Boas, Melville Herskovits, and Ruth Benedict, among others. She published "Hoodoo in America" in the *Journal of American Folklore* in 1931, which included one hundred pages of specific folktales and rituals. Much of this data would be included in *Mules and Men*, which was published during the first year of her graduate studies in anthropology at Columbia University and featured folklore from her field research in Florida and New Orleans between 1927 and 1929.

4. See Cotera (2008) for a comparative literary history of the ethnographic work of Ella Cara Deloria, Jovita Gonzalez, and Zora Neale Hurston in order to address their shared histories of marginalization within the field of anthropology. In particular, "'Lyin' Up a Nation': Zora Neale Hurston and the Literary Uses of the Folk" (71–101) provides a discussion regarding Hurston's collection of folklore that works to define her ethnographic commitments and tenuous authority as a native anthropologist.

5. For more on the relationship between Johnson and Hurston, see biographers Robert Hemenway ([1977] 1980) and Valerie Boyd (2003) as well as Carla Kaplan's collection of Hurston's letters (2002). The available correspondence between Hurston and Johnson can be traced in Carla Kaplan's *Zora Neale Hurston: A Life in Letters* (2002).

6. Powdermaker cites Herskovits's broader definition of acculturation and defines acculturation as "those phenomena that result when groups of individuals having different cultures come into continuous first-hand contact, with subsequent changes in the original cultural patterns of either or both groups" (Redfield et al. 1936, 149; Powdermaker [1939] 1993, 61n1). Herskovits authored the article along with Robert Redfield and Ralph Linton. The memo differentiates between acculturation, assimilation, and diffusion. Assimilation is considered "at times a phase of acculturation," and diffusion is described as "occurring in all instances of acculturation . . . but also constitutes only one aspect of the process of acculturation" (Redfield et al. 1936, 149–50).

7. Johnson also discusses the costs of a legal divorce as a significant constraint (1934, 74).

8. Herskovits would later cite passages from Johnson's work in *The Myth of a Negro Past* ([1941] 1990) as an example of one of the scholarly arguments that reflects and reproduces the myth that African Americans have no history.

9. Johnson states, "The plantation as represented in tradition and popular fancy is so far removed from the existing institution as to be but slightly related to the character of the folk that it bred" (1934, 1). Johnson describes the plantation of "romantic fiction" as idyllic in its representation of a carefree pastoral life of the enslaved living in abundant conditions (1). He goes on to say, "The actual plantation devoted to cotton was based on rigorous and dull routine. . . . Life, on the whole, was a grim business. Such were the imperatives of the economic conditions" (3).

10. As previously noted, Melville Herskovits argued that African survivals were found throughout the African diaspora. These survivals, he argued, explained some of the cultural practices (particularly religious, family patterns, language, and folktales) of African descendants in various geographic locales. Johnson's ethnography does include a section titled "Survivals"; however, he is not referencing the Herskovitsean concept of cultural survivals from Africa that the term typically suggests today. The section, instead, is devoted to a discussion of African American mortality in the wake of violence, illness, and poor access to health care.

11. Sterling Allen Brown is commonly known as a poet and folk life scholar of the Harlem Renaissance.

12. Thompson's endorsement is made in contrast to his summary rejection of Carter Godwin Woodson's *The Mis-Education of the Negro* ([1933] 1990). Thompson finds Woodson's work lacking in its combination of previous speeches and in its precepts for educating Black children in African and African American history. Following his review of Woodson's *The Mis-Education of the Negro*, Thompson writes, "Professor Johnson's book, on the other hand, is a serious sociological study of a rural Negro population in a limited area, done under the auspices of the Rosenwald Fund" (1935, 106). The Rosenwald Fund, or Julius Rosenwald Fund, (1917–1948) awarded grants, fellowships, and other significant awards in support of public education, agricultural, health institutions, and research that addressed race relations.

13. See Louise Lamphere's "Unofficial Histories: A Vision of Anthropology from the Margins," where she includes George Hunt for writing in an "authentic Kwakw'ala speech style" and includes Margaret Mead for her "problem-focused methodology" best revealed in *Coming of Age in Samoa* (Lamphere 2004, 129). Hurston, likewise, can be considered in these terms. However, in Lamphere's delineation, Hurston is placed within the second category of "minorities who were connected to anthropology in the same time period" (127). Despite Hurston's considerable fieldwork experience, publications in scholarly journals, scholarly endorsements by anthropologist Franz Boas and Melville Herskovits, as well as having published two popular ethnographies, she is defined as "connected" rather than having formally entered the discipline. Additionally, Hurston is excluded on the basis of class. Because she is not considered elite, Hurston is excluded from the first category of women who influenced anthropology during its formative period, so she is not recognized as a "formative" woman but as a "connected" minority. Although Lamphere's rhetorical mission is to include and recognize those from the margins, her delineations and descriptions work against her goals for inclusion. Along with Elsie Clews Parsons, Gladys Reichard, and Ella Deloria, Lamphere notes that Hurston contributed to "dialogical forms" in ethnographic writing (131).

14. E. Franklin Frazier argued that African cultural expressions and practices were largely decimated by slavery. He supported the view that Black people in America, although descendants of Africans, neither remembered nor consciously practiced African survivals that might significantly explain the distinctiveness of African American culture (see Mintz and Price [1976] 1992, 62–63). Hill argues that Hurston's description of African American culture offers a theory of culture as performative, where "everyday-life behavior" is viewed as dramatic action. This perspective, she argues, was influenced by Hurston's

interest in dramatizing folk culture for the theater (L. Hill 1996, 9). Also see Eve Dunbar's *Black Regions of the Imagination* (Dunbar 2013, 26–27).

15. I disagree with Hill's assertion that Hurston's ideas concerning mimicry fail to challenge assimilation and that her use of the term "mimicry" has to be considered ironically (L. Hill 1996, 8). Within the context of views concerning African American culture as a failed derivative of the larger American white culture, her assertion that "mimicry is an art itself" suggests that even in imitation of an "original" culture practice, there is a new, original cultural aesthetic that is produced.

16. Hurston's portrayal of the range of experiences she had in the lumber camp illustrates that she was thoroughly submerged into the daily life of the community and is a historically accurate representation of the myriad dangers of life in the lumber camps (Patterson 2005, 136–38).

17. Susan Meisenhelder's "Conflict and Resistance in Zora Neale Hurston's *Mules and Men*" (1996) provides an in-depth analysis of the specific social contexts of a number of prominent folktales that signify on race and labor in "Part 1" of the ethnography.

18. See Prahlad's *African American Proverbs in Context*. Prahlad defines a contextual theory of folklore as a four-part model that includes grammatical levels (literal meanings); situational levels (subtextual meanings dependent on exchanges between two or more individuals); group/social levels (where meaning is relatively shared across and between different social aggregates); and symbolic levels (involving psychological functions and values). These four parts "operate simultaneously when a proverb is spoken and, consequently, the job of the analyst is to discover in what ways meanings interact" (1996, 23–26).

19. Contemporary folklorist Sw. Anand Prahlad calls for an understanding of folklore in similar terms: "Folklore is a *contemporary*, dynamic phenomenon, integral to every person's life, not a holdover from some earlier, primitive stage of development" (1999, 573). Hurston published her collection of religious folklore in "Hoodoo in America," which provides one hundred pages of careful transcriptions of data and defines "hoodoo" or "conjure" as distinctive from Vodou and, at times and depending on regional contexts, related to spiritualism. The collection also provides some discussion of Bahamian obeah for "comparative purposes" (1931, 5).

20. See Arthur M. Kleinman's discussion of explanatory models in *Patients and Healers in the Context of Culture* (1980).

21. This aspect of Hurston's kinship challenges prevailing attitudes concerning her class status—that is, if one equates professional status with class and vice versa. In any case, Hurston had kinship ties that have not been fully explored (see Boyd 2003, 143). To what extent did her brother support her in her work (financial and otherwise)? And to what extent did this support sustain her independent scholarship beyond the patron-client relationships commonly referred to in discussions of her constrained scholarship?

22. A glossary and four appendices complete the framing of *Mules and Men*. The glossary provides definitions of the following terms or folklore concepts: "Jack" or "John," "woofing," "testimony," "John Henry," "long house," "Blue Baby," "Brer Rabbit," "the colored preacher," and "Georgia Skin Game." The work, social, convict, gaming, and children's songs she collected appear in the first appendix, and these include general notes on their

usage. Hurston also includes full piano arrangements for each song, suggesting that she expects readers to perform the songs themselves.

23. As far as I can determine, "Father Williams" is Joseph J. Williams, a missionary who published various works on Voodoo practices into the Caribbean. He wrote *Voodoo and Obeahs* (1932) and *Psychic Phenomena in Jamaica* (1934). Each text greatly relies on his firsthand accounts (and those of other foreign missionaries) to support his ethnological discussions.

24. Herskovits writes, "It is interesting to consider how important an effect the historical accident of the publication of these American Negro Brer Rabbit stories by Joel Chandler Harris has had upon folklorists working among African and New World Negroes. For if the entire body of Negro folklore be taken into account, it becomes readily apparent to what degree it is unjustifiable to assume, as Father Williams assumes, that Negro lore is restricted to accounts of animals" ([1941] 1990, 219).

25. R. S. Rattray published several volumes on Ashanti culture of Ghana.

26. "We do not really mean" is stated twice in Herskovits's review. The repetition of the phrase is possibly a colloquial expression that emphasizes its meaning. Although different in form, I think of Hurston's notations of the "Double Descriptive" in "Characteristics of Negro Expression" ([1934] 1995, 832). Williams also associates Hurston's work with stereotypical literary realistic works of Black culture by Roy Octavus Cohen. In rebuttal, Herskovits states, "One does not have to be a profound student of Negro life to understand that the stories of Octavus Roy Cohen are a travesty and a caricature on Negro life; and that while some persons of the type this writer portrays may exist somewhere, they are found more often in the pages of the *Saturday Evening Post*, where these stories usually appear, than in Negro communities of the United States" (Herskovits 1937b, 221).

27. Despite contemporary characterizations of Herskovits as primarily emphasizing survivals as static "vestiges" of an African past, he and Hurston shared similar understandings of culture as dynamic (Yelvington 2001, 240).

28. Powdermaker's focus on both Black and white respondents may have been one reason for not providing phonetic representations of language in her ethnography. Another reason may have been her lack of familiarity with the treatment of dialect as an important representation of language as culture. Yet another reason to consider is that she may have taken for granted the importance of dialect as a distinct cultural form—or African survival, in the case of African American culture—in American anthropology.

29. Whites are divided into aristocratic, middle-income, and poor. Housing patterns, housing conditions, employment, church affiliation, and social alliances are all noted as evidence of variations within the groups. Despite these differences, Powdermaker concludes that there is a general "homogeneity" that describes the white middle class who make up the majority of white residences within the town. Their homogenous culture, "conveyed by their residences[,] is borne out by the residents themselves, who display a marked unanimity of background, education, outlook, [and] life mode" ([1939] 1993, 15).

30. An exception here may be Powdermaker's deliberate consideration of "The Negro Response to the Situation," wherein she more pointedly considers Black attitudes to racial inequality in the town.

31. Powdermaker was aware of highly experimental modes of ethnography. See Powdermaker, Review of *Rebel Destiny*, by Melville Herskovits and Frances Herskovits (1935, 290–91).

32. An example of these interests in representing regional dialect is Mark Twain's *Huckleberry Finn* (1885) and a 1927 critical discussion of variations of dialect in his work by Katherine Buxbaum, "Mark Twain and American Dialect." Her reading of his work in this way comes during a period of increased interest in his work: "Critical appreciation seems to center just now around *Huckleberry Finn*, and no modern student of the work fails to mention enthusiastically its use of the vernacular" (1927, 236).

33. W.E.B. Du Bois critiques Powdermaker for "sticking almost too straitly to her subject and revealing in the finished *story* few obtrusions of the mass of irrelevant and contradictory data which she must have collected" (1939, 137). He also, revealingly, announces Powdermaker's work as the first to treat African American culture from an anthropological perspective. R. L. Duffus critiques Powdermaker's text for its "repressed" presentation (1939, BR3). Willard Waller stated, "*After Freedom* is a good job, and a particularly good literary job" (1940, 505). Charles S. Johnson, following a summary of the key discussions of the ethnography, stated, "An intimate realism is conveyed in the frequent documentary citations, rich in human values" (1939, 196). Horace Man Bond agrees with Johnson: "It is a merit of the book, and perhaps, a clue to the sharp picture it gives of institutions and personalities, that these factors are presented as they are in life—intertwined, lacking exclusive definition, with no one factor or theory explaining everything" (1939, 201).

34. Gertrude Fraser questions why *After Freedom* has been marginalized, noting that sociologist John Dollard's *Caste and Class in a Southern Town* (1937) received more critical attention within a contemporary survey (1983) of anthropological study in America (Fraser 1991, 404). (She references "Anthropologists View American Culture" [1983] by G. Spindler and L. Spindler, published in *Annual Review of Anthropology* 12: 49–78.) Compared to Powdermaker's *After Freedom*, Dollard's *Caste and Class* is a much more reflexive ethnography. Robert E. Park (who wrote the introduction to Charles Johnson's *Shadow of the Plantation*) praised *Caste and Class* as an "innovative" approach to the study of race relations. He also positively notes its reflexive presentation: "Because of the intimate nature of its observations, this volume has assumed something of the character of the autobiography of the observer" (Park 1937, 211).

35. Hemenway's ([1977] 1980) biography of Hurston may have begun this focus. His discussions of her fieldwork experiences are largely framed by a history (epistle) of Hurston's relationship with "Godmother" Mrs. Rufus Osgood. Hemenway's chapter "Grandmother and Big Sweet: 1927–1931" covers the years of Hurston's folklore research as published in *Mules and Men*. The chapter has much to say about this relationship and about Hurston's contributions to the field of folklore and studies of religious practice. Tiffany Ruby Patterson's chapter titled "Patronage: Anatomy of a Predicament," in *Zora Neale Hurston and a History of Southern Life* (2005), considers Mason, Fannie Hurst, and Hurston's publisher J. P. Lippincott as another trio of constraining patrons.

36. For example, the expansion of the paperback market occurs during this period.

37. DuCille actually refers to works about Black women being used in this way. By extension, any works that featured "others" would do.

38. This also begs the question that Carby raises as to why there is a renewed (and renewable) interest in Hurston's work as a romantic representation of the folk (1990, 90).

Chapter 6. "Burning Spots": Reading *Tell My Horse*

1. This assessment is supported by Genevieve West's discussion of the response to a series of lectures that Hurston gave regarding her work prior to its release. Attendees from the United States and Haiti expressed concern with her critique of America and Haiti (West 2005, 132–33).

2. Kevin Meehan, describing trends in receptions of Hurston's works, states, "Once we dethrone Hurston's roving narrator, we can then look for clues to the narrative politics of this background drama, which, in my view, has a strong anti-imperialist message" (2008, 59).

3. As with its marketing of *Mules and Men*, Lippincott's sensational and racist marketing shaped its critical reception (West 2005, 127–28). For an extended assessment of its popular and critical reception immediately following its publication, see West (2005, 127–44).

4. This sentence appears to begin Hurston's fourth argument, although it is not enumerated in the text.

5. Some ten years before, anthropologist Elsie Clews Parsons, who was a colleague of both Hurston and Woodson, briefly discussed the loa in her essay "Spirit Cult in Hayti" (1928). Parsons provides a song of Gede and brief notations that include "At the capital, Port-au-Prince, 'most people have the loi Gédé'" (Parsons 1928, 158).

6. See Robert Baron, "Amalgams and Mosaics, Syncretisms and Reinterpretations: Reading Herskovits and Contemporary Creolists for Metaphors of Creolization," *Journal of American Folklore* 116, no. 459 (2003): 88–115, for a discussion of Herskovits's use of the metaphors that falls short as a term to describe Vodou (105).

7. *Ôrìsà* (sometimes written as *Orisha*) is a Yoruba term for deity.

8. See also Amy Schmidt, "Horses Chomping at the Global Bit: Ideology, Systemic Injustice, and Resistance in Zora Neale Hurston's 'Tell My Horse,'" *Southern Literary Journal* 46, no. 2 (2014): 173–92. Schmidt states, "Significantly, while Hurston critiques Jamaica and Haiti for their exploitation of women, she also suggests that voodoo is a means to resist sexism, though the religion's resistance is typically characterized in relationship to racism and colonialism" (186).

9. It's worth noting an additional example of Hurston's conceptual and methodological authority within *Tell My Horse*. Hurston mentions Herskovits's field research efforts in Haiti, she comments on the brevity of his assistant's study, and she notes that they paid for a "staged dance." She then signifies that unlike his assistant, she is "too old a hand at collecting to fall for staged-dance affairs. . . . What I was actually doing was making general observations" (22–23). Herskovits's assistant was anthropologist Katherine Dunham. For more on Dunham's legacy, Elizabeth Chin, ed., *Katherine Dunham: Recovering an Anthropological Legacy, Choreographing Ethnographic Futures*, 2014.

10. See Diana Burnett for her reading of Hurston as a pioneer of Africana Religious Studies (2016, 255). She likewise notes Mikell's observation regarding Hurston moving beyond the influence of Herskovits (Mikell 1982, 226).

Epilogue

1. See Guy-Sheftall's "Black Women's Studies: The Interface of Women's Studies and Black Studies" (1992) for a history of the emergence of Black women's studies in the United States.

2. Farah Jasmine Griffin, "That the Mothers May Soar and the Daughters May Know Their Names: A Retrospective of Black Feminist Literary Criticism," *Signs* 32, no. 2 (2007): 483–507.

3. See Barbara Smith, "Reply to Deborah Chay," *New Literary History* 24, no. 3 (1993): 653–56. Smith underscores how her statement was not written as an "intellectual exercise" (653). Additionally, she states, "'Toward a Black Feminist Criticism' was not written for an academic journal, but for one of the earliest and most important lesbian feminist literary magazines, *Conditions: Two*" (653–654).

4. See Alice Walker, *Gathering Blossoms Under Fire: The Journals of Alice Walker 1965–2000* (2022). This collection of Walker's journals, edited by Valerie Boyd, was published published as this book went into production.

5. See Moya Bailey, *Misogynoir Transformed: Black Women's Digital Resistance* (2021), for her discussion of the ways "that Black women and Black nonbinary, agender, and gender-variant folk" work to resist and transform misogynoir in digital spaces.

6. Harrison and Harrison's *African American Pioneers in Anthropology* (1999) was published two years before Irma McClaurin's *Black Feminist Anthropology: Theory Politics, Praxis, and Poetics* (2001) was published. See also Ira E. Harrison, Deborah Johnson-Simon, and Erica Lorraine Williams, *The Second Generation of African American Pioneers in Anthropology* (2019).

7. This includes a focus that omits diverse class experiences within the Black community. Hurston, for example, does not demand stories on the upper class, which are "an interesting problem" to consider. Instead, she says, a "realistic story around a Negro insurance official, dentist, general practitioner, undertaker and the like would be most revealing" ([1950] 1995, 954). This point is taken up in Carla Freeman's *Entrepreneurial Selves: Neoliberal Respectability and the Making of a Caribbean Middle Class* (2014).

8. McClaurin describes the work of Martin R. Delaney's "Principia of Ethnology: The Origins of Race and Color, with an Archaeological Compendium of Ethiopian and Egyptian Civilization from Years of Careful Examination and Enquiry" (1879) as "the earliest anthropological work written by an African American" (McClaurin 2001, 11).

9. See Hurston's "How It Feels to Be Colored Me" ([1928] 1995).

10. In the same essay, Hurston quips, "Sometimes, I feel discriminated against, but it does not make me angry. It merely astonishes me. How *can* any deny themselves the pleasure of my company! It's beyond me." ([1928] 1995, 829; Hurston's emphasis).

References

Archival Sources

Carl Van Vechten Papers Relating to African American Arts and Letters. James Weldon Johnson Collection. Yale Collection of American Literature Beinecke Rare Book and Manuscript Library.

James C. Freeman Private Archive

Lomax Collection, Prints and Photographs Division, Library of Congress, Washington, DC.

Works Cited

Abu-Lughod, Lila. 1993. *Writing Women's Worlds: Bedouin Stories*. Berkeley: University of California Press.

Apter, Andrew. 1991. "Herskovits' Heritage: Rethinking Syncretism in the African Diaspora." In *Syncretism in Religion: A Reader*, edited by Anita M. Leopold and Jeppe S. Jensen, 160–84. London: Routledge.

Association to Preserve the Eatonville Community, Inc., "About Zora Neale Hurston." https://zorafestival.org/about/zora-neale-hurston/. Accessed June 22, 2022.

Awkward, Michael. (1988) 2000. "Appropriative Gestures: Theory and Afro-American Literary Criticism." In *African American Literary Theory: A Reader*, edited by Winston Napier, 331–38. New York: New York University Press.

———. 1991. *Inspiriting Influences: Tradition, Revision, and Afro-American Women's Novels*. New York: Columbia University Press.

Baber, Willie L. 1999. "St. Clair Drake: Scholar and Activist." In Harrison and Harrison, *African American Pioneers in Anthropology*, 191–212.

Bailey, Moya. 2021. *Misogynoir Transformed: Black Women's Digital Resistance*. New York University Press.

Baker, Houston A., Jr. 1987. "In Dubious Battle." *New Literary History* 18 (Winter): 363–69.

Baker, Lee D. 1998. *From Savage to Negro: Anthropology and the Construction of Race, 1896–1954*. Berkeley: University of California Press.

Bambara, Toni Cade. 1970. *The Black Woman: An Anthology*. New York: New American Library.

———. (1981) 1998. "Some Forward Remarks." Foreword to Hurston, *The Sanctified Church*, 9–13.

Baron, Robert. "Amalgams and Mosaics, Syncretisms and Reinterpretations: Reading Herskovits and Contemporary Creolists for Metaphors of Creolization." *Journal of American Folklore* 116, no. 459 (2003): 88–115.

Behar, Ruth. 1995. "Introduction: Out of Exile." Introduction to Behar and Gordon, *Women Writing Culture*, 1–29.

———, and Deborah A. Gordon, eds. 1995. *Women Writing Culture*. Berkeley: University of California Press.

Bell, Roseann P., Bettye J. Parker, and Beverly Guy-Sheftall, eds. 1979. *Sturdy Black Bridges: Visions of Black Women in Literature*. Garden City, NY: Anchor/Doubleday.

Bell-Scott, Patricia, ed. 1991. *Double Stitch: Black Women Write about Mothers and Daughters*. Boston: Beacon Press.

Bernreuter, Robert G. 1929. Review of *Coming of Age in Samoa*, by Margaret Mead. *American Journal of Psychology* (July): 489.

Blanchard, Albert C. 1934/1935. "Some Aspects of Mortality in Florida, 1921–1930." *Social Forces* 13, no. 1 (October–May): 73–79.

Bloom, Harold. 1986a. Introduction to Bloom, *Zora Neale Hurston (Modern Critical Views)*, 1–4.

———. 1986b. *Zora Neale Hurston (Modern Critical Views)*. New York: Chelsea House Publishers.

B. M. 1929. Review of *Coming of Age in Samoa*, by Margaret Mead. *Pacific Affairs* (April): 225–26.

Boas, Franz. 1920. "The Methods of Ethnology." *American Anthropologist* 22, no. 4: 311–21.

———. (1928) 1986. *Anthropology and Modern Life*. New York: Dover Publications.

———. (1932) 1983. "The Aims of Anthropological Research." *Science* 76, no. 1983 (December): 605–613.

———. (1935) 1978. Preface to Hurston, *Mules and Men*, by Zora Neale Hurston.

Bolles, A. Lynn. 2001. "Seeking the Ancestors, Forging a Black Feminist Tradition in Anthropology." In McClaurin, *Black Feminist Anthropology*, 24–48.

Bond, Horace Man. 1939. Review of *After Freedom*, by Hortense Powdermaker. *Annals of the American Academy of Political and Social Science* 205 (September): 201–202.

Bontemps, Arna, ed. 1972. *The Harlem Renaissance Remembered: Essays, edited with a Memoir by Arna Bontemps*. New York, Dodd, Mead.

Boyce Davies, Carole. 1994. *Black Women, Writing, and Identity: Migrations of the Subject*. London: Routledge.

———, and Molara Ogundipe-Leslie, eds. 1995. *Moving beyond Boundaries*. Vol. 2. *Black Women's Diasporas*. Washington Square: New York University Press.

Boyd, Valerie. 1988. "Looking for Alice." *Ms.* (March-April): 90+.

———. 2003. *Wrapped in Rainbows: The Life of Zora Neale Hurston*. New York: Scribner.

Brown, Karen McCarthy. (1991) 2010. *Mama Lola: A Vodou Priestess in Brooklyn*. Berkeley: University of California Press.

Brown, Sterling A. 1936. Review of *Shadow of the Plantation*, by Charles S. Johnson. *Journal of Negro History* 21, no. 1: 70–73.

Burnett, Diana. 2016. "Illuminating the Legacy of Zora Neale Hurston: Visionary, Architect, and Anthropologist of Africana Religious Subjectivities." *Journal of Africana Religions* 4, no. 2: 255–66.

Buxbaum, Katherine. 1927. "Mark Twain and American Dialect." *American Speech* 2, no. 5: 233–36.

Carby, Hazel V. 1987a. "The Quicksand of Representation: Rethinking Black Cultural Politics." In Carby, *Reconstructing Womanhood*, 163–75.

———. 1987b. *Reconstructing Womanhood: The Emergence of the Afro-American Woman Novelist*. Oxford: Oxford University Press.

———. 1989. "The Canon: Civil War and Reconstruction." *Michigan Quarterly Review* 28, no. 1: 35–43.

———. 1990. "The Politics of Fiction, Anthropology, and the Folk: Zora Neale Hurston." In *New Essays on Their Eyes Were Watching God*, edited by Michael Awkward, 71–93. Cambridge, UK: Cambridge University Press.

Chin, Elizabeth, ed. 2014. *Katherine Dunham: Recovering an Anthropological Legacy, Choreographing Ethnographic Futures*. Santa Fe: School for Advanced Research Press, 2014.

Christian, Barbara. 1980. *Black Women Novelists: The Development of a Tradition, 1892–1976*. Westport, CT: Greenwood Press.

———. 1986. "We Are the Ones That We Have Been Waiting For: Political Content in Alice Walker's Novels." *Women's Studies International Forum* 9, no. 4: 421–26.

———. 1987. "The Race for Theory." *Cultural Critique*, no. 6: 51–63. https://doi.org/10.2307/1354255/.

———. (1987) 2000. "The Race for Theory." In *African American Literary Theory: A Reader*, edited by Winston Napier, 280–89. New York: New York University Press.

———. 2007. "But What Do We Think We're Doing Anyway: The State of Black Feminist Criticism(s) or My Version of a Little Bit of History." In *New Black Feminist Criticism, 1985–2000*, edited by Gloria Bowles, M. Giulia Fabi, and Arlene R. Keizer, 5–19. Urbana: University of Illinois Press.

Chubb, Thomas Caldecot. 1936. Review of *Mules and Men*, by Zora Neale Hurston. *North American Review* 241, no. 1: 181–83.

Clifford, James. 1983. "On Ethnographic Authority." *Representations* 2 (Spring): 118–46.

———. 1986. "Introduction: Partial Truths." Introduction to Clifford and Marcus, *Writing Culture*, 1–26.

———, and George E. Marcus, eds. 1986. *Writing Culture: The Poetics and Politics of Ethnography*. Berkeley: University of California Press.

Cole, Johnnetta B. 2001. Foreword to McClaurin, *Black Feminist Anthropology*, ix-xi.

Collins, Derek. 1996. "The Myth and Ritual of Ezili Freda in Hurston's *Their Eyes Were Watching God*." *Western Folklore* 55, no. 2: 137–54.

Combahee River Collective. (1977) 1982. "A Black Feminist Statement." In *But Some of Us Are Brave*, edited by Gloria T. Hull, Patricia Bell Scott, and Barbara Smith, 13–22. New York: Feminist Press.

Condé, Maryse. 1998. "O Brave New World." *Research in African Literatures* 29, no. 3: 1–7.

Corse, Sarah M., and Monica D. Griffin. 1997. "Cultural Valorization and African American Literary History: Reconstructing the Canon." *Sociological Forum* 12, no. 2: 173–203.

Cotera, María Eugenia. 2008. *Native Speakers: Ella Deloria, Zora Neale Hurston, Jovita González, and the Poetics of Culture*. Austin: University of Texas Press, 2008.

DiMaggio, Paul. 1982. "Cultural Capital and School Success: The Impact of Status Culture Participation on the Grades of U.S. High School Students." *American Sociological Review* 47, no. 2: 189–201.

Dollard, John. 1937. *Caste and Class in a Southern Town*. New Haven, CT: Yale University Press.

Dorst, John. 1987. "Rereading *Mules and Men*: Toward the Death of the Ethnographer." *Cultural Anthropology* 2, no. 3: 305–318.

Douglass, Frederick, Western Reserve College, and African American Pamphlet Collection. (1854) 2006. "The Claims of the Negro, Ethnologically Considered: An Address before the Literary Societies of Western Reserve College, at Commencement, July 12, 1854." [Rochester, NY: Printed by Lee, Mann & Co., 1854]. Library of Congress. http://memory.loc.gov/ammem/aapchtml/aapchome.html/.

Drake, Claire. 1978. "Reflections on Anthropology and the Black Experience." *New Perspectives on Black Education*. Spec. issue of *Anthropology and Education Quarterly* 9, no. 2: 85–109.

Drewal, Henry John. 2008. "Mami Wata: Arts for Water Spirits in Africa and Its Diasporas." *African Arts* 41, no. 2: 60–83.

Du Bois, W.E.B. (1926) 1995. "Criteria of Negro Art." In *The Portable Harlem Renaissance Reader*, edited by David Levering Lewis, 100–105. New York: Penguin Books.

———. 1939. "*After Freedom*—A Cultural Study of the Deep South." Review of *After Freedom*, by Hortense Powdermaker. *Social Forces* 18, no. 1: 137–39.

duCille, Ann. 1993. *The Coupling Convention: Sex, Text, and Tradition in Black Women's Fiction*. New York: Oxford University Press.

———. 1994. "The Occult of True Black Womanhood: Critical Demeanor and Black Feminist Studies." *Signs* 19, no. 3: 591–629.

———. 2005. "The Mark of Zora: Reading between the Lines of Legend and Legacy." *Scholar and Feminist Online* 3, no. 2. https://sfonline.barnard.edu/hurston/ducille_01.htm/.

———. 2006. "On Canons: Anxious History and the Rise of Black Feminist Literary Studies." In *The Cambridge Companion to Feminist Literary Theory*, edited by Ellen Rooney, 29–52. Cambridge, UK: Cambridge University Press.

Duck, Leigh Anne. 2004. "'Rebirth of a Nation': Hurston in Haiti." *Journal of American Folklore* 117, no. 464: 127–46.

Duffus, R. L. 1939. "The Racial Problem in the Deep South." Review of *After Freedom*, by Hortense Powdermaker. *New York Times*, February 5, BR3.

Dunbar, Eve. 2013. *Black Regions of the Imagination: African American Writers between the Nation and the World*. Philadelphia: Temple University Press.

Durrow, Heidi W. 2008. "Dear Ms. Larsen, There's a Mirror Looking Back." *PMS: Poem/Memoir/Story* 8: 101–109.

———. 2010. *The Girl Who Fell from the Sky: A Novel*. Chapel Hill, NC: Algonquin Books.

Dutton, Wendy. 1993. "The Problem of Invisibility: Voodoo and Zora Neale Hurston. *Frontiers: A Journal of Women Studies* 13, no. 2: 131–52.

Eagleton, Terry. 1987. *Literary Theory: An Introduction*. Minneapolis: University of Minnesota Press.

Ebron, Paulla A. 2001. "Contingent Stories of Anthropology, Race, and Feminism." In McClaurin, *Black Feminist Anthropology*, 211–32.

Elliott, Michael A. 2002. *The Culture Concept: Writing and Difference in the Age of Realism*. Minneapolis: University of Minnesota Press.

Erlich, Victor. 1969. *Russian Formalism: History Doctrine*. The Hague: Mouton.

Evans, Mari. 1970. *I Am a Black Woman*. New York: Morrow.

Exum, Pat Crutchfield, ed. 1974. *Keeping the Faith: Writing by Contemporary Black American Women*. New York: Fawcett Publications.

Fauset, Arthur Huff. (1925) 1997. "American Negro Folk Literature." In *The New Negro: Voices of the Harlem Renaissance*, edited by Alain Locke, 238–44. New York: Simon and Schuster.

Foreman, P. Gabrielle. 1990. "Looking Back from Zora, or Talking Out Both Sides My Mouth for Those Who Have Two Ears." *Black American Literature Forum* 24, no. 4: 649–66.

Foster, Frances Smith. 1993. *Written by Herself: Literary Production by African American Women, 1746–1892*. Bloomington: Indiana University Press.

———. 2006. "Forgotten Manuscripts: How Do You Solve a Problem Like Theresa?" *African American Review* 40, no. 4: 631–45.

Franklin, V. P., and Bettye Collier-Thomas. 1996. "Biography, Race Vindication, and African American Intellectuals: Introductory Essay." *Journal of Negro History* 81, nos. 1/4: 1–16.

Fraser, Gertrude. 1991. "Race, Class, and Difference in Hortense Powdermaker's 'After Freedom: A Cultural Study in the Deep South.'" *The Legacy of Hortense Powdermaker*. Spec. issue of *Journal of Anthropological Research* 47, no. 4: 403–416.

Freeman, Carla. 2014. *Entrepreneurial Selves: Neoliberal Respectability and the Making of a Caribbean Middle Class*. Durham, NC: Duke University Press.

Freeman, Derek. 1983. *Margaret Mead and Samoa: The Making and Unmaking of an Anthropological Myth*. Cambridge, MA: Harvard University Press.

Freeman Marshall, Jennifer. [Marshall, Jennifer Freeman]. 2013. "In Search of Heidi Durrow within a Black Woman's Literary Tradition: On Reading *The Girl Who Fell from the Sky*." *Forum for World Literature Studies* 5, no. 1: 27.

Gates, Henry Louis, Jr. 1987a. Foreword to Holloway, *The Character of the Word*.

———. 1987b. "'What's Love Got to Do with It?': Critical Theory, Integrity, and the Black Idiom." *New Literary History* 18 (Winter 1987): 345–62.

—————. 1988. *The Signifying Monkey: A Theory of African-American Literary Criticism*. New York: Oxford University Press.

—————, ed. 1990. Introduction to *Reading Black, Reading Feminist: A Critical Anthology*, edited by Henry Louis Gates Jr., 1–17. New York: Meridian.

—————. 1993. Preface to *Zora Neale Hurston: Critical Perspectives Past and Present*, edited by Henry Louis Gates Jr. and K. A. Appiah, xi–xv. New York: Amistad Press.

Gayles, Gloria Jean Wade. 1984. *No Crystal Stair: Visions of Race and Sex in Black Women's Fiction*. New York: Pilgrim Press.

Gordon, Deborah. 1988. "Writing Culture, Writing Feminism: The Poetics and Politics of Experimental Ethnography." *Inscriptions* 3–4. https://culturalstudies.ucsc.edu/inscriptions/volume-34/2598-2/.

—————. 1990. "The Politics of Ethnographic Authority: Race and Writing in the Ethnography of Margaret Mead and Zora Neale Hurston." In *Modernist Anthropology: From Fieldwork to Text*, edited by Marc Manganaro, 146–62. Princeton, NJ: Princeton University Press.

—————. 1993. "The Unhappy Relationship of Feminism and Postmodernism in Anthropology." *Constructing Meaningful Dialogue on Difference: Feminism and Postmodernism in Anthropology and the Academy: Part 2*. Spec. issue of *Anthropological Quarterly* 66, no. 3 (July): 109–117.

Griffin, Farah Jasmine. 2007. "That the Mothers May Soar and the Daughters May Know Their Names: A Retrospective of Black Feminist Literary Criticism." *Signs* 32, no. 2: 483–507.

Grosvenor, Vertamae. 2004. "Alice Walker on Zora Neale Hurston's 'Spiritual Food.'" *Intersections: Crafting a Voice for Black Culture*. National Public Radio. April 26. Transcript. http://www.npr.org/templates/story/story.php?storyId=1849395/.

Guy-Sheftall, Beverly. 1992. "Black Women's Studies: The Interface of Women's Studies and Black Studies." *Phylon* 49, nos. 1/2: 33–41.

—————. 1995a. "The Evolution of Feminist Consciousness among African American Women." Introduction to Guy-Sheftall, *Words of Fire*, 1–24.

—————. 1995b. *Words of Fire: An Anthology of African-American Feminist Thought*. New York: New Press.

Haas, Robert. 2000. "Might Zora Neale Hurston's Janie Woods Be Dying of Rabies? Considerations from Historical Medicine." *Literature and Medicine* 19, no. 2: 205–228.

Hahn, Robert A., and Arthur Kleinman. 1983. "Belief as Pathogen, Belief as Medicine: 'Voodoo Death' and the 'Placebo Phenomenon' in Anthropological Perspective." *Medical Anthropology Quarterly* 14, no. 4: 3, 16–19.

Hale, Dorothy J. 1994. "Bakhtin in African American Literary Theory." *ELH* 61, no. 2: 445–71.

Handler, Richard. 1985. "On Dialogue and Destructive Analysis: Problems in Narrating Nationalism and Ethnicity." *Journal of Anthropological Research* 41, no. 2: 171–82.

Harper, Frances Ellen Watkins. 1990. *A Brighter Coming Day: A Frances Ellen Watkins Harper Reader*. Edited by Frances Smith Foster. New York: Feminist Press.

Harper, Frances Ellen Watkins, Hollis Robbins, and Henry Louis Gates. 2010. *Iola Leroy; or, Shadows Uplifted*. New York: Penguin Books.

Harris, Joel Chandler. (1880) 1982. *Uncle Remus: His Songs and His Sayings*. New York: Penguin Press.

Harrison, Faye. 1992. "The Du Boisian Legacy in Anthropology." *Critique of Anthropology* 12, no. 3: 239–60.

———. 1995. "Writing Against the Grain: Politics of Difference in the Work of Alice Walker." In Behar and Gordon, *Women Writing Culture*, 233–45.

Harrison, Faye V., and Ira E. Harrison, eds. 1999. *African American Pioneers in Anthropology*. Urbana: University of Illinois Press.

Harrison, Ira E., Deborah Johnson-Simon, and Erica Lorraine Williams, eds. 2019. *The Second Generation of African American Pioneers in Anthropology*. Urbana: University of Illinois Press.

Hazzard-Donald, Katrina. 2013. *Mojo Workin': The Old African American Hoodoo System*. Urbana: University of Illinois Press.

Hemenway, Robert. 1972. "Zora Neale Hurston and the Eatonville Anthropology." In Bontemps, *Harlem Renaissance Remembered*, 190–214.

———. (1977) 1980. *Zora Neale Hurston: A Literary Biography*. Urbana: University of Illinois Press.

Henderson, Mae Gwendolyn. 1989. "Speaking in Tongues: Dialogics, Dialectics, and the Black Woman Writer's Literary Tradition." In Gates, *Reading Black, Reading Feminist*, 116–42.

Hernández, Graciela. 1995. "Multiple Subjectivities and Strategic Positionality." In Behar and Gordon, *Women Writing Culture*, 148–65.

Herskovits, Melville J. (1937a) 2007. *Life in a Haitian Valley*. Princeton, NJ: First Markus Wiener Publishers, 2007.

———. 1937b. Review of *Mules and Men*, by Zora Neale Hurston. *Folklore* 48: 219–21.

———. 1937c. "The Significance of the Study of Acculturation for Anthropology." *American Anthropology* 39, no. 2: 259–64.

———. 1939. "Cottonville and the Race Problem." Review of *After Freedom*, by Hortense Powdermaker. *The Nation*, September 16, 298–99.

———. (1941) 1990. *The Myth of the Negro Past*. Boston: Beacon Press.

———, and Frances S. Herskovits. 1934. *Rebel Destiny: Among the Bush Negroes of Dutch Guiana*. New York: McGraw Hill.

Hill, Lynda Marion. 1996. *Social Rituals and the Verbal Art of Zora Neale Hurston*. Washington, DC: Howard University Press.

Hill Collins, Patricia. (1990) 2009. *Black Feminist Thought: Knowledge, Consciousness, and the Politics of Empowerment*. New York: Routledge.

Holloway, Karla F. C. 1987. *The Character of the Word: The Texts of Zora Neale Hurston*. New York: Greenwood Press.

hooks, bell. (1981) 2015. *Ain't I a Woman: Black Women and Feminism*. New York: Routledge.

———. 1990. "Saving Black Folk Culture: Zora Neale Hurston as Anthropologist and Writer." In *Yearning: Race, Gender, and Cultural Politics*, 135–43. Boston: South End Press.

———. 1995. "Zora Neale Hurston: A Subversive Reading." In Boyce Davies and Ogundipe-Leslie, *Moving beyond Boundaries*, 2: 244–55.

Howard, Lillie P. 1977. "Marriage: Zora Neale Hurston's System of Values." *CLA Journal* 21, no. 2: 256–68.

———. 1980. *Zora Neale Hurston*. Boston: Twayne Publishers.

———. 1993. *Alice Walker and Zora Neale Hurston: The Common Bond*. Westport, CT: Greenwood Press.

Hull, Gloria T., Patricia Bell Scott, and Barbara Smith, eds. 1982. *All the Women Are White, All the Blacks Are Men, but Some of Us Are Brave: Black Women's Studies*. Old Westbury, NY: Feminist Press.

Hurston, Zora Neale. (1928) 1995. "How It Feels to Be Colored Me." In Wall, *Zora Neale Hurston: Folklore, Memoirs, and Other Writings*, 826–29.

———. 1931. "Hoodoo in America." *Journal of American Folklore* 44, no. 174: 317–417.

———. 1934. *Jonah's Gourd Vine*. Philadelphia: J. B. Lippincott Co.

———. (1934) 1995. "The Characteristics of Negro Expression." In Wall, *Zora Neale Hurston: Folklore, Memoirs, and Other Writings*, 830–46.

———. (1935) 1978. *Mules and Men*. Bloomington: Indiana University Press.

———. (1937) 1978. *Their Eyes Were Watching God*. Urbana: University of Illinois Press.

———. (1937) 1998. *Their Eyes Were Watching God*. New York: Perennial Classics.

———. (1938a) 1990. "Art and Such." In Gates, *Reading Black, Reading Feminist: A Critical Anthology*. New York: Penguin Group.

———. (1938b) 1990. *Tell My Horse: Voodoo and Life in Haiti and Jamaica*. New York: Harper and Row.

———. (1938c) 1995. *Tell My Horse: Voodoo and Life in Haiti and Jamaica*. In Wall, *Zora Neale Hurston: Folklore, Memoirs, and Other Writings*, 269–555.

———. 1939. *Moses, Man of the Mountain*. Philadelphia: J. B. Lippincott.

———. (1941) 1995. "Seeing the World as It Is." *Dust Tracks on a Road: An Autobiography*. In Wall, *Zora Neale Hurston: Folklore, Memoirs, and Other Writings*, 782–95.

———. (1942) 1995. *Dust Tracks on a Road*. In Wall, *Zora Neale Hurston: Folklore, Memoirs, and Other Writings*, 558–808.

———. 1947. Review of *Voodoo in New Orleans*, by Robert Tallant. *Journal of American Folklore* 60, no. 238: 436–38.

———. 1948. *Seraph on the Suwanee: A Novel*. New York: Scribner's.

———. (1950) 1995. "What White Publishers Won't Print." In Wall, *Zora Neale Hurston: Folklore, Memoirs, and Other Writings*, 950–55.

———. 1981. *The Sanctified Church*. Berkeley, CA: Turtle Island Foundation.

———. 1985. *Spunk: The Selected Short Stories of Zora Neale Hurston*. Berkeley, CA: Turtle Island Foundation.

———. 2011. "From 'HEROD THE GREAT.'" *Callaloo* 34, no. 1: 121–25.

———. 1975. "Saving the Life That Is Your Own: The Importance of Models in the Artist's Life." Public lecture. Modern Language Association, San Francisco, California, December.

———. 2018. *Barracoon: The Story of the Last "Black Cargo."* Edited by Deborah G. Plant with a foreword by Alice Walker. 1st ed. New York: Amistad/HarperCollins Publishers.

————, Jean Lee Cole, Charles Mitchell, C. Lok Chua, Lin Yutang, Ira Dworkin, Jesse Alemán, Shelley Streeby, Kathleen Tamagawa, and Greg Robinson. 2008. *Zora Neale Hurston: Collected Plays.* Piscataway, NJ: Rutgers University Press.

————, Genevieve West, and Tayari Jones. 2020. *Hitting a Straight Lick with a Crooked Stick: Stories from the Harlem Renaissance.* 1st ed. New York: HarperCollins Publishers.

————. 2022. *You Don't Know Us Negroes: And Other Essays.* Edited and with an introduction by Genevieve West and Henry Louis Gates Jr. 1st ed. Amistad/HarperCollins Publishers.

"ism." *Webster's II New College Dictionary.* 1995.

Jakobson, Roman. 1956. "Two Aspects of Language and Two Types of Aphasic Disturbances." In Roman Jakobson and Morris Halle, *Fundamentals of Language.* The Hague: Mouton de Gruyter.

James, Stanlie M., Frances Smith Foster, and Beverly Guy-Sheftall, eds. 2009. *Still Brave: The Evolution of Black Women's Studies.* New York: Feminist Press.

JBHE Foundation, Inc. 2001. "Black Authors Don't Know They Have Entered the Literary Canon Until They See a Cliffs Notes Version of Their Work." *Journal of Blacks in Higher Education* 32 (Summer): 25.

Jennings, LaVinia Delois. 2013. *Zora Neale Hurston, Haiti, and* Their Eyes Were Watching God. Evanston, IL: Northwestern University Press.

Johnson, Barbara. 1984. "Metaphor, Metonymy, and Voice in *Their Eyes Were Watching God.*" In *Black Literature and Literary Theory,* edited by Henry Louis Gates Jr., 205–219. New York: Methuen.

————. (1985) 1986. "Thresholds of Difference: Structures of Address in Zora Neale Hurston." In *"Race," Writing, and Difference,* edited by Henry Louis Gates Jr., 317–28. Chicago: University of Chicago Press.

————. (1987) 1991. *A World of Difference.* Baltimore: Johns Hopkins University Press.

Johnson, Charles S. 1934. *Shadow of the Plantation.* Chicago: University of Chicago Press.

————. 1939. "A Study in Black and White." Review of *After Freedom,* by Hortense Powdermaker. *New Republic,* June 21, 195–96.

Jordan, June. 1974. "Notes toward a Balancing of Love and Hatred." *Black World* 23, no. 10: 4–8.

Joyce, Joyce A. 1987a. "The Black Canon: Reconstructing Black American Literary Criticism." *New Literary History* 18 (Winter): 335–44.

————. 1987b. "'Who the Cap Fit': Unconsciousness and Unconscionable in the Criticism of Houston Baker, Jr., and Henry Louis Gates, Jr." *New Literary History* 18 (Winter): 371–83.

Kaplan, Carla, ed. 2002. *Zora Neale Hurston: A Life in Letters.* New York: Anchor Books.

Karem, Jeff. 2011. *The Purloined Islands: Caribbean-US Crosscurrents in Literature and Culture, 1880–1959.* Charlottesville: University of Virginia Press.

Kendrick, B. B. 1935. Review of *Shadow of the Plantation,* by Charles S. Johnson. *Annals of the American Academy of Political and Social Science* 177 (January): 290.

Kingston, Maxine Hong. 1982. "Cultural Mis-readings by American Reviewers." In *Asian and Western Writers in Dialogue: New Cultural Identities*, edited by Guy Amirthanayagam, 55–65. London: Macmillan.

Kleinman, Arthur M. 1980. *Patients and Healers in the Context of Culture*. Berkeley: University of California Press.

Kolodny, Annette. 1975. "Some Notes on Defining a 'Feminist Literary Criticism.'" *Critical Inquiry* 2, no. 1: 75–92.

Lamothe, Daphne. 1999. "Vodou Imagery, African American Tradition, and Cultural Transformation in Zora Neale Hurston's *Their Eyes Were Watching God*." *Callaloo* 22, no. 1: 157–75.

———. 2008. *Inventing the New Negro: Narrative, Culture, and Ethnography*. Philadelphia: University of Pennsylvania Press.

Lamphere, Louise. 2004. "Unofficial Histories: A Vision of Anthropology from the Margins." *American Anthropologist* 106, no. 1: 126–39.

Landes, Ruth. 1935. Review of *Shadow of the Plantation*, by Charles S. Johnson. *Journal of American Folklore* 48, no. 188: 202.

Larsen, Nella. 1928. *Quicksand*. New York: A. A. Knopf.

———. 1929. *Passing*. New York: A. A. Knopf.

Lee, Spike, dir. 1986. *She's Gotta Have It*. Island Pictures.

Lionnet, Francoise. (1989) 1990. "Autoethnography: The An-Archic Style of *Dust Tracks on a Road*." In Gates, *Reading Black Reading Feminist*, 382–414.

Locke, Alain. (1925) 1997. *The New Negro: Voices of the Harlem Renaissance*. New York: Touchstone.

———. (1938) 1993. "Alain Locke: *Opportunity*, June 1, 1938." In Gates and Appiah, *Zora Neale Hurston: Critical Perspectives*, 18.

Long, Howard H. 1935. Review of *Shadow of the Plantation*, by Charles S. Johnson. *Journal of Negro Education* 4, no. 1: 123–25.

Lowe, John. 1997. *Jump at the Sun: Zora Neale Hurston's Cosmic Comedy*. Urbana: University of Illinois Press.

Lutz, Catherine. 1990. "The Erasure of Women's Writing in Sociocultural Anthropology." *American Ethnologist* 17, no. 4: 611–27.

———. 1995. "The Gender of Theory." In Behar and Gordon, *Women Writing Culture*, 249–66.

Marcus, George E., and Dick Cushman. 1982. "Ethnographies as Texts." *Annual Review of Anthropology* 11: 25–69.

———, and James Clifford. 1985. "The Making of Ethnographic Texts: A Preliminary Report." *Current Anthropology* 26, no. 2: 267–70.

———, and Michael M. J. Fischer. 1986. *Anthropology as Cultural Critique: An Experimental Moment in the Human Sciences*. Chicago: University of Chicago Press.

Mascia-Lees, Frances E., Patricia Sharpe, and Colleen Ballerino Cohen. 1989. "The Postmodernist Turn in Anthropology: Cautions from a Feminist Perspective." *Signs* 15, no. 1: 7–33.

Mason, Theodore O., Jr. 1988. "Between the Populist and the Scientist: Ideology and Power in Recent Afro-American Literary Criticism; or, 'The Dozens' as Scholarship." *Callaloo* 36 (Summer): 606–615.

McClaurin, Irma, ed. 2001a. *Black Feminist Anthropology: Theory, Politics, Praxis, and Poetics.* New Brunswick, NJ: Rutgers University Press.

———. 2001b. "Forging a Theory, Politics, Praxis, and Poetics of Black Feminist Anthropology." Introduction to McClaurin, *Black Feminist Anthropology*, 1–23.

———. 2012. "Zora Neale Hurston: Enigma, Heterodox, and Progenitor of Black Studies." *Fire!!!* 1, no. 1: 49–67.

McDowell, Deborah E. 1980. "New Directions for Black Feminist Criticism." *Black American Literature Forum* 14, no. 4: 153–59.

———. (1980) 1995. "New Directions for Black Feminist Criticism." In *"The Changing Same": Black Women's Literature, Criticism, and Theory*, 16–23. Bloomington: Indiana University Press.

———. (1984) 1995. "The Changing Same: Generational Connections and Black Women Novelists—*Iola Leroy* and *The Color Purple*." In McDowell, *"The Changing Same": Black Women's Literature, Criticism, and Theory*, 34–57.

———. 1995a. *"The Changing Same": Black Women's Literature, Criticism, and Theory.* Bloomington: Indiana University Press.

———. 1995b. "Transferences: Black Feminist Thinking: The 'Practice' of 'Theory.'" In McDowell, *"The Changing Same": Black Women's Literature, Criticism, and Theory*, 156–75.

McGee, R. Jon, and Richard L. Warms. 1996. 1st ed. *Anthropological Theory: An Introductory History.* Mountain View, CA: Mayfield Publishing.

———. 2020. *Anthropological Theory: An Introductory History.* 7th ed. Lanham, MD: Rowman and Littlefield.

McKay, Nellie. 1990. "'Crayon Enlargements of Life': Zora Neale Hurston's *Their Eyes Were Watching God* as Autobiography." In *New Essays on Their Eyes Watching God*, edited by Michael Awkward, 51–70. Cambridge, UK: Cambridge University Press.

McNeill, B. C. 1936. Review of *Mules and Men*, by Zora Neale Hurston. *Journal of Negro History* 21, no. 2: 223–25.

Mead, Margaret. (1928) 2001. *Coming of Age in Samoa: A Psychological Study of Primitive Youth for Western Civilization.* New York: First Perennial Classics.

Meehan, Kevin. 2008. "Decolonizing Ethnography: Spirit Possession and Resistance in *Tell My Horse*." *Obsidian* 9, no. 1: 59–73.

Meisenhelder, Susan. 1996. "Conflict and Resistance in Zora Neale Hurston's *Mules and Men*." Journal of American Folklore 109, no. 433: 267–88.

Mikell, Gwendolyn. 1982. "When Horses Talk: Reflections on Zora Neale Hurston's Haitian Anthropology." *Phylon* 43, no. 3: 218–30.

———. 1983. "The Anthropological Imagination of Zora Neale Hurston." *Western Journal of Black Studies* 7, no. 1: 27–35.

———. 1988. "Zora Neale Hurston." In *Women Anthropologists: A Biographical Dictionary*, edited by Ute Gacs et al., 160–66. New York: Greenwood Press.

————. (1990) 1999. "Feminism and Black Culture in the Ethnography of Zora Neale Hurston." In Harrison and Harrison, *African American Pioneers in Anthropology*, 51–69.

Mintz, Sidney W. 2007. Introduction to Herskovits, *Life in a Haitian Valley*, v–xii. Princeton, NJ: Markus Wiener Publishers.

————, and Richard Price. (1976) 1992. *The Birth of African-American Culture: An Anthropological Perspective*. Boston: Beacon Press.

Mitchell, Ernest Julius, II. 2013. "Zora's Politics: A Brief Introduction." *Journal of Transnational American Studies* 5, no. 1. http://escholarship.org/uc/item/38356082/.

Mitchell-Kernan, Claudia. 1971. *Language Behavior in a Black Urban Community*. Monographs of the Language-Behavior Laboratory. Berkeley: University of California, Berkeley, No. 2.

Moraga, Cherrie, and Gloria Anzaldúa. 2015. *This Bridge Called My Back: Writings by Radical Women of Color*. Albany: SUNY Press.

Morgan, L. H. (1877) 1963. *Ancient Society*. New York: Meridian Books.

Morrison, Toni. (1970) 1994. *The Bluest Eye*. New York: Plume.

————, ed. 1974. *The Black Book*. New York: Random House.

————. (1987) 2004. *Beloved: A Novel*. New York: Vintage Books.

————. 1989. "Unspeakable Things Unspoken: The Afro-American Presence in American Literature." *Michigan Quarterly Review* 28, no. 1: 1–34.

————. 2004. Foreword to *Sula*. New York: Vintage International.

————. 2009. "'Black Book' Captures African-American Experience." Interview by Michelle Norris. *All Things Considered*. NPR. December 10. https://www.npr.org/templates/story/story.php?storyId=121289328/.

Moylan, Virginia Lynn. 2011. *Zora Neale Hurston's Final Decade*. Gainesville: University Press of Florida.

Moynihan, Daniel. 1965. *The Negro Family: The Case for National Action*. Washington, DC: U.S. Government Printing Office.

Nicholls, David G. 1999. "Migrant Labor, Folklore, and Resistance in Hurston's Polk County; Reframing *Mules and Men*." *African American Review* 33, no. 3: 467–79.

Painter, Nell Irvin. 1997. *Sojourner Truth: A Life, a Symbol*. 1st ed. New York: W. W. Norton.

Parascandola, J. 1996. From MCWA to CDC—Origins of the Centers for Disease Control and Prevention." *Public Health Reports* 111, no. 6: 549–51.

Park, Robert E. 1934. Introduction to *Shadow of the Plantation*, by Charles S. Johnson. Chicago: University of Chicago Press.

————. 1937. Review of *Caste and Class in a Southern Town*, by John Dollard. *The Annals of the American Academy of Political and Social Science* 193, no. 1: 210–11.

————. 1940. "After Freedom: The Portrait of a Community in the Deep South." Review of *After Freedom*, by Hortense Powdermaker. *American Journal of Sociology* 45, no. 4: 612–13.

Parsons, Elsie Clews. 1928. "Spirit Cult in Hayti." *Journal de La Société Des Américanistes* 20: 157–79.

Patterson, Tiffany Ruby. 2005. *Zora Neale Hurston and a History of Southern Life*. Philadelphia: Temple University Press.

PBS. 2008. "Zora Neale Hurston: Jump at the Sun." *American Masters*. August 26.

Perry, Ruth, and Martine Watson Brownley, eds. 1984. *Mothering the Mind*. New York: Holmes and Meier.

Perry, William James. 1923. *Children of the Sun*. London: Methuen.

Peterkin, Julia. (1928) 1998. *Scarlet Sister Mary: A Novel*. Athens: University of Georgia.

Peterson, Dale E. 1993. "Response and Call: The African American Dialogue with Bakhtin." *American Literature* 65, no. 4:761–75.

Plant, Deborah G. 1995. *Every Tub Must Sit on Its Own Bottom: The Philosophy and Politics of Zora Neale Hurston*. Urbana: University of Illinois Press.

———. 2003. "The Benedict-Hurston Connection." *CLA Journal* 46, no. 4: 435–56.

———. (2007) 2011. *Zora Neale Hurston: A Biography of the Spirit*. Westport, CT: Praeger Publishers.

Plummer, Brenda Gayle. 1982. "The Afro-American Response to the Occupation of Haiti, 1915–1934." *Phlyon* 43, no. 2: 125–43.

Powdermaker, Hortense. 1935. Review of *Rebel Destiny*, by Melville Herskovits and Frances Herskovits. *Annals of the American Academy of Political and Social Science* 177 (January): 290–91.

———. (1939) 1993. *After Freedom: A Cultural Study in the Deep South*. Madison: University of Wisconsin Press.

Prahlad, Sw. Anand. 1996. *African-American Proverbs in Context*. Jackson: University Press of Mississippi.

———. 1999. "Guess Who's Coming to Dinner: Folklore, Folkloristics, and African American Literary Criticism." *African American Review* 33, no. 4: 565–75.

Pryse, Marjorie. 1985. "Zora Neale Hurston, Alice Walker, and the 'Ancient Power' of Black Women." Introduction to *Conjuring: Black Women, Fiction, and Literary Tradition*, edited by Marjorie Pryce and Hortense J. Spillers. Bloomington: Indiana University Press, 1985.

Puckett, Newbell Niles. 1926. *Folk Beliefs of the Southern Negro*. Chapel Hill: University of North Carolina Press.

Ramsey, Alvin. 1974. "Through a Glass Whitely: The Televised Rape of *Miss Jane Pittman*." *Black World* 23, no. 10: 31–38.

Redfield, Robert, Ralph Linton, and Melville J. Herskovits. 1936. "Memorandum for the Study of Acculturation." *American Anthropologist* 38, no. 1: 149–52.

Renda, Mary A. 2001. *Taking Haiti: Military Occupation and the Culture of U.S. Imperialism, 1915–1940*. Chapel Hill: University of North Carolina Press, 2001.

Richard, Guthrie. 2011. *Publishing: Principles and Practice*. London: Sage Publications.

Roberts, John. 1980. "*Mules and Men* by Zora Neale Hurston; *Their Eyes Were Watching God* by Zora Neale Hurston." *Journal of American Folklore* 93, no. 370: 463–66.

Rodriguez, Cheryl. 2001. "A HomeGirl Goes Home: Black Feminism and the Lure of Native Anthropology." In McClaurin, *Black Feminist Anthropology*, 233–57.

Rowe, John Carlos. 2000. *Literary Culture and U.S. Imperialism: From the Revolution to World War II*. Oxford: Oxford University Press.

Sadoff, Dianne F. 1985. "Black Matrilineage: The Case of Alice Walker and Zora Neale Hurston." *Signs* 11, no. 1: 4–26.

Schmidt, Amy. 2014. "Horses Chomping at the Global Bit: Ideology, Systemic Injustice, and Resistance in Zora Neale Hurston's 'Tell My Horse,'" *Southern Literary Journal* 46, no. 2: 173–92.

Schmidt, W. 1933. *High Gods in North America*. Oxford: Clarendon Press.

Showalter, Elaine. 2001. *Inventing Herself: Claiming a Feminist Intellectual Heritage*. New York: Scribner.

Smith, Barbara. (1977a). 2009. "A Black Feminist Statement: *The Combahee River Collective*." In *Still Brave: The Evolution of Black Women's Studies*, edited by Stanlie Myrise James, Frances Smith Foster, and Beverly Guy-Sheftall, 3–11. New York: Feminist Press.

———. (1977b) 2000. "Toward a Black Feminist Criticism." In *African American Literary Theory: A Reader*, edited by Winston Napier, 132–46. New York: New York University Press.

———. 1978. "Sexual Politics and the Fiction of Zora Neale Hurston." *Radical Teacher*, no. 8: 26–30.

———, ed. 1983. *Home Girls: A Black Feminist Anthology*. New York: Kitchen Table/ Women of Color Press.

———. 1989. "A Press of Our Own Kitchen Table: Women of Color Press." *Frontiers: A Journal of Women Studies* 10, no. 3: 11–13.

———. 1993. "Reply to Deborah Chay." *New Literary History* 24, no. 3: 653–56.

Smith, David Lionel. 1991. "The Black Arts Movement and Its Critics." *American Literary History* 3, no. 1: 93–110.

Smith, Grafton Elliot. 1933. *The Diffusion of Cultures*. London: Watts and Company.

Smitherman, Geneva. 1977. *Talkin and Testifyin: The Language of Black America*. Boston: Houghton Mifflin, 1977.

Southerland, Ellease. 1974. "The Novelist-Anthropologist's Life/Works: Zora Neale Hurston." *Black World* 23, no. 10: 20–29.

———. 1979. "The Influence of Voodoo on the Fiction of Zora Neale Hurston." In Bell et al., *Sturdy Black Bridges*, 171–83.

Spillers, Hortense J. 1985. "Afterword. Cross-Currents, Discontinuities: Black Women's Fiction." In *Conjuring: Black Women, Fiction, and Literary Tradition*, edited by Marjorie Pryse and Hortense J. Spillers, 249–61. Bloomington: Indiana University Press.

———. 2004. "A Tale of Three Zoras: Barbara Johnson and Black Women Writers." *Diacritics* 34, no. 1: 94–97.

Stacey, Judith. (1988) 1991. "Can There Be a Feminist Ethnography?" In *Women's Words: The Feminist Practice of Oral History*, edited by Sherna Berger Gluck and Daphne Patai, 111–19. New York: Routledge.

Stevens, George. 1937. "Negroes by Themselves." Review of *Their Eyes Were Watching God*, by Zora Neale Hurston. *Saturday Review of Literature*. September 18. Pg. 3.

Strathern, Marilyn. 1987. "An Awkward Relationship: The Case of Feminism and Anthropology." *Reconstructing the Academy*. Special issue of *Signs* 12, no. 2: 276–92.

Tate, Claudia. 1983. *Black Women Writers at Work*. New York: Continuum.

Taylor, Clyde. 1972. "Black Folk Spirit and the Shape of Black Literature." *Black World* 21, no. 10: 31–41.

"Their Eyes Were Watching *Their Eyes Were Watching God.*" 2005. Studio briefing. March 9. MovieWeb. https://movieweb.com/studio-briefing-march-9th-2005/. Accessed May 1, 2008.

Thompson, Holland. 1935. Review of *The Mis-Education of the Negro*, by Carter Godwin Woodson; and *The Shadow of the Plantation*, by Charles S. Johnson. *Journal of Southern History* 1, no. 1: 105–106.

Trefzer, Annette. 2000. "Possessing the Self: Caribbean Identities in Zora Neale Hurston's *Tell My Horse.*" *African American Review* 34, no. 2: 299–312.

Tucker, Cynthia. 1991. "Lost and Found." *Atlanta Journal-Constitution*. February 3. M1.

Turner, Darwin T. 1971. "Zora Neale Hurston: The Wandering Minstrel." In *In a Minor Chord: Three Afro-American Writers and Their Search for Identity*. Carbondale: Southern Illinois University Press, 89–120.

Tylor, E. B. 1865. *Researches into the Early History of Mankind and the Development of Civilization.* London: J. Murray.

Visweswaran, Kamala. (1988a) 2007. "Defining Feminist Ethnography." *Inscriptions* 3–4. Center for Cultural Studies, February 2007. https://culturalstudies.ucsc.edu /inscriptions/volume-34/kamala-visweswaran/.

———. 1988b. "Race and the Culture of Anthropology." *American Anthropologist* (March), 70–83.

———. 1997. "Histories of Feminist Ethnography." *Annual Review of Anthropology* 26: 591–621.

Walker, Alice. 1968. *Once.* New York: Harcourt, Brace, and World.

———. (1972) 1983. "A Talk: Convocation 1972." In Walker, *In Search of Our Mothers' Gardens*, 33–41.

———. 1973a. "Everyday Use." In Walker, *In Love and Trouble*, 47–59.

———. 1973b. *In Love and Trouble: Stories of Black Women.* New York: Harcourt Brace Jovanovich Publishers.

———. 1973c. "The Revenge of Hannah Kemhuff." In Walker, *In Love and Trouble*, 60–80.

———. 1973d. *Revolutionary Petunias and Other Poems.* New York: Harcourt Brace Jovanovich.

———. (1974) 1983. "In Search of Our Mothers' Gardens: The Creativity of Black Women in the South." In Walker, *In Search of Our Mothers' Gardens*, 231–43.

———. 1975. "In Search of Zora Neale Hurston." *Ms.* March 1975, 74–89.

———. (1975a) 1983. "In Search of Zora Neale Hurston" (later retitled "Looking for Zora"). In Walker, *In Search of Our Mothers' Gardens*, 93–116.

———. (1975b) 1983. "Saving the Life That Is Your Own: The Importance of Models in the Artist's Life." In Walker, *In Search of Our Mothers' Gardens*, 3–14.

———. 1977. "Zora Neale Hurston: A Cautionary Tale and a Partisan View." Foreword to Hemenway, *Zora Neale Hurston: A Literary Biography*, xi-xviii.

———, ed. 1979a. *I Love Myself When I Am Laughing . . . and Then Again When I Am Looking Mean and Impressive: A Zora Neale Hurston Reader.* New York: Feminist Press.

———. 1979b. "On Refusing to Be Humbled by Second Place in a Contest You Did Not Design: A Tradition by Now." Dedication to Walker, *I Love Myself When I Am Laughing . . .*, 1–5.

———. 1983a. "From an Interview." In Walker, *In Search of Our Mothers' Gardens*, 244–72.

———. 1983b. *In Search of Our Mothers' Gardens: Womanist Prose*. San Diego: Harcourt Brace Jovanovich Publishers.

———. 1989. *The Temple of My Familiar*. San Diego: Harcourt Brace Jovanovich Publishers.

———. 2004. *Now Is the Time to Open Your Heart*. New York: Random House.

———. 2022. *Gathering Blossoms under Fire: The Journals of Alice Walker, 1965–2000*. Edited by Valerie Boyd. New York: Simon and Schuster.

Wall, Cheryl A. 1982. "Zora Neale Hurston: Changing Her Own Words." In Gates and Appiah, *Zora Neale Hurston: Critical Perspectives*, 76–97.

———, ed. 1989. *Changing Our Words: Essays on Criticism, Theory, and Writing by Black Women*. New Brunswick, NJ: Rutgers University Press.

———, ed. 1995a. *Women of the Harlem Renaissance*. Bloomington: Indiana University Press, 1995.

———, ed. 1995b. *Zora Neale Hurston: Folklore, Memoirs, and Other Writings*. New York: Library of America.

———, ed. 1995c. *Zora Neale Hurston: Novels and Short Stories* New York: Library of America.

———. 1995d. "Zora Neale Hurston's Traveling Blues." In *Women of the Harlem Renaissance*, 139–99. Bloomington: Indiana University Press.

———, ed. 1998. "*Mules and Men* and Women: Zora Neale Hurston's Strategies of Narration and Visions of Female Empowerment." In *Critical Essays on Zora Neale Hurston*, edited by Gloria L. Cronin, 53–70. New York: G. K. Hall.

———. 2001. "Histories and Heresies: Engendering the Harlem Renaissance." *Meridians* 2, no. 1: 59–76.

———. 2005a. "In Search of Our Mothers' Gardens and Our Fathers' (Real) Estates: Alice Walker, Essayist." In *Worrying the Line: Black Women Writers, Lineage, and Literary Tradition*, 209–234. Chapel Hill: University of North Carolina Press.

———. 2005b. *Worrying the Line: Black Women Writers, Lineage, and Literary Tradition*. Chapel Hill: University of North Carolina Press, 2005.

———. 2016. "The Writer as Critic in the Emergence of Black Feminism." In *Black Feminist Literary Criticism: Past and Present*, edited by Karla Kovalova and Cheryl A. Wall, 17–28. Frankfurt am Main: Peter Lang.

Wallace, Michele. 1979. *Black Macho and the Myth of the Superwoman*. New York: Dial Press.

———. (1988) 1990. "Who Owns Zora Neale Hurston? Critics Carve Up the Legend." In *Invisibility Blues: From Pop to Theory*, 172–86. London: Verso.

———. 1989. "Variations on Negation and the Heresy of Black Feminist Creativity." In Gates, *Reading Black, Reading Feminist*, 52–67.

Waller, Willard. 1940. "*After Freedom*—A Cultural Study in the Deep South." Review of *After Freedom*, by Hortense Powdermaker. *American Anthropologist* 42, no. 3: 504–505.

Walters, Keith. 1999. "'He Can Read My Writing but He Sho' Can't Read My Mind': Zora Neale Hurston's Revenge in *Mules and Men*." *Journal of American Folklore* 112, no. 445: 343–71. https://doi.org/10.2307/541367/.

Washington, Mary Helen. (1937) 1998. Foreword to *Their Eyes Were Watching God*, by Zora Neale Hurston. New York: Perennial Classics, 1998. ix–xvii.

———. 1972. "The Black Woman's Search for Identity." *Black World* 21, no. 10: 68–75.

———. 1974. "Black Women Image Makers." *Black World* 23, no. 10: 10–20.

———, ed. 1975. *Black-Eyed Susans: Classic Stories by and about Black Women*. Garden City, NY: Anchor Press.

———. 1979. "Zora Neale Hurston: A Woman Half in Shadow." Introduction to Walker, *I Love Myself When I Am Laughing . . .*, 7–25.

———. 1984. "I Sign My Mother's Name: Alice Walker, Dorothy West, Paule Marshall." In Perry and Brownley, *Mothering the Mind*, 142–63.

———. (1987) 1993. "'I Love the Way Janie Crawford Left Her Husbands': Emergent Female Hero." In Gates and Appiah, *Zora Neale Hurston: Critical Perspectives*, 98–109.

———. (1990) 1998. Foreword to Hurston, *Their Eyes Were Watching God*. New York: Perennial Classics.

Wax, Murray. 1956. "The Limitations of Boas's Anthropology." *American Anthropologist* 58, no. 1: 63–74.

Weber, Bruce. 2002. "Joy and Blues In Florida's Piney Woods." *New York Times*. April 25, 2002, late ed.: E1.

Weedon, Chris. 2000. *Feminist Practice and Poststructuralist Theory*. 2nd ed. Oxford: Blackwell Publishers.

West, M. Genevieve. 2005. *Zora Neale Hurston and American Literary Culture*. Gainesville: University Press of Florida.

———. 2010. "Part Two: 'The Country in the Woman' and 'She Rock.'" *Amerikastudien/ American Studies* 55, no. 4, Universitätsverlag WINTER Gmbh, 583–86.

———. 2014. "'Youse in New Yawk': The Gender Politics of Zora Neale Hurston's 'Lost' Caroline Stories." *African American Review* 47, no. 4: 477–93.

White, Evelyn C. *Alice Walker: A Life*. 1st ed. New York: Norton, 2004.

Williams, Brackette F., and Drexel G. Woodson. (1939) 1993. "Hortense Powdermaker in the Deep South: The Conundrum of Race, Class, and Gender 'After Freedom' for Anthropology and African American Studies Today." Introduction to Powdermaker, *After Freedom: A Cultural Study in the Deep South*, ix–xl.

Williams, Joseph. 1936. Review of *Mules and Men*, by Zora Neale Hurston. *Folklore* 47: 329–34.

Williams, Sherley Ann. 1978. Foreword to Hurston, *Their Eyes Were Watching God*. Urbana: University of Illinois Press, v–xv.

Wolf, Diane L. 1996. "Situating Feminist Dilemmas in Fieldwork." In *Feminist Dilemmas in Fieldwork*, 1–55, Boulder, CO: Westview Press.

Woodson, Carter G. (1933) 1990. *The Mis-Education of the Negro*. 1st Africa World Press ed. Trenton, NJ: Africa World Press.

[Woodson, Carter G.] 1934. Review of *Rebel Destiny*, by Melville J. Herskovits and Frances Herskovits. *Journal of Negro History* 19, no. 3 (July): 334–36.

———. 1937. Review of *Life in a Haitian Valley*, by Melville J. Herskovits. *Journal of Negro History* 22, no 3: 366–69.

———. 1939a. Review of *After Freedom*, by Hortense Powdermaker. *Journal of Negro History* 24, no. 2 (April): 219–20.

———. 1939b. Review of *Tell My Horse*, by Zora Neale Hurston. *Journal of Negro History* 24, no. 1: 116–18.

Wright, Richard. (1937a) 1995. "Blueprint for Negro Writing." In *The Portable Harlem Renaissance Reader*, edited by David Levering Lewis, 194–205. New York: Penguin Books.

———. (1937b). 1993. "Richard Wright: New Masses, October 5, 1937." In Gates and Appiah, *Zora Neale Hurston: Critical Perspectives*, 16–17.

Yelvington, Kevin A. 2001. "The Anthropology of Afro-Latin America and the Caribbean: Diasporic Dimensions." *Annual Review of Anthropology* 30: 227–60.

"Zora Neale Hurston." Women on Stamps: Part 3. Smithsonian National Postal Museum. https://postalmuseum.si.edu/exhibition/women-on-stamps-part-3-literature-from-abolition-to-civil-rights/zora-neale-hurston/. Accessed July, 5, 2022.

Zumwalt, Rosemary Lévy. 1988. *American Folklore Scholarship: A Dialogue of Dissent*. Bloomington: Indiana University Press.

Index

Black vernacular. *See* African American and regional vernacular; African American vernacular and dialogue, Hurston's use of

Black Woman, The: An Anthology (Bambara), 184, 192

"Black Woman's Search for Identity, The" (Washington), 30–31

"Black Women Image Makers" (Washington), 33, 185

Black women writers, invisibility of, 39, 40, 48, 204n46

Black World (journal), 24, 30–34, 44, 69, 86, 199n8

Bloom, Harold, 60, 202n30

"Blueprint for Negro Writing" (Wright), 11, 203n34

Bluest Eye, The (Morrison), 7, 81–82

Boas, Franz, influence on Hurston, 105, 130, 170, 181; critics on, 98, 106, 112, 162, 195n1

Boas, Franz, *Mules and Men* preface by, 137–38, 144–46, 158, 212n2; on cultural representation, 113, 145, 157, 162, 170; Mikell on, 108; in *Modern Critical Views*, 60

Boasian anthropology, 106, 118, 130–31, 135, 169, 207n14; culture concept and, 126; folklore and, 95, 96; grand theories and, 130, 144; racial differences challenged in, 170–71; Wax on, 103–4

Bohannon, Laura, 119

Bolles, A. Lynn, 6, 183, 191

Bond, Horace Man, 216n33

Bontemps, Arna, 37, 201n23

book jackets: blurbs and endorsements on, 43–44, 104, 163, 204n39; images of Hurston on, 13, 15–17; misidentified "smiling woman" on, 197n23; of *Tell My Horse*, 104; of *Their Eyes Were Watching God*, 43, 44, 204n39

Boyce Davies, Carole, 74, 83–84, 198n33, 202n31

Boyd, Valerie, 12, 196n12, 202n27

Briggs, Jean, 119

Brooks, Gwendolyn, 33, 42, 84, 197n19, 198n33

Brown, Karen McCarthy, 89–93, 151

Brown, Sterling A., 143, 213n11

"But What Do We Think We're Doing Anyway?" (Christian), 183, 188

Buxbaum, Katherine, 216n32

canon, Hurston's work as. *See* literary canon, Hurston's work in; Walker, Alice, Hurston's restoration and

"Canon, The: Civil War and Reconstruction" (Carby), 68–69

canon formation, 202n25; anthologies' importance in, 24, 47–48, 198n33, 209n17; anthropological canon, 96, 115, 118–19, 130; Black feminist anthropology, 188–89; Boyce Davies on, 83–84, 202n31; canon debates, 3–6, 25, 27, 53–59, 67–70, 126–27; Carby on, 68–69, 125, 211n38; feminist anthropology, 119–20, 124–27, 129–30, 132; Mead and, 107, 127, 130; Mikell on, 107; Morrison on, 67–68, 69, 125, 126, 132, 211n38; white male American, 44

"Can There Be a Feminist Ethnography?" (Stacey), 122

Carby, Hazel, 3, 5, 70, 195n3, 200n16, 217n37; on Black feminist criticism, 81; on canon formation, 68–69, 125, 211n38; Hernández on, 111, 209n19; on Hurstonism, 74, 75–76

Case for the Negro Family, The: The Case for National Action (Moynihan), 198n2

Caste and Class in a Southern Town (Dollard), 216n34

Catholicism, 178, 180

Changing Our Words: Essays on Criticism, Theory, and Writing by Black Women (Wall, ed.), 206n17

"Changing Same, The: Generational Connections and Black Women Novelists-*Iola Leroy* and *The Color Purple*" (McDowell), 74–75

"Characteristics of Negro Expression" (Hurston), 85, 144, 197n17, 215n26

Character of the Word, The: The Texts of Zora Neale Hurston (Holloway), 62

Chinaberry Tree, The (Fauset), 4

Chopin, Kate, 38

Christian, Barbara, 3, 53, 205n9; "But What Do We Think We're Doing Anyway?," 183, 188; Foreman on, 77; Morrison and, 68; on new theories, 56, 60, 67, 70; poststructuralism and, 55, 61, 125, 187; "Race for Theory," 25–26, 51, 54–56, 58, 59, 125, 187, 202n25; "We Are the Ones That We Have Been Waiting For," 187

"Claims of the Negro, Ethnologically Considered, The: An Address before the Literary Societies of Western Reserve College, at Commencement, July 12, 1854" (Douglass), 132

Clifford, James, 115–17, 118, 123, 207n14; experimental ethnography and, 211n36; feminist anthropologists' response to, 120, 126

CliffsNotes, 23

Cohen, Colleen Ballerino, 123

Cohen, Roy Octavus, 215n26

Cole, Johnetta B., 192

Colette, 202n31

collectivism, 188

Collins, Derek, 89

Collins, Patricia Hill, 192

Color Purple, The (Walker), 29, 46, 74–75, 187

Columbia University, 106

Combahee River Collective, 184–85, 186

Comedy: American Style (Fauset), 4

Coming of Age in Samoa (Mead), 98–99, 100, 102–3, 107, 180, 213n13

Conditions (journal), 186, 218n3

Conjuring: Black Women, Fiction, and Literary Tradition (Spillers), 75, 206n2

Cooke, Michael, 40

Corse, Sarah M., 5, 71, 198n34

"'Crayon Enlargements of Life': Zora Neale Hurston's *Their Eyes Were Watching God* as Autobiography" (McKay), 76–77, 206n21

Crisis, The (NAACP magazine), 4

"Criteria of Negro Art" (Du Bois), 11, 203n34

critical reception of Hurston's anthropological work, 6, 9, 87, 95–132, 191; anthropology canon, 2, 5, 28, 96, 133; legitimacy questions, 117, 210n28. *See also* experimental ethnography; Gordon, Deborah; Hernández, Graciela; Mikell, Gwendolyn; *Mules and Men*, critical reception; poststructuralist readings of Hurston's anthropological work; *Tell My Horse*, critical reception

critical reception of Hurston's literary work, 2, 24; anthropology lens, 84–93, 120; by Black men during Harlem Renaissance,

4, 7–8, 10, 130, 203n34; in *Black World*, 24, 30–34, 44, 69, 199n8; literary theory changes influence, 52–53; motherhood theme in, 45–46, 204nn41–42; popularity arguments (Hurstonism), 3–5, 12, 195n3; before Walker, 30–35; Walker and Hurston paired in, 46–47, 200n12. *See also* Gordon, Deborah; Mikell, Gwendolyn; poststructuralist scholarship; signifying texts; Walker, Alice, Hurston's restoration and

cultural artifacts, 85, 108

cultural authenticity, 7; "authentic" Blackness, 42, 44, 47–48, 57, 58, 198; challenges to, 26, 69, 145, 171; cultural realism, 210n34; *Mules and Men*, 144, 213n13; *Their Eyes Were Watching God*, 5, 26, 47, 58, 73; Walker on Hurston's, 25, 29, 35, 44; "writing against culture," 123, 132, 210n35

"Cultural Valorization and African American Literary History: Reconstructing the Canon" (Corse and Griffin), 5

culture, African American, 41, 144–45; "authentic" Blackness, 42, 44, 47–48, 57, 58, 198; Boas and, 113, 126, 145, 157, 162, 170; mimicry in, 144, 214n15; *Mules and Men* works against stereotypes, 133, 135, 150–51, 156, 157; slavery's effects on, 141–42, 212n8; white influence on, 142, 143, 161–62. *See also* African American and regional vernacular; African survivals

Culture Concept, The (Elliot), 210n34

Cushman, Dick, 119

Daemonic Genius (Margaret Walker), 203n33

Davis, Ossie, 22

Day, Caroline Bond, 191

"Dear Ms. Larsen, There's a Mirror Looking Back" (Durrow), 80, 81

deconstructionist theories, 53, 54. *See also* poststructuralist scholarship

Dee, Ruby, 22

"Defining Feminist Ethnography" (Visweswaran), 118, 210n30

Delaney, Martin R., 192, 218n8

Deloria, Ella, 127

Derrida, Jacques, 53

Dessa Rose (Williams), 65

dialogue, Hurston's use of. *See* African American vernacular and dialogue, Hurston's use of

Diggs, Irene, 191

Dollard, John, 216n34

domestic violence, 32

Dorst, John, 152

Double Stitch: Black Women Write about Mothers and Daughters (Bell-Scott, ed.), 204

"double voiced" and double consciousness concepts, 53, 86

Douglass, Frederick, 132, 192

Du Bois, W.E.B., 11, 53, 192, 203n34, 216n33

duCille, Ann, 3, 195nn2–3, 200n16, 206n20, 217n37; on Black feminist studies, 46–47, 204n44; on circulation of Hurston's out of print works, 196n7; on Hurstonism, 4, 6, 35, 74; "Mark of Zora, The," 199n3

Duck, Leigh Anne, 168

Duffus, R. L., 216n33

Dunbar, Eve, 214n14

Dunham, Katherine, 191, 217n9

Durrow, Heidi, 26, 80–83

Dust Tracks on a Road (memoir, Hurston), 12–13, 86–87, 170–71, 201n23

Eagleton, Terry, 57

Eatonville, Florida, 20, 45, 86, 195n1, 197n25, 201n23, 204n37

Ebron, Paulla, 191

education of Hurston, 104, 109–10, 208n9; at Barnard and Columbia, 106, 111–12, 170, 212n3. *See also* Boas, Franz, influence on Hurston

Elliot, Michael A., 210n34

Ellison, Ralph, 23, 63, 197n19

"Erasure of Women's Writing in Sociocultural Anthropology, The" (Lutz), 211n39

Erzulie (Ezili) *loa (lwa)* (Haitian Vodou gods), 178, 179, 207n16; Guede (Gede), 174–77, 181, 193, 217n5; Lasyrenn, 89, 90–93. *See also* Vodou

essentialism and erasure of Black women's experience and intellectual work, 59, 66, 75, 79, 97, 124–25, 205n10. *See also* invisibility and omission of Black literary and cultural work

ethnocentric bias, 101–2, 208n11

ethnographic authority of Hurston, 6, 27, 108, 121, 170; defining elements, 111, 114, 117–18; influences on, 104, 117; *Mules and Men* and, 134, 135, 156; scholars define, 98–99; *Tell My Horse* and, 96, 168, 207n1

ethnographies, poststructuralism and, 6, 88, 119, 123–24

"Ethnographies as Texts" (Marcus and Cushman), 119

ethnographies of Hurston, 6, 96–105, 132, 207nn1, 14; *Dust Tracks on a Road* as, 87; feminist anthropology and, 115; Gordon on, 98–105; Hernández on, 111–13; influence on, 114, 122, 162, 212n3, 216n35. *See also Mules and Men* (Hurston); *Tell My Horse: Voodoo and Life in Haiti and Jamaica* (Hurston)

ethnography, conventional methodology, 115, 124, 166, 170–72, 217n9; Herskovits and, 180; Hurston's critique of Tallant, 171–72; poststructuralist debates, 88, 123; Powdermaker and, 158–59. *See also* anthropology, discipline of; experimental ethnography

Etienne, Isabel (Mambo Madame), 173

Evans, Mari, 41, 196n10, 199n4

"Everyday Use" (Walker), 201n19

evolutionary theories, 103, 106, 208n12

experimental ethnography, 116–21, 131, 164; African Americanists and, 97, 133, 210n27; *After Freedom*, 157–63; Behar and, 127; feminist ethnography, 116–17, 118–21, 210n27, 211n36; Johnson, Charles and, 136, 162; "Postmodernist Turn in Anthropology" on, 123, 211n36; Powdermaker and, 136, 216n31. See also *Mules and Men*, historical contexts of

Exum, Pat Crutchfield, 185

Eyes (musical adaptation of *Their Eyes Were Watching God*), 196n10, 199n4

Fauset, Arthur Huff, 211n1

Fauset, Jessie Redmon, 4, 40, 75, 76, 77–78, 83

"female" language concerns, 48–49, 204n47

"Feminism and Black Culture in the Ethnography of Zora Neale Hurston" (Mikell), 108–9, 209n14

Were Watching God, 23, 34, 51, 71, 198n34, 204n38. *See also* canon formation; Walker, Alice, Hurston's restoration and literary theory, 3, 52–55; African American literary theory, 53–54, 56, 62, 70, 210n27; "Race for Theory, The," 25–26, 51, 54–56, 58, 59, 125, 187, 202n25. *See also* Black feminist literary studies; poststructuralist scholarship

Locke, Alaine, 7, 8, 10, 11, 12, 98, 162

Lomax, Alan, 18

Lomax Collection, 17, 21

Long, Howard H., 143

"Looking Back from Zora, or Talking Out of Both Sides of My Mouth for Those Who Have Two Ears" (Foreman), 77–78, 190, 206n21

"Looking for Alice" (Boyd), 202n27

"Looking for Zora" (Walker). *See* "In Search of Zora Neale Hurston" (aka "Looking for Zora") (Walker)

Lorde, Audre, 3, 41

"Lost and Found" (Tucker), 45, 202n26, 203n36

"lost and found" Hurston stories by Walker, 35, 36, 40, 45, 201n17, 203n36

Lowe, John, 16–17

lumber camps, 146–47, 214n16

Lutz, Catherine, 126, 211n39

"'Lyin' Up a Nation': Zora Neale Hurston and the Literary Uses of Folk" (Cotera), 212n4

Madhubuti, Haki, 52

"Making of Ethnographic Texts, The: A Preliminary Report" (Clifford and Marcus), 116

Malinowski, Bronislaw, 126

Mama Lola: A Vodou Priestess in Brooklyn (Brown), 89–93, 151

Marcus, George E., 115–17, 119, 120, 123, 210n34, 211n36

Margaret Mead and Samoa: The Making and Unmaking of an Anthropological Myth (Freeman), 102

"Mark of Zora, The" (duCille), 199n3

"Mark Twain and American Dialect" (Buxbaum), 216n32

Marshall, Paule, 33, 40

Mascia-Lees, Frances E., 123–24, 211n37

masculine subjectivity, 120–21

Mason, Charlotte Osgood "Godmother," 10, 98, 162, 203n36, 209n18; contractual terms with Hurston, 8, 109; Gordon on, 99, 112; Hemenway on, 216n35

Mason, Theodore, 56

matrilineal heritage. *See* foremother status

McClaurin, Irma, 6, 13–14, 129, 189–91, 196n15

McDowell, Deborah, 3, 48–49, 70, 97, 124–25, 204n47; on Hurstonism, 74–75

McGee, R. Jon, 130

McKay, Nellie, 74, 76–77, 206n21

Mead, Margaret, 98–100, 102–5, 126, 208n1, 208n6, 213n13; canon formation and, 107, 127, 130; erasure from *Writing Culture,* 125; Herskovits critiques methods of, 180

Meehan, Kevin, 217n2

Meisenhelder, Susan, 147, 148

mentors and patrons, 42, 112, 118, 209n18; influence on ethnographies, 114, 122, 162, 212n3, 216n35; Locke, 7, 10, 11, 12, 98, 162; *Tell My Horse* and, 8, 99–100, 104, 105, 109, 181. *See also* Boas, Franz, influence on Hurston; Mason, Charlotte Osgood "Godmother"

Meridians: feminism, race, and transnationalism (journal), 205n1

"Metaphor, Metonymy, and Voice in *Their Eyes Were Watching God*" (Johnson), 58–60

Meyer, Annie Nathan, 8

Michigan Quarterly Review, 68–69

Mikell, Gwendolyn, 6, 105–11, 208n5, 209n15; on Haiti, 106–7, 209n13; Hernández on, 111–12; on *Mules and Men,* 105–9; on *Tell My Horse,* 105, 107, 108–9, 179

mimicry, 144, 214n15

Mintz, Sidney, 179

Mis-Education of the Negro, The (Woodson), 213n12

misogynoir, 218n5

Mitchell, Ernest Julius, 168–69

Mitchell-Kernan, Claudia, 204n45

Modern Critical Views (Bloom), 60

Modernist Anthropology: From Fieldwork to Text, 98

Moe, Henry Allen, 174

JENNIFER L. FREEMAN MARSHALL is an associate professor in the Department of English and Interdisciplinary Studies at Purdue University.

THE NEW BLACK STUDIES SERIES

Beyond Bondage: Free Women of Color in the Americas   *Edited by David Barry Gaspar and Darlene Clark Hine*

The Early Black History Movement, Carter G. Woodson, and Lorenzo Johnston Greene
Pero Gaglo Dagbovie

"Baad Bitches" and Sassy Supermamas: Black Power Action Films   *Stephane Dunn*

Black Maverick: T. R. M. Howard's Fight for Civil Rights and Economic Power
David T. Beito and Linda Royster Beito

Beyond the Black Lady: Sexuality and the New African American Middle Class
Lisa B. Thompson

Extending the Diaspora: New Histories of Black People   *Dawne Y. Curry, Eric D. Duke, and Marshanda A. Smith*

Activist Sentiments: Reading Black Women in the Nineteenth Century
P. Gabrielle Foreman

Black Europe and the African Diaspora   *Edited by Darlene Clark Hine, Trica Danielle Keaton, and Stephen Small*

Freeing Charles: The Struggle to Free a Slave on the Eve of the Civil War
Scott Christianson

African American History Reconsidered   *Pero Gaglo Dagbovie*

Freud Upside Down: African American Literature and Psychoanalytic Culture
Badia Sahar Ahad

A. Philip Randolph and the Struggle for Civil Rights   *Cornelius L. Bynum*

Queer Pollen: White Seduction, Black Male Homosexuality, and the Cinematic
David A. Gerstner

The Rise of Chicago's Black Metropolis, 1920—1929   *Christopher Robert Reed*

The Muse Is Music: Jazz Poetry from the Harlem Renaissance to Spoken Word
Meta DuEwa Jones

Living with Lynching: African American Lynching Plays, Performance, and Citizenship, 1890–1930   *Koritha Mitchell*

Africans to Spanish America: Expanding the Diaspora   *Edited by Sherwin K. Bryant, Rachel Sarah O'Toole, and Ben Vinson III*

Rebels and Runaways: Slave Resistance in Nineteenth-Century Florida
Larry Eugene Rivers

The Black Chicago Renaissance   *Edited by Darlene Clark Hine and John McCluskey Jr.*

The Negro in Illinois: The WPA Papers   *Edited by Brian Dolinar*

Along the Streets of Bronzeville: Black Chicago's Literary Landscape
Elizabeth Schroeder Schlabach

Gendered Resistance: Women, Slavery, and the Legacy of Margaret Garner
Edited by Mary E. Frederickson and Delores M. Walters

Racial Blackness and the Discontinuity of Western Modernity   *Lindon Barrett, edited by Justin A. Joyce, Dwight A. McBride, and John Carlos Rowe*

Fannie Barrier Williams: Crossing the Borders of Region and Race   *Wanda A. Hendricks*

The Pekin: The Rise and Fall of Chicago's First Black-Owned Theater   *Thomas Bauman*

Grounds of Engagement: Apartheid-Era African American and South African Writing
Stéphane Robolin

Humane Insight: Looking at Images of African American Suffering and Death
Courtney R. Baker

The University of Illinois Press
is a founding member of the
Association of University Presses.

_____

University of Illinois Press
1325 South Oak Street
Champaign, IL 61820-6903
www.press.uillinois.edu